S0-AJW-091

Why We Left

An Anthology of American Women Expats

Compiled and Edited
by Janet Blaser

Why We Left: An Anthology of American Women Expats
Collected essays of 27 women happily living in Mexico

Copyright © 2019 by Janet Blaser
All rights reserved. This book may not be used or reproduced in any manner without permission in writing from the author. The only exception is for the use of quotations in a book review.

Cover designed by Marysol Galvan Pelayo

Janet Blaser
Visit the author's website at www.whyweleftamerica.com
and her Facebook page, @whyweleftamerica

Printed in the United States of America

First Printing: February 2019

For Spike, Vrinda & Dennis,
with love

"I have an idea that some men are born out of their due place. Accident has cast them amid strangers in their birthplace, and the leafy lanes they have known from childhood or the populous streets in which they have played remain but a place of passage. They may spend their whole lives aliens among their kindred and remain aloof among the only scenes they have ever known. Perhaps it is this sense of strangeness that sends them far and wide in the search for something permanent to which they may attach themselves. Perhaps some deep-rooted atavism urges the wanderer back to lands which his ancestors left in the dim beginnings of history. Sometimes a man hits upon a place to which he mysteriously feels that he belongs. Here is the home he sought, and he will settle amid scenes that he has never seen before, among men he has never known, as though they were familiar to him from his birth. Here at last he finds rest."

—*The Moon and Sixpence*
by W. Somerset Maugham

Table of Contents

Why We Left

An Anthology of
American Women Expats

Introduction

I moved to Mexico in 2006, driving alone from California with only a few months preparation and planning. I didn't know anyone else who had done this—friends said I was either courageous or crazy—and I didn't know anyone in Mazatlán, where I was headed. What I did know is that the deep happiness I'd felt while there on vacation was something I hadn't felt in a long, long time (if ever) and was something I definitely needed and wanted in my life.

And so I made that momentous move. Since then, more than a decade has passed, and I can't imagine ever living in the U.S. again. For sure, there's been lots of stumbling—the language, the customs, starting a business—but even more, there's been smooth sailing. I smile more, relax easily, am more patient and open to that very Mexican concept of "mañana." I don't stress about the small stuff and watch curiously those who do. When I visit family now I increasingly feel like a "stranger in a strange land," a fish out of water, a visitor. I've evolved, I think, into a better person.

During the time I've lived in Mexico, I've met many other expats, from the U.S., from Canada, from Europe and elsewhere. One afternoon I started thinking about how different we all were— why we came, how we got here, what it took, why we stayed, what our lives look like now. I wondered if there was a common denominator, a thread that somehow connected us all to this Mexican adventure we were so happily having.

I began in the most simple way to look for women to tell their stories, posting on Facebook expat pages all over Mexico, reaching thousands of people. From those that responded I asked for a short description of who they were and chose a representative cross-section of women of varying ages, marital and financial status, loca-

11

tion and length of time in Mexico. All were eager to share their experiences. We were off!

Like me, the other 26 women you'll hear from in this book have recreated their lives and themselves in Mexico. Some were seeking adventure; some wanted an affordable, beautiful place to retire; others found business or career opportunities that wouldn't have been possible north of the border. They are all ages, from millennials to elders; some are married, some single, some with young children or children who've grown up in both worlds. Some planned and saved for years, while others made a spur-of-the-moment decision. They come from all walks of life, from all over America, and settled throughout Mexico: in the fabled colonial cities, the coastal tropics, beachfront tourist towns, the mountain villages. Some are "newbies," with only a year or two under their expat belts, while others have stopped counting the years as their life in Mexico has become their norm.

As you read you'll see similarities, too; most notably that everyone is happy and no one regrets their decision to move to Mexico. At the same time, each story is so different I found it impossible to read all of them straight through; I needed time between them to consider and contemplate and reflect.

My hope is that this book does two things: That it inspires others who may be feeling an urge, an itch, something deep down that just won't go away, to live a different life, outside of the proverbial box, where happiness is easier to come by. And secondly, that it applauds the grand adventures these women are having.

As for me, I can look at who I've become and point to this one decision—to move to Mexico and become an expat—as a crucial turning point in my own personal evolution. These essays speak to the truth of that experience: the challenge of our struggles, the delight of our joys and our gratitude for all of it. We've been humbled and we've seen moments to be proud of. But mostly we've wondered and considered, time and again, what the heck we were doing, and how glad we were to be doing it.

1. "The Bug"

Virginia Saunders
Puerto Vallarta, Jalisco

I remember when I first got the bug.

After a morning of sightseeing in Arles, we were having a late lunch on the Place du Forum. Our rosé was delicious, so we ordered a *pichet*, thinking it would be two more glasses. But it turned out to be four.

Oh well. If there's one thing we've learned in our travels, it's to just go with the flow. So we ditched our itinerary and just let the afternoon unfold.

Across from us, Le Café La Nuit looked the same as it did when Van Gogh painted it, and there was a small market on the square. As we nursed our wine, tables of Frenchmen talked animatedly about politics, and smartly dressed women stopped by for a pastis and a pastry.

I thought, "This is the life!" and started to wonder if it could be our life. I was making a good living as the creative director of an advertising agency in Southern California, and I'd begun to think about retirement, although I was only 55 at the time.

We left Arles and headed for Avignon and Aix-en-Provence, but I couldn't shake the feeling that there was a simpler life more enjoyable than the one we were living. And I resolved to start investigating the possibility.

Back home, things were stressful at work. My agency had been bought by the largest advertising agency holding company in the world. And because my boss's final compensation would be based on our performance over the next three years, maximizing profit became the lens through which everything was viewed. We hired a shiny new CFO to play bad cop regarding money matters, and set some very aggressive revenue goals, which through a combination of luck and pain we managed to achieve. I was working much harder than I wanted to, but my quarterly bonuses removed some of the sting.

Molly and I were able to take two trips outside the country a year, usually for three weeks at a time. And by 2010, we were exploring less-visited destinations like Corsica, Catalonia and the Basque Country—always with an eye toward moving abroad.

Coming back to California was predictably a letdown. Although there are many things I love about the Golden State, we were isolated out in the suburbs and the cost of living was crippling.

After a particularly bleak homecoming, we sat down and made a wish-list of what we'd want in a home base. For Molly, living by the beach, preferably a surf beach, was tops, while I wanted good infrastructure, great food and a welcoming expat community.

Like most people interested in living abroad, I subscribed to International Living and pored over the articles every month. Costa Rica seemed to tick most of our boxes, so we did a research trip in 2012 to San José, the Océ Peninsula and Tamarindo. Even though I knew that 100+ degree temperatures and flat surf were unusual for March, I knew pretty quickly I couldn't be happy living there.

When I returned to work that year, some personnel changes and a new reporting structure made things really difficult for me. So after eight years, I quit my job. Because I'd lasted significantly longer than any of my predecessors, my boss thought he'd need at least half a year to find a suitable replacement. He asked me to stay through September, and since I didn't have a plan, I agreed. To his credit, he gave me a generous severance package and treated me fairly.

I spent that six months trying to figure out where we'd like to live and how to make a living without a day job. I figured I'd be able to make enough money freelancing to make ends meet, and at first, that was true.

Using our wish list as a guide, we came up with a short-list of places we might like. We loved Biarritz and San Sebastian, but when it came to cost of living, neither was what you'd call a bargain. Portugal seemed to hit all our buttons, especially Cascais, which was a 30-minute train ride from Lisbon and had surfing, beautiful beaches, good restaurants and an International Women's Club.

By the time we visited in 2015, I was pre-sold and ready to move. We loved Cascais, but also thought Carvoeiro or Praia da Luz could work. I liked everything about Portugal, especially the proximity to the rest of Europe. But not being a cheap, easy flight to Paris meant it was difficult and costly to get back to the Pacific Northwest, where Molly's elderly parents lived.

Her mother was going to need care and her father would need help managing that process and downsizing. After really thinking things through, we concluded that it didn't make sense for us to move that far away. So we started to look closer to home.

My freelance business had fallen off a cliff. A decade before, being able to craft a great headline was a skill you could take to the bank. But now that everyone's marketing budget was skewed heavily toward Google and Facebook ads, ads practically wrote themselves. All you had to do was add a noun or a verb to your keyword. *Et voila.*

Once we started to see more money going out than coming in, we doubled down on our search.

We liked the idea of Mexico, so when Molly's niece invited us to her December wedding in Cabo San Lucas, we decided to spend a few extra days checking out San Jose del Cabo. With dozens of galleries, a charming hotel and lots of romantic restaurants, the town was lovely. But it was about a 25-minute walk to the beach, and the oceanfront hotels were all-inclusive, which made it hard to grab a beer or a meal on the shore. For us, this was a deal-breaker. So it was back to the drawing board.

By now, I was doing quite a bit of research online, and I had stumbled across a blog by Tricia Lyman. She and her husband were looking for the perfect place to retire abroad and in the process had checked out Panama, Costa Rica, Nicaragua and Ecuador and ended up saying, "We don't like any of these places as much as we like Puerto Vallarta—let's try that."

Tricia's blog, "Lyman's Journey," was a fascinating read, full of helpful information. She had also started a Facebook page called "Puerto Vallarta: Everything You Need or Want to Know" that was an absolute godsend. I spent the next month or so reading Tricia's blog and researching Puerto Vallarta. Molly and I had both been to P.V. in the mid-1980s, and then once on a cruise in 2006. But we weren't that familiar with it, although our impressions were positive.

We decided to do a six-day research trip, which closed the deal. We stayed a few nights downtown and a few nights in the Marina, so we could check out several neighborhoods. It was hard to resist the ocean-front promenade, the lively restaurant scene on Basilio Badillo and the incredible sunsets that seemed to be a nightly event. There was no expat event during our visit, but Sara Wise, the organizer, agreed to meet us for a drink and let us pick her brains. She and her husband were a big help.

We had no intention of renting a place on that trip, but we wanted to look at as many properties as we could so we'd know what fair market value was and how much we would realistically need to budget for. We saw more than a dozen places, but most of them wouldn't work for us for one reason or another. Many involved a steep, uphill climb. Others were open-air affairs without walls. One even had bats living in the laundry room. Most wouldn't accept a big dog.

Discouragement set in. So when the agent showed us a lovely place in the Zona Romantica in our price range—one that took dogs—we went ahead and pulled the trigger. We agreed to begin the lease on May 1, about six weeks in the future. Flying back to California, we were both equal parts excited and overwhelmed. There was so much to do and so little time. I'd been thinking about moving outside the country for nearly 10 years, but when the rubber met the road, I felt completely unprepared.

Once we got organized, the to-do list was daunting. In no particular order, we needed to:

- Get our house ready to sell
- Prepare for house guests coming from England in early April
- Find solutions for banking, mail service and working remotely
- List our house
- Figure out how to transport the stuff we were taking to Puerto Vallarta
- Figure out how to get our dogs to Puerto Vallarta
- Figure out how to get rid of the stuff we weren't taking
- Get health insurance

We'd moved twice in the past for my work. Since I was always starting a new job in a few weeks, I never had time to go through my belongings. We just packed everything up and hit the road. Once we arrived at the new place, we'd unpack the boxes that contained the things we used and leave the others to gather dust in the basement or garage. When I finally opened up all the boxes to see what we had, I was shocked at all the things we'd hauled from one coast to the other that we didn't want or need.

We classified everything one of three ways: 1) Things we were definitely moving with us; 2) Things we were on the fence about; and 3) Things we were getting rid of. As time went by, the vast majority of items in the second category moved to the third.

We planned to take our two dogs on the plane with us, one in a carrier under the seat and one below in a kennel. This limited the number of other things we could realistically take with us in one trip. We realized that we'd need to fly down twice: once to take down a load, and the second time to bring everything else and the dogs.

Doing a deep dive into your possessions is an emotional and time-consuming proposition. You can't throw away notes from your high school boyfriend without reading them first. You fall down one rabbit hole after another, and before you know it, four hours have passed and you've only been through two boxes.

As time passed, we got more disciplined (or more panicked) depending on your point of view. Thoughtful consideration gave way to snap judgements about what to keep and what to toss.

I'd inherited some things from my family I thought might be of some value—a 12-place setting of Limoges china, sterling flatware for eight, some Karastan rugs—but after getting quotes from sites like classicreplacements.com, it didn't seem to be worth the effort. When we realized that getting rid of our stuff would be time-consuming and not as lucrative as we'd hoped, we looked at the alternatives. Having an estate sale seemed like the best option. We found several companies in our area, consulted Yelp to see which ones were highly rated, then went to a couple of sales to see how organized they were.

We were impressed by the reviews and organization of one of the companies and called them to come out and give us an estimate. They were excited because most of their sales were for families who were trying to deal with the possession of elderly parents who had passed away. Consequently, a lot of the items were dated and undesirable.

The estate sale couple was very enthusiastic to do our sale, especially when we told them we planned to sell our cars, a Jaguar XK8 convertible and a Volkswagen CC. They charged a 30% commission but agreed to sell the cars for 20%. They had a fairly big database of customers, and they knew who collected what, which seemed like a good strategy. The other big plus was that they promised to take away everything that didn't sell. This was essential because as we got down to the wire, timing became critical. We were having the sale on Saturday and Sunday and the new owners of our house were taking possession at 5 p.m. on Monday.

While having an estate sale was an expeditious solution for us, we definitely left some money on the table. We ended up selling the Jaguar to someone we knew, but they charged us the commission anyway because they had "marketed" it. The new owners of our house ended up buying a lot of our antiques at the sale, so we also ending up paying a commission on that. And one of the people working at the sale showed up and bought the twice-used Kitchenmaid mixer and Cuisinart for $70 before the sale even began.

If I had it to do over again, this would be my advice: Ask all your friends over and give them first dibs on your stuff. If you feel okay about giving it away, do. If you want something for it, make them a fair offer. Don't invite the estate sale people over until you've given your friends first crack at your things, because they'll expect whatever you show them to be included in the sale.

Unless you've really stayed on top of things, you likely have more paperwork than you realize. At this point, we'd been together for 18 years, and we had every canceled check, every pay stub, every tax return and every credit card bill we'd ever received. Sadly, you can't just throw this stuff away because much of it has Social Security numbers and other personal information. Shredding turned out to be a part-time job. We had scores of boxes full of paperwork, and shredding was expensive. Our local high school had a fundraiser that let you shred a banker's box of paper for $10. We had to make more than one trip.

Our friends from Britain were visiting us in early April and we didn't feel like we could list our house until they'd gone. We'd met with our realtor and she suggested we move all our knick-knacks out into the garage so the house would appear larger and uncluttered. This gave us a chance to start going through our things.

We were hopeful that our house would sell quickly, and it did. We listed on Thursday, said we would look at offers on Sunday, and sold it to the highest bidder for $20,000 over asking that weekend, which was a big relief.

Now the timing was really tight because we needed to make another trip to Puerto Vallarta to take down a load of stuff. Our lease began on May 1, so we flew down the first week of May with four gigantic suitcases that we unpacked and left in our rental. There was an expat Happy Hour at Langostino's during our brief visit, and we were able to have dinner with Tricia and Mike Lyman, who have become dear friends. We stayed a couple of nights at the condo we'd rented and then flew back to finish up.

I'd read that a Schwab checking account was a good solution for banking in Mexico because they had great customer service and would rebate any ATM fees. I used the proceeds from the sale of the house to open a brokerage and checking account there.

The local Residence Inn took dogs, so we arranged to move there on the Friday night before the garage sale. We planned to stay there until we moved to a hotel at LAX the night before our flight to Puerto Vallarta. Some friends had moved into a local VRBO when they were in-between houses, which might have been a better option for us.

The dogs needed health certificates for immigration. We paid $350 to get them from our local vet, but we weren't sure they would work because they weren't issued by the Department of Agriculture. We ended up buying a second set from a different vet that turned out to be the same thing.

There were many friends we wanted to say goodbye to, so during this time, we were also juggling drinks and dinner with those near and dear to us. Because of the distances involved and the traffic, getting together in Southern California is never easy, and as much as we wanted to see people, it was another challenge, especially since we'd sold both our cars.

Our final day before heading to LAX was a busy one. We found two more boxes of paperwork that needed to be shredded and ran into something we didn't really know what to do with—the ashes from our past dogs who had died. Both of them had enjoyed the water, so we went to Westlake and said a few words as we scattered them into the lake. I'm reasonably certain this was illegal, but it seemed like the right thing to do at the time.

We had four suitcases, two of which were enormous, one dog kennel, one dog carrier and two carry-ons. We got all our stuff in the hotel van and got a porter to help us haul it to the place where we checked in the dogs. Alaska Airlines was great, but I was nervous about our Border Collie going below. And I was concerned that our little fellow was going to bark and get us thrown off the flight. He's not a service animal, so we couldn't take him out of his carrier. We gave him Rescue Remedy a few days before the flight, but it just seemed to agitate him, so we brought some treats and hoped for the best.

He was a trooper, so that was one hurdle down. But I was still worried about getting through Customs. They'd searched our bags every time we'd gone through, and I wasn't sure what would happen to the dogs while the agents inspected our belongings. I'd read all sorts of horror stories about people spending hours at Animal Control because they had the wrong paperwork or because the paperwork was okay, but the color of the ink was wrong. So I was anxious about that part of the journey.

When we landed, we got through Customs pretty quickly. We'd packed our clothes in those vacuum bags, and that made it much faster for customs to look through our things.

I took Riley to Animal Control and the gal who examined him couldn't have been nicer. She was just finishing up with him when Molly brought Lily over in her kennel. Molly's not very big, but she managed to hoist Lily in her kennel—which must have weighed about 75 pounds—off the baggage carousel by herself. We spent less than 30 minutes at Animal Control, gathered up the bags and dragged them to the exit where a driver from Superior Tours was waiting for us. Half an hour later, we were on the balcony of our condo.

The Romantic Zone was a little crazy. The annual Drag Race— one of many fun Pride Week events—was underway, so there were lots of people in the streets. After a full day of travel, we didn't think the dogs were up to that, but we thought a beach walk was in order. As we sat admiring the sunset, a young woman came to pat our dogs and ended up inviting us to a dinner party the next evening. Molly and the woman exchanged numbers, and the next night, we went to a lovely get-together in a beautiful flat with a gorgeous view of the church and its crown. That night, we met Gabby and Lee, a young couple who'd just moved down from North Carolina. They have also become good friends.

Although we'd informed the leasing agent that our Border Collie weighed fifty pounds—we'd even attached a photo to our application—two weeks after moving in we were asked to leave. Turns out the condo bylaws didn't allow pets that weighed more than 25 pounds. Since they were fining us every day we were there, we were scrambling to find a new home. Not that many rentals take large dogs, but we found a place in Amapas with amazing views and a huge infinity pool. It wasn't perfect, but we were happy to end our search.

We were introduced to someone who helps expats manage their health care and we bought health insurance for a fraction of what we'd paid in California. We got check-ups, opened a Mexican bank account and learned basic Spanish, which is an ongoing process.

It's hard to believe that was two years ago. Our life here has exceeded our expectations in almost every way. Some things are more challenging, many things less so. And over time, we've figured out how to simplify most tasks.

Adjusting to retirement wasn't as easy as I'd expected. I foundered a little with no clear purpose. And having no possessions to define us was also disorienting—most people identify with their belongings more than they realize. But before long, I really enjoyed not being asked what I did for a living, and I liked that no one cared what brand of watch you wore. Most of all, I enjoyed walking everywhere, or hopping on a bus or into a taxi.

With no real responsibilities or obligations, we've been free to reinvent ourselves and our lives. Tending to my mental, physical and spiritual health has been my top priority, and living here has opened up so many opportunities in those areas. We hike, we swim, we paddleboard, we take Pilates and painting classes, we walk on the beach, we volunteer, we read, we write, we cook, we paint, we sweat in the sauna, we spend time with friends. What we don't do is sit in traffic, worry about how we'll afford health insurance or dread Mondays.

Both of us are healthier, thinner, fitter, happier and mellower than we've ever been. We love the people, the culture, the food, the music, the lifestyle, the birds, the flowers, the sunsets—you name it. Hardly a day goes by that one of us doesn't say "pinch me" to the other.

We know that we're blessed and we feel extremely fortunate to be in the position we're in. Our friends here come from every background and circumstance imaginable. They're young, old, American, Canadian, European, gay, straight, married, single, retired, working or telecommuting. But one thing we all have in common is that our lives here are better than they were before.

If you've thought about making this journey yourself, there are plenty of women you can reach out to who would love to help. Don't worry too much about timing. When it's right, things will all fall into place.

As a copywriter and creative director, Virginia Saunders created advertising campaigns for some of the most sophisticated marketers in the world, including American Express, Royal Caribbean International, Westin Hotels and Resorts, Sony, and DirecTV. Currently based in Puerto Vallarta, Mexico, when she's not writing, she's enjoying all this beautiful destination has to offer with her partner and their rescue dog Riley.

2. "Welcome to Palapa-Ville"

Wendy Wyatt
Cozumel, Quintana Roo

My mother practically begged me not to move to Mexico. "It's so dangerous, why do you want to go there?" she said. "I'll never see you again. How will you survive?!" Eventually, that changed to, "So, I can still just pick up the phone and call you? I can really fly there in a few hours?" My father and my sister were a little taken aback too, but then they were 100% on board after just a few minutes. "A free place for me to come visit in Mexico? On the Caribbean? You should do it!"

My husband and I have been in Paamul, Mexico, for five weeks today, but we started making plans a few years ago. It all began as a dream to leave public service when I turned 57 and would be able to properly retire from my job as a registered dietitian working at the Veteran's Healthcare Administration. We don't have children, only our precious dogs, so that made planning a little easier but still not as easy as I'd thought. I knew we wanted to be on or near the beach, and I'd only visited the Mayan Riviera a few times, mostly at all-inclusive resorts, where I rarely left the property.

On a Sunday afternoon in 2016, not long after the Pulse nightclub shooting in Orlando, Florida, where 49 people were killed and 53 wounded, and only a year after a white supremacist murdered nine African-American churchgoers in my own hometown, I Googled "real estate in Mexico." I was tired of crying nightly while I watched the news or in the morning on my way to work. Selfish, senseless murders were taking a toll on me. Not to mention the fact that I was soon to start walking into a job every day and seeing a picture of the new commander in chief who I was deeply ashamed of.

I narrowed down my search to Quintana Roo, which I'd visited before. Lots of nice places and lots of expensive places that I thought were out of reach, so I sorted by price. First on the list was a house with beach access for $35,000 U.S. dollars. Really?! The next was $40,000, then $42,000, $50,000, etc. I thought, this can't be right, there must be an error. I started looking at the photos more closely and discovered one of the strangest things I'd ever seen. These were RVs with a house built around them. What? That was insane. I shared the website with my husband Heath and my dear friend and old roommate Nan. They were called "Mayan Mansions." We had a good laugh about the name but I was really intrigued.

Over the next year I kept going back to that website and dreaming. My husband was also dreaming and studying Spanish. He's an artist and can work from anywhere. I wasn't so lucky; there's not a V.A. in Mexico. Our plan was still in place—retire at 57, which was nine years away at that point—and then buy a home in another (less expensive) country. Then Nan suggested a destination party for her sixtieth birthday which was a few months away. I jumped onboard and said, "Hell yeah, let's go to Mexico!"

In March of 2017, not long after the new administration had taken over and sidelined my government promotion for more than a month (things were not going my way, to say the least), we took off for Nan's week-long birthday party with 15 of our friends. The party in Soloman Bay, Quintana Roo, turned into an opportunity for my husband and I to search for real estate. I finally talked him and Nan into driving over to the strange RV park neighborhood to check out the "Mayan Mansions." After eating lunch at a restaurant and walking on the beautiful beach we snuck into the park.

All three of us fell in love with the neighborhood, the crazy RV houses and the eclectic bunch of people who lived there: musicians, artists, contractors, photographers, healthcare workers, school teachers and more. They were from the U.S., Canada, Europe, Africa and other places with one thing in common: their love for a country other than the one they were born in. Most of them were snowbirds (people who only stay during the winter months) and that's what we were thinking of doing at first: Buy a place, visit for a few weeks a year and in eight years we can retire and move full-time to Mexico. Problem was, I only got two weeks of vacation a year so we wouldn't be using the house that often and the rules prevented us from renting to anyone when we weren't there.

After hours and hours and weeks and weeks of discussions about just taking off and moving and not waiting to retire, my husband finally said these magic words, "If we get down there and don't like it, we just pack up and go back home." It was really that simple!

We bought our palapa in May of 2017. I retired six weeks before my 50th birthday and moved from a 2,500 square-foot house with all the bells and whistles, including a brand-new kitchen, a dock and a boat on a marsh in Charleston, South Carolina, to an RV with a palapa roof in Mexico. And if I decide I don't like it, I can always go back home.

But getting here was not easy. It took us about a year to settle everything, get vested in my job, sell our house, my car, furniture, etc. before we were able to move. During this time one of our Charleston neighbors suggested we start a VLOG about our journey. This was the perfect opportunity to give Heath a new project. (You can check it out on YouTube - search for "Mexicoing with Heath and Wendy.") If you're considering a move to Mexico, there's lots of information, or if you just want to be entertained by a couple of yahoos who decided to leave their life and start anew, check it out.

The first thing to know about being an American purchasing a home in Mexico is that there are no rules. You cannot own the land within 50 kilometers of any Mexican border (or the ocean) unless you're Mexican, allegedly. You also supposedly cannot take out a loan from a Mexican bank and hold a mortgage on your home. We decided to sell everything in the U.S. except some precious items and basic necessities to finance our new endeavor and the move to Mexico. Sounds easy? Not so fast.

To start with, we were buying our place in Mexico, steps from the Caribbean (so within 50 kilometers from a border), from a Canadian couple (snowbirds) who were currently in Canada. So how do you make it actually happen and how do you know you own it? Trust. Plain and simple. Not to say that people don't get swindled every day, because I know they do. Along with keeping good records of every transaction, we just had to believe that the couple we were buying from were honest people. Turns out they are. Then there's the question of not owning the land; we bought a house but not the land it's sitting on. Again, it boils down to trust.

We made arrangements to meet the Canadians in Mexico to complete the transaction in fall of 2017. Simple. We meet and overlap our visits so we can finish the paperwork, pay a transfer fee and turn it into the office who owns the land. Well. This is Mexico, and we learned our first lesson about *mañana*. In our neighborhood we have a land lease that includes your basic utilities and 24-hour security. We paid for two years up front and have documentation from the owner of the land stating exactly that. We had also started paying for insurance on the house just after we bought it. The man who's holding the insurance policy will be here tomorrow, the office said. OK, tomorrow /*mañana* it is.

Mañana comes and goes, and again *mañana* comes and then the next *mañana* and then you start freaking out. Time is running out, we have a flight scheduled, I have to go back to work. Finally, another *mañana* comes and the transfer fee is paid and we have an insurance policy in hand. We're the proud owners of a home in the U.S. and in Mexico.

Our plan was to be in Mexico by my 50th birthday. We set a departure date for the first week of March so we could be there by mid-April. Now, to get out of the U.S. home and into our new retirement home in Mexico. We had to sell the house. I loved my house and most everything in it. How could I possibly part with all this stuff? I needed it all, or at least I thought I did.

Look around your home. What's precious to you? I started a list. Definitely my retro bar and '50s diner table from my kitchen, the sofa, my sleep-number mattress, Heath's grandmother's china and silver, letters I'd received over the years, my high school annuals, Heath's paintings, all our photographs, Heath's camera collection, my record collection, our CD collection, my books. Definitely taking our dogs, Gertie and Granny. Seems easy enough.

That's when we started thinking about how we were going to get all this "stuff" and our fur-babies to Mexico. Get a U-Haul? Not an option. (Where do you return your U-Haul in Mexico?) Fly? Not putting my dogs in a cargo hold. What about making them therapy dogs so they can just fly with us? Not an option with our dogs. (If you met them you'd know why.) We decided we were going to drive to the Yucatán Peninsula from South Carolina. Even if we drove straight through without stopping, that was 50 hours with two dogs, a pick-up truck and a pull-behind trailer.

We kept thinking, no problem, we got this. The more research we did about driving across the U.S. / Mexico border and the roads we'd be driving on, the more we realized that taking a trailer and keeping all our possessions safe on this journey was just not feasible. It was time to rethink what "precious" meant. The list began to narrow. We decided to keep a few things in storage in the U.S. Because, like Heath said, "We can always go back."

The "taking it to Mexico list" became very short. We planned to pack a suitcase each for the journey, dog food, dog beds and dog toys. I bought clear plastic totes and packed our clothes and shoes, my favorite kitchen tools, a set of dishes, Grandma's silver (which are now our everyday utensils), a medicine box, a pared-down version of Heath's art supplies and a few small kitchen appliances. We also brought our favorite artwork that would withstand the heat and humidity, some books, three tool boxes, fishing gear, a computer, printer and scanner. Doesn't sound like a lot but when you're packing it into the bed of a truck, wow! We also numbered every box and made a manifest with all the items in each box in English and Spanish, along with the value in U.S. dollars and pesos.

At this point we were thinking, planning, researching and stressing out about crossing the border with all our stuff, worrying about the best route to take, crossing the border, what it was going to be like when we got there, crossing the border, were the dogs going to adjust, crossing the border, getting health records for the dogs, crossing the border, do we get residential status or tourist visas, crossing the border, practicing Spanish every day and crossing the border. It was honestly the only thing I could think about. I had nightmares of tidal waves washing over our new home and not being able to find the dogs or my husband. I was waking up for hours at a time in the middle of the night. I was sleep-deprived, exhausted and now menopausal. (Seriously?! Now?) At this point I was still working and hadn't even considered telling my boss about my plans. In fact, the plans still didn't feel real to me yet, even though it was all I could think of. Work continued as if I was going to be there for the next 10 years.

I finally told work I was leaving. My last day was March 2, and we hit the road on March 7. After about 10 days of taking our time, visiting friends and family, and driving the Natchez Trace, we made it to Austin, Texas, where we had an appointment to secure the health certificates for the dogs.

We arrived in Laredo, Texas the following day where we'd originally planned to cross the border. After discussing this with several other expats we'd met in Palapa-ville and online, we decided the best place to cross was at the Columbia crossing. We set out at 5:30 a.m. on a Sunday and arrived at the Columbia crossing at 6 a.m. only to find out it didn't open until 8 a.m. Really?! All this planning and now we had to turn around and drive back to Laredo, where the crossing is open 24/7. That became our new plan.

We arrived in the dark not knowing what to expect. My Spanish was still pretty crappy at best; it was a good thing Heath had been studying more than me. The checkpoint guard asked for our passports and had us pull over. He asked Heath to open the back of the truck. When he looked in, all he could say was, "That's a lot of stuff." He asked us what we had and Heath said we had a list, which, of course, we couldn't find. After about five minutes of frantically searching the cab of the truck we found it. He read through the list, glanced around the bed of the truck and sent us on our merry way.

Now where to? Finally, we found our way to the immigration building, a few blocks from the crossing. I surveyed the parking lot and surprisingly, there were several other loaded down trucks with U.S. citizens crossing the border into Mexico. A couple hours later and we were back on the road. Everyone had told us to get through the crossing and away from the border towns as quickly as possible in the daylight, due to illegal activity, the cartel, *banditos*, etc. They also say leave space at red lights between you and the car in front in case you need an escape, and whatever you do, don't drive at night. All this sounds very scary but we had absolutely no problems. Again, not to say this kind of stuff never happens but it didn't happen to us. Besides, you can be massacred at a country music concert in Las Vegas, your children can be murdered at their elementary school in Connecticut, or, in our hometown, you could be shot in the back at a traffic stop by a police officer or slaughtered by a racist for going to Bible study.

Anyway, after a scenic eight-hour drive through the mountains we arrived at our first Airbnb in San Miguel de Allende, Guanajuato. What a beautiful town! If you ever have the opportunity, I highly recommend going there, but don't take a truck. You can refer to our YouTube videos if you want to see why.

We had originally decided to take our time traveling to our destination, but after a couple weeks of living out of a suitcase, some bad weather and packing in and out with two dogs every day we decided to speed things up. I have to tell you there are some shady hotels in Mexico and finding a dog-friendly place is not always easy. Having everything you own in the back of your truck and leaving it parked on the street or in a parking lot that's not secure was not something we wanted to do either. We thought we could just look on the internet and find something, right? But you'll find great reviews for some really strange places. In Mexico, it's common to drive into a single car parking garage, enter your hotel room through the garage, and pay by the hour through the little window in your bathroom while you rifle through the sex toy menu. Let me tell you, after checking the bed for bed bugs, I slept in my clothes on top of the covers at that place. We followed this with a stay at a Hampton Inn in Villahermosa, Tabasco. The Hampton Inn never seemed so exotic. Then we spent a few days in Campeche at another Airbnb with a fantastic host in a beautiful town. *Muy tranquilo*! I was still pinching myself and couldn't believe I didn't have to get up and go to work the next day. Instead, the next day we would arrive in our new home.

We have been in our palapa now for about six weeks. I can see the Caribbean from my living room where I'm typing this. I have a lovely woman cleaning my house today for about $25 bucks and I may go paddleboarding in a few minutes. I have a massage scheduled every few weeks for about $25 U.S.

Not every day is like this, however. I've had so many mosquito bites I can't begin to count them, my hair has become a tangled, frizzy mess (and I have straight hair), I've been infected with pinworms, had three days of Montezuma's revenge, had an assassin bug land in my hair last night, and am just now recovering from a rash on my butt from wearing a wet swimsuit too many days in a row.

But I wouldn't trade this experience for anything. Everyone we've met (with the exception of one super-pushy restauranteur) has been very pleasant; not always on time, but pleasant. Things move at a much slower pace here and I'm starting to catch on. Mexican time is different—no one's really in a hurry. Things can be done *luego* or *mañana*. People do what they want in the moment, and everyone seems happier for it. And I totally get the whole *siesta* thing (not that everyone does it, but I do). It's pretty freaking hot here, and it can really zap your energy. It's actually a pretty good idea to take a break in the middle of the day, aka siesta time.

When we left the States to come to Mexico I was worried about things like getting sick, health insurance, finding a doctor, a veterinarian, dentist, etc. Well, in our three short months here, Heath had to have a metal shaving removed from his eyeball and along with the post-op medication it cost about $78 U.S. dollars. We also had a doctor make a house call (this seems to be pretty much the norm) to check out my rash and check Heath's blood pressure—to the tune of a whopping $38 U.S. dollars. And in both instances we were able to see the doctor on the day we called to make the appointment. What is America doing wrong with healthcare?

I took my first trip back to the U.S. last week. It made this adventure seem like a dream. On the plane ride there I actually started to worry about getting sick in the U.S. and how I would pay for medical care. By day two I was homesick for Palapa-Ville. I was missing my husband, my dogs, the rain dripping through the palapa roof, hanging my clothes on the laundry line (I'd never hung out laundry before moving here; it's sort of cathartic,

33

you should try it!) and the iguanas that guard the laundry line, paddleboarding, the sound of the wind rustling through the palms, the barking geckos, morning walks and the greetings of *"Hola!"* and *"Buenos dias!"* from the men roofing the palapas. Don't get me wrong—I also miss my non-frizzy U.S. hair, sweet pickle relish, real Q-Tips, good linens and a store where I can buy everything on my shopping list in one place. But where's the fun in that?

They're doing something right here. I feel like this country is more free than the United States and if you're not involved in the drug trade and are cautious about what you're doing and when and where, you're safe.

I video-conference with Ginger, my best friend of 35 years, almost weekly. She's the person who introduced me to my husband/best friend, as well my old roommate/new Mexican neighbor, Nan. She has always been the adventurous, outgoing one in our friendship and has been very supportive from the beginning of this journey. After we arrived, though, she confided she never believed I would actually follow through with this crazy idea of moving to a trailer in another country. We've had several visitors (and some nay-sayers) who've come to visit us since we arrived. And guess what? Every single one of them says, "I get it now. I understand why you left and why you chose Mexico."

I'm so glad we got here before they put up that damn wall to keep us Americans out of Mexico.

Wendy Wyatt is currently retired and has been living in the Riviera Maya with husband Heath and two fur babies, Gertie and Granny, since March 2018. Born and raised in Tennessee, she graduated from the nutrition & food science program at the University of Tennessee. She also worked as a registered dietitian for 25 years and as the nutritionist for the weight loss surgery program for the Veteran's Healthcare Administration in Charleston, South Carolina. Wendy remains interested in the field of nutrition, health and the science of food and cooking. When not trying to learn Spanish, she enjoys running and biking with Gertie, paddleboarding with Granny and doing everything in between with Heath. Follow them on YouTube at "Mexicoing with Heath & Wendy."

3. "Living My Dream"

Glen Rogers
San Miguel de Allende, Guanajuato
& Mazatlán, Sinaloa

I once overheard a friend telling someone that "Glen is always reinventing herself." Although I wasn't sure it was true at the time, I liked the idea. And as I'm writing this, it appears to be true.

My first trip to Mexico was on my 15ᵗʰ wedding anniversary; we went to Playa del Carmen via Cancun. At that time, it was just a small beachfront community with a few fish restaurants and beach bars offering tequila where you sat on swings instead of bar stools. We visited the Mayan pyramid of Tulum on the coast, then drove further into the Yucatán to visit Chichen Itza, a highlight of the trip. Those were the days when this famous archeological site received only a few hundred visitors a day compared to the current count of 4,000 a day. Although I saw some incredible sites, this had to be the worst vacation of my life—and it wasn't Mexico's fault. I swore to myself I would divorce the man as soon as I returned to California. However, I hung in there another five years before jumping off into a new life.

I never felt an affinity with Mexico; my sights were always set on Europe. My secret fantasy was to have a second studio in the South of France or Italy. As an artist, I imagined myself following in the footsteps of Picasso and his crowd, spending my time in various studios depending on the season. Although I had friends who regularly traveled to Mexico and spoke highly of Oaxaca's fabulous *Día de los Muertos* (Day of the Dead) celebration and Mexico City's world-class museums, still I had not even a glimmer of interest.

A couple of years later, living the artist life in Oakland, California, I visited a psychic to see what my future would bring. She was very insightful, gave me lots to think about, and at the end of the session, asked for questions. I wanted to know if she envisioned me in that studio in South of France. "No," she said, "I see you in Mexico." Her vision included me looking down from a balcony to the street below. (A fact that has come to pass.) Although her reading momentarily piqued my interest, I didn't make any moves towards Mexico and pretty much forgot about it for several years.

I was enjoying a rich and productive life in the San Francisco Bay Area, exhibiting my paintings and prints as well as designing and installing public art projects. During this time, I often got together with girlfriends for weekend travel adventures and finally began feeling the pull to Mexico. One of our group secured an invitation to stay at the home of a mutual artist friend who had a home in Mazatlán. Although I'd had a contentious relationship with this woman for many years, I decided to bury the hatchet and let it go in order to enjoy my re-entry into Mexico. She was nothing but gracious and introduced me to the city, local artists and the surrounding areas. Through her eyes, I saw the possibilities.

We visited in April, one of the most beautiful months of the year in Mazatlán, and I have to say, it was love at first sight. Here was the place of my dreams—a historical city on the ocean that even *looked* like my dream of the South of France! It was only a three-hour flight from the Bay Area, housing was still very inexpensive and the town looked like New Orleans by-the-sea. Add to that my discovery that in the indigenous Nahuatl language, Mazatlán meant "land of the deer"—my personal animal totem—and I was in.

I went to see a realtor the next day as if in a trance and said, "Find me a little house." For under $30,000 USD, I bought a place in beautiful Centro Histórico, then referred to as Viejo (Old) Mazatlán. My realtor later told me I got the prize for the fastest sale. There was nothing special about this small one-bedroom house, but it had been recently renovated and was ready to move in. I loved that it was situated on Calle Venus (Goddess of Love!) and its close proximity to the heart of the city and Olas Altas beach. It was a great location, and you know what they say: "Location, location, location." Soon after, I added a second-floor studio with skylights and a terrace. I spoke little to no Spanish at the time, but with help from my new friends, both expats and Mexican, it came together pretty easily. Contractors are referred to as *maestros* in Mexico, and this one really lived up to his moniker. Within three months, I had a spacious, new, light-filled studio.

It was 1999 when I made that first trip to Mazatlán and bought the house on Calle Venus. My intention at the time was to keep my place in Oakland and come down occasionally—just like my fantasy. But as life happens, on one of my trips down, I was introduced to a music professor from the art school and pretty quickly fell in love. We maintained a long-distance relationship until finally I had to question our living apart. There was also another element to the equation. I'd been working with an architect as an artist consultant for 10 years on Art & Architecture projects in schools in the Bay Area. We created amazing projects such as art fences, stairwell barriers and tile projects in collaboration with students and teachers. It had been an incredible introduction to the public art field but I was ready to move on and work independently. Since these projects provided my bread and butter, I had to come up with a creative solution to reinvent myself. I decided to move to Mexico, rent out my house in Oakland and continue applying for public art opportunities.

Once I settled into Mazatlán, gone was the hustle and bustle of everyday life in the United States. Gone was the dependency on my car and the two-hour plus commute to job sites around the Bay Area. I was delighted with my new lifestyle of walking everywhere, including to the local market, or *mercado*, to buy fresh fish, fruit and vegetables. The Plaza Machado, a couple of blocks away, was just coming to life again after years of dormancy, with outdoor cafes and strolling musicians. The newly renovated Angela Peralta Theatre was a jewel and offered free or very inexpensive cultural performances, including the symphony, opera, ballet and modern dance. The beach and the beautiful Sea of Cortez were just a few blocks from my home and an 11-mile ocean front boardwalk, the *malecon*, hugged the shore where I could walk, ride my bicycle or meet friends to watch the sunset. What was not to love? I had found my Paradise: a beautiful, inexpensive place for an artist to live and work.

I was very content with my life, very productive in the studio, and like any other city I lived in, I became involved in the local art scene. However, I soon realized that Mazatlán's one downfall was its lack of art galleries, museums and opportunities for visual artists. But it was also a blank slate—you could create what you wanted. With the help of the City's cultural organization, I put together an Open Studio event in Centro Histórico based on my experiences in San Jose, California. This was an annual event to highlight the local talent of painters, sculptors, photographers and more. As in other cities, visitors pick up a map and go on a self-guided tour visiting artists in their studios and, if they like, they can purchase art directly from the artist. It was such a success that after two years, the event morphed into a monthly Artwalk from November through May during Mazatlán's high season. Fifteen years later, this highly acclaimed tour is still going strong, now organized by the city's Cultural Department and supported by the Office of Tourism and local businesses.

One day I was helping a friend who wanted to buy a house in Mazatlán when we stumbled upon an old two-story home in my neighborhood that was built in the late 1800s. The house was "For Sale By Owner" (*Trato Directo*), so we got a tour by a cousin of the owners. We walked through the space and out the back door into a big yard with trees, a patio and a garden that made my heart stop—all things I was missing in my little house. I held my breath until my friend said he wasn't interested, and then I blurted out, "Good, this is *my* house!" It needed some TLC, for sure—in fact it was flat-out ugly—but I could see the possibilities. I envisioned the upstairs as my studio—three spacious, light-filled rooms with its own street entrance—and that balcony to look down on the street below that the psychic predicted years before. The downstairs had 20-foot ceilings and original beams, called *vigas*, but no sign of a kitchen and the bathroom was in bad shape. The façade had been modified to a 1950s contemporary with ugly green stone and the original arched windows and doorways were plastered over. Friends who saw it thought I was crazy. It was not a pretty picture.

Although it took two years to purchase the property because of unclear titles (a common occurrence in Mexican real estate), it was well worth the wait. After a lot of *mañanas* and *proxima semanas* (next week), my Mexican boyfriend convinced me that I would never get that house until I went to Mexico City and met the owners face-to-face. He was right. I flew to Mexico City, and with a friend as translator, met with the couple and their attorney to sign the papers.

Viejo Mazatlán had been virtually abandoned in the 1970s and there were many ruins begging to be restored. By the time I arrived, INAH, the *Instituto Antropología y História*, had declared the area a historical district and required a permit to renovate. I wanted to comply with the rules, but the young sergeant at arms did not make it easy. When I wanted to re-create the arches inside my home, he said there were no arches in Mazatlán, even though one could clearly see the delineation under the cracked plaster. But after a while, he left me alone with my local *maestro* (contractor) to transform this ugly duckling into a swan. I loved the challenge and enjoyed designing everything from the kitchen and bathrooms, with gorgeous Talavera tiles, to the iron work, where I incorporated my sculptural motifs. Using lots of orange, yellows and reds on the walls throughout the home, I warmed up this neglected beauty and brought her back to life. The last detail was to finish the patio and gardens and add a lap pool with my signature spiral design in the tile work. I sometimes hear complaints and remorse from other expats about renovating in Mexico, but I had a great experience and made a lasting ally with my *maestro*, Tino, who will still come running at my smallest request.

Now that I had a larger studio, I could offer workshops in monotype printing as a way to support myself. This was a specialty of mine in the Bay Area and I had envisioned setting up my studio for classes here. This was dependent upon moving my etching press, which literally weighs a ton, from California. I bought a small open-air trailer that I attached to my van and, with a girlfriend, drove it down across the border at Nogales. Going through the border has been a scary thing for me after a bad experience moving art for an exhibition. Basically I learned to be creative with the true value of my contents. With my press in tow, I went through the "nothing to declare" lane. Of course I was stopped and had to pay duty on the press, but it was less painful than going the official route. Getting the press up to the second-floor studio was another challenge but was solved by hiring five of the local car wash guys from down the street to push and pull this huge, heavy hunk of steel up the stairwell.

I had my first "Monotype in Mazatlán" workshop in 2007, specifically marketed to printmakers from California who wanted an art vacation. I've now expanded this fulfilling and successful venture to other great Mexican cities like Oaxaca, Guanajuato and San Miguel de Allende, and also Peru.

Unlike Puerto Vallarta and other popular Mexican destinations, there were no real art galleries in Mazatlán when I arrived and still there are very few. After living there for almost 10 years, I'd bought a little house to renovate for a rental, and then, at the last minute, decided to try it as an exhibition space. For four years, I ran Luna: Arte Contemporáneo, a gallery where I exhibited my own work as well as my favorite area artists. Owning a business in Mexico had new and different challenges: getting a working visa, hiring an accountant and reporting to the local tax authorities. I had a lot of support from friends who volunteered and we staged monthly exhibitions that were well-attended and much-anticipated. These were exciting times!

Through the gallery, I organized a number of interesting events that benefited the local artists and got a lot of attention in the community. We did steamroller printing in the street with the help of the Cultural Department, who secured the steamroller. Large four-foot woodcuts were created by 20 artists and later displayed at Luna, the Angela Peralta Gallery and the Día de Muertos celebration. The public enjoyed seeing the printing process unfold before their eyes. I also organized some international artist exchanges; two were with Bluseed Studios out of New York, who brought their handmade paper process to share with both professional and student artists. A select group of Mazatlán artists also had the opportunity to visit their studio in Saranac Lake where they participated in workshops, stayed with local families and enjoyed swimming, kayaking and hiking. When I was invited to produce an art event for Mazatlán's International Week, I brought in artists from GAP/Global Art Project who held beginner and advanced workshops and exhibited work at the Museo de Arte. In both exchanges, the local and international artists interacted and learned from each other, sharing their culture and art techniques. With all of these activities, I found that getting publicity for art events in Mexico was a lot easier than in the U.S. The newspapers embraced the arts and often gave us full-color spreads. I sent out press releases and participated in press conferences (in my broken Spanish) and was given nothing but respect and acceptance from the Mexicans. What a change from being virtually ignored in the Bay Area!

After 18 years in Mazatlán, I had accomplished so much as an artist and arts organizer in this community that I began to get the itch for a new challenge, a new market for my work and a new place to live. It was time to reinvent myself. The long hot summers with humidity in the high 90s were also beginning to wear me down and so I was looking for a place with a more temperate climate. I looked at Oaxaca, a city I love, but although it had the right climate and a great art scene, I couldn't picture myself there. So, following my intuition, I turned my sights on San Miguel de Allende. I'd visited there a number of times for short visits but never had an interest in moving there. When I began looking around, I honestly didn't consider it as an option, thinking that it was out of my price range. But surfing the real estate sites I found a small house that caught my attention. I went there to check it out and rather impulsively made an offer. That was two years ago, and last summer I relived my first experience in Mexico and built a second-floor studio on my new home in San Miguel de Allende.

San Miguel has been an artist's haven since the 1940s and continues to attract artists, writers and creatives. The Bellas Artes and the Instituto de Allende originally established the reputation as an artist colony and today they still provide an anchor for the arts. There are galleries everywhere but La Fabrica Aurora, a renovated textile mill, with its collective of galleries and artist studios, has become a focal point. There's always an art opening or performance to attend or an Artwalk in one of the surrounding *colonias*. There's an international writer's conference that attracts a sophisticated crowd and the city boasts a plethora of artisan crafts from all over Mexico. I'm also attracted to San Miguel because it's a spiritually-minded community with plenty of options for yoga, meditation, full moon ceremonies, etc. It's a beautiful town situated in the mountains near Mexico City and is filled with classic Old World charm like cobblestone streets and colonial architecture.

I chose my new place in the San Antonio neighborhood of San Miguel partly because it hosts an Artwalk once a year which draws hundreds of visitors and collectors. I've participated twice now and it's a great way for me to introduce my work. I had an etching press built in Veracruz for the new studio and now offer monotype workshops in San Miguel as well. I've met fellow artists through San Miguel Printmakers and other venues and have participated in a number of gallery exhibitions. This year, I'm bringing the Plastic Madness / *Locura del Plástico* exhibition I organized in Mazatlán to San Miguel, inviting local artists to create artwork from found plastic to raise the awareness of this global problem. As a member of the San Miguel Literary Sala, I've had a place to introduce my book, *Art & Sacred Sites: Connecting with Spirit of Place*, and to give readings and promote book sales. I'm finding that San Miguel is a small and friendly town where it's easy to meet people and get involved in the community.

I now have the best of both worlds, from the beach to the mountains, with studios in Mazatlán and San Miguel. I load up my car with art, my cat and clothes and make the 10-hour drive between cities in order to stay connected and maintain both households. I take the toll roads (*cuotas*) which provide a smooth and safe ride, and always take a friend for company. At this point, I'm staying the winter in San Miguel (against local logic) because that's when the town expands with gringos and the event calendar fills up. I'm adjusting to the cold weather, sometimes as low as 20 degrees Fahrenheit in the evenings and mornings, and outfitting myself with a new wardrobe of sweaters and jackets. The days are glorious and sunny and I have good heaters to combat the cold. I can easily rent out my two homes while I'm gone or use them for international house exchanges—so far, San Francisco, Barcelona and the South of France.

Moving to Mexico is one of the best decisions I ever made, and as a single woman, some would even say courageous. I tend to make decisions intuitively and follow the mantra, "Jump and the net will appear," made famous by Julia Cameron in her book, "The Artist's Way." Living in my adopted country is a constant challenge and not for the faint-hearted. We expats have to learn the system and go with the flow, from dealing with immigration to signing up for local utilities. It's true, I miss simple pleasures like browsing in bookstores and going shopping for something on a whim. On the other hand, I have affordable health insurance and a doctor and a vet who both make house calls at 6 p.m. on a Saturday night. I had no Spanish when I moved, but I continually study the language to eke out my somewhat fluent version.

Living in Mexico has been a wonderful journey that still delights and keeps me on my toes. Because it's affordable, it has provided me a way to live my dream of being a full-time artist. I'm continually motivated and inspired by my surroundings, the people and the Mexican way of life.

Glen Rogers is an artist/educator who approaches life with an adventurous spirit and a reverence for Mother Earth. Her life journey is one of art and discovery.

Originally from Mississippi, she lived in the San Francisco Bay Area before relocating to Mazatlán, Mexico in 2002 where she lived full-time until 2016. She has since made her home in San Miguel de Allende where she has developed a studio and now splits her time between the two cities. Her enthusiasm for art in community has inspired her to create projects and curate numerous exhibitions like The Monotype Marathon in San Jose, CA and First Friday Artwalk and Steamroller Printing in Mazatlán. Her recent project is Plastic Madness, a travelling exhibition, featuring works created from throw-away plastics to focus on this global problem.

Glen's book, "Art & Sacred Sites: Connecting with Spirit of Place," continues to connect her with audiences at museums, galleries, and community centers. Glen teaches monotype printing workshops in San Miguel de Allende and organizes Art Vacations to Oaxaca, Guanajuato and Peru. As a painter, printmaker, and public sculptor, her artwork has been exhibited internationally in museums and galleries and is in many public and private collections. Glen has an MFA in printmaking and is a member of California Society of Printmakers. Visit her website and blog www.glenrogersart.com, www.artandsacredsites.com.

4. "Raising a Polyglot"

Roxanna Bangura
Veracruz City, Veracruz

I swear the more time I spend here in Mexico the more reasons I have for my move, from how family-oriented Mexico is to how I've lost nearly 30 pounds because of all the fresh food. At this point, I should say "we." My daughter Amaris, who is now 10, is my right and left hand and my main motivation for moving to Mexico.

From the time she was an infant, Amaris was exposed to Krio (my mother's language), English, Twi (her dad's language) and Spanish. I would play programs for her in Spanish and when she was three I contracted a family friend who used to teach in Monterrey, Mexico. It was important that my child be fluent in multiple languages; I believe being a polyglot is an essential life skill to have.

I have a Mandarin tutor for Amaris, and she will also learn French and have an International Baccalaureate education, which has world-wide recognition. An IB diploma will position her to attend just about any university globally. These were nearly impossible goals for me to accomplish for her in the U.S. due to the higher cost of living. Amaris will have the opportunity to be mentored by a pilot who happens to be a woman, and learn to ride horses and travel around Mexico and Latin America. I'm willing to make this effort on her behalf because I want her to have as many options as possible in life in terms of career and experiences. I don't want my daughter to have limitations. I want her to be able to be free, independent and smart. Boxes and pigeonholes should never apply to her. This is why I had the nerve to pick up stakes and move to Mexico.

That said, the actual notion to move from the U.S. came to fruition in the fall of 2016, and we moved in June 2017, when Amaris finished third grade. Prior to that time I was a single mom whose marriage ended in 2013. I desperately wanted to move abroad but was stuck working two and three jobs to make ends meet. I simply did not know how I could move with my daughter.

In my 20s I lived and traveled in Europe and West Africa and always enjoyed immersing myself in other cultures. Fast forward to my early 30s and motherhood and marriage. I suppressed my passion for travel and life abroad during my marriage because I thought I could no longer pursue those things that made me happy. My marriage was really a slow death. I was depressed and just going through the motions, but I was deeply dissatisfied with my life. When my marriage ended I wanted to leave the U.S. again but was clueless as to how I could do it.

I used exercise as therapy and worked multiple jobs to take care of my daughter and myself. Although I managed to hold on to my house for another two years, eventually I also lost that to the bank. My daughter and I had to move in with my mother, which was a big setback. I made sure to get various health and wellness certificates and even looked into becoming an Occupational Therapist. All of this took money, which I did not have. I was at a really low point and it was hard to see my way out.

The one thing that was a constant was living vicariously through the various immigrant/expats abroad sites on social media. I used resources like Facebook to find immigrant and expat groups to gather intel on life abroad. The most influential group for me was Black Americans Living Abroad. I read stories from highly educated, cosmopolitan people who were black like me and I wanted to be just like them again. I wanted expansion and experiences similar to theirs. So as providence would have it, I connected with a sister in Mexico and became intrigued with the country. I read voraciously about Mexico, engaged in my local Mexican community and became a pest asking unending questions to my friend from Puebla who lives in the U.S. I became fixated on Mexico and knew it was going to be home for me and my daughter. For nine months, all my energy and focus was on our move. I had dreams that needed to be accomplished for my daughter, and I knew that Mexico would make them a reality.

I sold and gave away a lot of things, and packed and repacked up until the day of departure. When we first arrived in Mexico we spent a week in the capital, Mexico City, because I wanted to get acclimated with our adopted country's capital. We enjoyed the hustle and bustle of such a large city and found people to be friendly and helpful, especially while using the vast subway system.

Initially I chose Veracruz to live because I have a sister here who held my hand during and after the transition. We were able to stay with her for three weeks and she helped me find housing and work, (I teach all subjects in English at a private school and online) as well as a school for Amaris. At first Amaris attended a public school which was ideal for her to acquire Spanish since there were no English speakers. Now she attends a bi-lingual school because it's important for her to keep up with her Anglophone education as well.

I'm also connected to Veracruz because of the history of the enslaved West Africans in the area. An African freedom fighter and former enslaved individual by the name of Yanga (he founded Yangatown in Veracruz one of the first freetowns in Latin America) is believed to be from Guinea, which is where my paternal grandfather is from. Essentially all of these factors led me to Veracruz.

We've now been living in Veracruz for 15 months and have more or less adjusted to life here, but there are times when we miss fellowshipping with our community. The small city that we live in is very homogenous so we stick out like sore thumbs. People are openly curious and downright nosey when it comes to our presence here. Since we live in an area that doesn't attract many foreigners from the U.S. and Canada, Amaris and I are the cause of gossip and speculation. People inform me of my routines and where I work and what businesses I frequent. As a New Yorker this freaks me out and is so intrusive, but it's normal here. Almost without fail people want to touch our hair or take a photo with us, which is off-putting and annoying at times. Amaris has learned to assert herself and tell people NO when they ask (and sometimes not) to touch her hair.

I'm thinking I will buy property in Mexico but I don't know exactly where as of yet; I'm having a ball exploring the country. So far we've made several more trips to Mexico City, and have been to Veracruz Port, Cordoba, Puebla, Hildalgo and Chiapas. We've even gone to Guatemala. There are too many places to name that we want to visit. We're learning about life here and I look forward to many more years in *mi nuevo pais.*

Finally, I want to say that living in a culture and country that's not your own is fascinating, thrilling, exciting and hard. We have challenges and must push through. I remind myself of why I chose to live in Mexico and I press on. I will forever cherish our time here.

Roxana Bangura was born and raised in New York and received her journalism degree from Utica College of Syracuse University. After graduation, she began following her dream of traveling the world, working and living in London and going regularly to Paris and elsewhere in France. Upon returning to the U.S., Roxana worked for the federal Equal Opportunity Commission and for an organization with members of parliament from around the world, and also in the Roman Senate and other European and African governments. She travelled to Ghana and Ivory Coast in West Africa as part of conferences on development.

She is the proud mother of a 10-year-old girl and is determined that she be multi-lingual. Roxana says, "I'm here in Mexico to ensure a bright future for her." Follow the adventures of Roxana and Amaris on "The Roxana Bangura" channel on YouTube (https://www.youtube.com/channel/UCp_yrT9yYC1ah-R7XTSFrKg) and "The Bangura Chronicles" on Facebook and Pateron. https://web.facebook.com/thebangurachronicles/

5. "Exit Strategy"

Lina Weissman
Sayulita, Nayarit

"Salad bar?"
"We're going to the tropics ..."
"But people like salad. Remember, no editing!"
"OK, agreed. On the list."
"Tequila bar, delivery service, maybe some catering."
"I think we should stay away from food."
"No editing."
"Right, sorry. On the list."

My husband and I started this exit strategy conversation for at least a year before we moved to Mexico. While we certainly took the conversations seriously, neither of us ever chose to say out loud that there was no chance in hell we could move permanently. God knows what happened to this list that followed us to Mexico, hanging on our refrigerator for years, but it was the beginning of our crazy fantasy, mostly born out of desperation and boredom, to simply be living another life.

Sitting in front of my computer 12 years and a lifetime later, I find myself looking back at a journal/blog I kept about our experiences. Note that 2008, the year we moved, was before Facebook took over the world, so I wrote a blog both to record our experiences and to share them with family and friends who totally thought we were nuts. Most still do. As I look at this blog now, I'm almost brought to tears by how beautifully stupid and curious we were. I look at the pictures of my husband, son and the crazy number of animals we ended up fostering (don't even go there) and can see in our faces that sense of adventure for which we were craving.

However, I see more; I think I'm actually just seeing it now. I notice the sense of peace, of freedom, a sense of belonging that we seemed to have found so early in our relocation to another country. I wonder why I haven't noticed that before. Many animals, two homes, plenty of disasters and a lot of learning later, I think we still experience a sense of wonder, of challenge and, yes, of peace, almost every day. This is why we still call Sayulita our home.

I notice I always tell my story starting at the end. I think I do this to assure the listener that there can be a happy ending to risking your career at its peak, your marriage and your child's health, welfare and education for what can sometimes appear as a selfish act. So, to put you at ease, rest assured that we live in a lovely home, we're both still working and have tons of fun together, we're honored to be part of an amazing community and, most importantly, our now bilingual son just successfully finished his first year of university. Please know the rest of the story has twists and turns along the way. Chronology can be boring so don't expect that. Living in Mexico is not a logical or linear process; neither is my story.

It was the beginning of our third year of full-time living in Mexico when I started to actually feel like we really, really lived here. I noticed all those feelings of newness had faded somehow as our lives in our adopted country continued. My need to document and photograph strange events waned, as they simply became less strange. I felt comfortable finding things, knowing how to pay bills, how to solve minor nuisances. I could almost pretend my natural cravings for dark chocolate and good wine had been replaced by the desire for salt and lime. The school year was beginning, the tropical summer rains were raging, bug-of-the-week season was in full swing and power outages were simply a part of life. We were feeling pretty blessed.

To celebrate our community being back together again after summer vacations, we had a big pot-luck at the house. While the adults were eating and drinking inside, the kids were running up and down the street playing in the rain and enjoying the river (otherwise known as our street) during a particularly heavy tropical storm. Suddenly, the kids came running in screaming that we all needed to come out to the street as the rain was picking up and a parked car was beginning to float. We quickly put our shoes on and followed the kids outside. I'd never seen our street so full of water; a car parked nearby was indeed already being overtaken. Many of us had experienced several tropical storms by then and were past the shock phase of seeing the kind of damage that could be done. We grabbed shovels and chains and a friend went around the corner to get his big truck that had a winch. Working together, we dug the car out of what was quickly becoming a mud pit and moved it to a side street that was a bit higher. As quickly as we'd reacted, we went back inside and continued the party. I think the kids gave up on playing in the mud and went upstairs. We were becoming experts at living abroad, or so we thought.

The following night, I remember being woken up by a big rumble that made me think the earth had broken in half. I told myself it was probably just a fallen tree, which happens all the time during tropical storms. However, the rumbles continued and seemed to be getting closer. I got out of bed and looked in front of our house. I still vividly remember the fear in my bones as I witnessed large boulders from the canyon up the street being swept down in a torrent of water that appeared to be several feet high and rising quickly. Because of the storm the night before, everyone in our neighborhood had moved all the cars normally parked on the street to higher ground, so the boulders didn't have much to impede their progress.

I quickly ran to wake up the family so we could decide what to do. My son was nine at the time. We went downstairs to inspect the situation. The water was about three inches from our front door and already beginning to seep in the back patio doors. My son grabbed the squeegee—an important household item in the tropics—and my husband and I each got brooms. We spent the rest of this long, dark night keeping the water out of the house, picking up rugs and furniture on the first floor and keeping an eye on the front door. In reality, if the street water had gotten high enough to come in the front door, there was nothing we could have done. The storm stopped a bit before dawn and we all retreated upstairs to finally get a little sleep.

A spooky silence hung over the town the next morning as we all put on our rain boots and coats and walked around to see the damage. Our road was about two feet higher and filled with mud and rocks; another inch and a half and all of this would have been in our house. Our back hillside had collapsed and fallen into our pool and back patio. The house across the street was completely flooded and filled with a few inches of mud. Needless to say, there was no electricity, cell or internet in the whole town. That first day was spent helping neighbors dig out front doors and vehicles. Most couldn't access clean water as the electricity was off so pumps weren't working. At the end of the day, we still felt isolated but also lucky—we had access to water in our pool, our house was spared and we were able to help others. We slept a well-deserved rest.

When we woke up the next morning, we realized the real damage the storm had caused. As folks started to get past their own trauma, they began to learn and share what had happened to others. Homes located in Tamarindo and Nangal, the poorer neighborhoods along the main river, were completely flooded, and belongings and people had washed downstream. Luckily, all had survived and then returned home to find mud and silt deposited often up to window sills in their homes. Those just a block away from the river experienced a street elevation of three to four feet, which quickly took over their homes and yards.

Within 48 hours, we organized crews to dig out homes with shovels, and once the electricity was back on, we used power washers to try and clean out the mud and the mold and bugs that the mud had quickly attracted. We literally went home by home. School was obviously not happening during this time and my son's days included digging mud from homes less fortunate than ours. After a few days, maggots set in to the remaining homes that still had mud in them and the work had to be abandoned. Instead, we created a kind of emergency donation center where folks could bring clothes, shoes and food to be given to those in need. I still remember the families I brought food to, and I have a special place in my heart for one family who'd lost about 80% of their home in the Tamarindo area. They did accept some food, but when I tried to give them shoes for their child, they explained they thought others were actually more in need and perhaps they could contribute a pair of their own child's shoes as she had two pairs.

I realize I'm telling this story to illustrate just how different life can be in a foreign country, especially when you least expect it. During this flood, the swine flu epidemic, the washing out of the Ameca Bridge (which connects the states of Nayarit and Jalisco), impending hurricane threats and many more disasters, there was a complete and utter lack of official support, and folks simply fended for themselves. All your expectations are shattered. During the floods, I think we, and the other foreigners, kept waiting for the "cavalry" to show up, some sign of government or not-for-profit presence. We wondered, where were the Red Cross helicopters!? None of those things happened then or during any other community crisis.

The local Mexicans never expected official help and didn't wait for it. They took care of themselves and were grateful for what they had. Government support is not only not expected, it's often not wanted, as officials are simply not trusted.

The day I had to explain how to interact with Mexican police officers to my then 10-year-old son was a doozie! Most of our time spent here in Mexico as a family has probably been spent like families all over the world. We shop for food, pay our bills, work, enjoy family time, discipline our child, do homework and make plans for the future. There have been plenty of times I've probably forgotten we were actually in Mexico or raising a son in another country. Even now, it can take life's extremes, both good and bad, to help remember where I live. I've seen sunsets that must have been painted by hand. I've experienced intense and true connections with individuals from all over the world. I've seen a turtle giving birth and been there to help ensure that her little ones make it back to sea a year later. I've seen a friend die in a Mexican hospital that should not have. And I've seen a friend saved in a Mexican hospital that I think an American doctor would have given up on.

Probably now I should actually tell you my story. Folks always want to know how I moved here, the actual moment and decision.

For me, this wasn't so clear; I kind of moved here by accident, as in the definition of a non-intentional act. I was living quite a lovely life in Northern California; both my husband and I had full-time jobs we enjoyed, our son was enrolled in a wonderful public school and we had just remodeled our second home and had a terrific, close group of friends. My husband was a teacher at the time and we'd heard the union was about to stop giving out sabbaticals due to budget cuts. He had a lot of seniority and was eligible. I was working too many hours in a rewarding but very stressful job. While we both felt grateful for the life we'd built, I had spent the last two years of my life finding relaxation in reading about other people's adventures, starting with "Shooting to Boh" and ending with, I'm embarrassed to say, "Eat Pray Love." I wrote and submitted my husband's sabbatical application because I was just that desperate.

When the sabbatical was accepted, I went into my boss's office and told him about this amazing year-long adventure we wanted to have and offered to either quit or work part-time remotely; up to him. After getting over the initial shock, my offer to work part-time was accepted. The "Coolest Boss Ever" award was thus created.

I arrived in Sayulita in July, the beginning of the rainy season. My husband, son and I lived in a 600 sq. foot home we'd built several years earlier. We'd traveled in Mexico for almost 20 years before finding Sayulita and deciding it was a place we could eventually retire to. We built a small home to rent and stay in when we visited. Part of the reason we decided to stay for the year when we did was to help open an ecologically-minded, bilingual school in town. Our son was enrolled in the fourth grade for that year.

Somewhere in the first two months I somehow decided this was where we really needed to live. I cannot actually remember the moment, it just seeped in. I didn't share this thought with anyone, though, not even my family.

Shortly after my son started school, we built a chicken coop and got baby chicks. In Mexico, one does not order chicks online. One mentions to someone who lives in San Ignacio that having some chicks would be awesome and they show up. My son's new school had no after-school activities at the time so he paraded home with

54

kids every day to sit on a bale of hay and play with the chicks. Those first few weeks we had to keep a close eye on the chicks as the *malla*, or fencing, we'd used was just not small enough to keep them safely inside and the cat who'd adopted us seemed to always be nearby. You can do the math.

While watching the chicks one day, my husband had what we fondly refer to as the "chicken epiphany:"

"Lina, I just had a thought."

"What's that?"

"We need to stay here."

"What do you mean?"

"We need to move here, like really, not go back."

"Yeah, I know," I responded, because I already did.

And so we stayed.

When I first moved to Sayulita, it was pretty much still a small fishing village. All the roads were dirt, national tourism didn't really exist and foreign tourism was limited to a short season of December through March. Everybody knew everybody; it was a regular small town with all the politics, *chisme* (rumors, gossip) and limited resources you find in small towns anywhere. I spent the better part of my first year here making soap, laundry detergent, crackers, bagels, etc. Pretty much anything that was not a corn tortilla, a cucumber, onion or any kind of pepper could simply not be found here. I used to joke that part of me had always wanted to live in the 1800s, and well, here was my chance. There was no local government ... okay, maybe there still isn't. I referred to Sayulita as the "Wild West" partly to poke fun and partly to honor its craziness.

Sayulita then, and somewhat today, functions despite itself. But from the beginning, Sayulita held for me something I was unable to find in the U.S. or in my 20 years of traveling; there's an international community here that holds a collective sense of tolerance and is truly invested in quality of life, the outdoors and alternative approaches to solving problems. While Sayulita now boasts an abundance of real restaurants, a full-fledged tourism industry and some paved streets, it's still my town. When I first moved abroad, someone told me the locals wouldn't accept me for at least five years. I absolutely swear to you it was just about that five-year mark when the locals started looking at me differently. Blank gazes suddenly turned into knowing glances as folks nodded and said "*Adios!*" as we passed by each other and sometimes there were random hugs and kisses in greeting. I'm sure many people were thinking, "We might be stuck with that *gringa*," or "When the hell is she leaving?!"

One of my favorite Mexican moments happened during Mother's Day two years ago. I was meeting a friend in front of El Club and got there first. In the lot across the street, they were clearly setting up for a Mother's Day event: a stage, sound system, chairs and everything. Mexicans do celebrations big! A few minutes after I got there, a group of mothers arrived in a car and started handing out individually wrapped roses to all moms joining the event or walking by. They were all chatting and hugging and just celebrating the day. I was thinking about how people here really embrace holidays, particularly those connected to family.

I was sitting in my car watching this like a fly on the wall and women were all around me; I was kind of invisible. Then it hit me; No matter how long I live here, I will really never be a part of this. Language and culture divides are huge and I just have to get what I can and appreciate from afar. The second that popped into my head, the group of women suddenly looked at me, walked over to my car, knocked on the window to get my attention, handed me a rose and said, "Happy Mother's Day!" While Americans build walls and mistake noise for joy, Mexicans build bridges and celebrate life. We have much to learn.

About four months into our adventure in Sayulita, I wrote a list of "Top Ten" likes and dislikes about our move. I'm shocked how many of them are still true!

Things That I Love
- Having chickens
- Not being cold
- Hanging laundry outside to dry
- Walking through town and knowing folks
- Having time to do things

- Exploring new areas
- Learning Spanish
- Meeting characters and drop-outs
- Going to exercise classes
- Doing something completely different we never thought we could do

Things That Are Way Annoying
- Bugs, bugs everywhere
- Sweating through everything
- Not ever getting whites white (how do the local moms do it?!)
- Leaving friends at home
- Having it be too hot to do things
- Not understanding enough about the culture to not make a fool of myself
- Not knowing enough Spanish to really communicate everything
- Meeting weirdoes who think they're cool
- Running into scary dogs with no one watching them
- Thinking that our adventure might be over someday

After almost 12 years of living here full-time, I no longer fear that our adventure will be over. I'm living my "bucket list." Like most working folks and parents, I still have to remember to take time to enjoy, but I now have the time to take if I want it—and the perspective to know the world will not fall apart if I do. (Oh, and the local moms finally told me that a combination of salt, lime and sun can make anything white again.) Even after so much time here, I still feel frustrated that I can't fully express myself in Spanish. But it's more than that; the longer I live here and the more Spanish I speak, the further apart our cultures seem to be.

I know that's not what you expected to hear, but it's my experience. The subtleties of language and culture are not to be underestimated. It's easy to translate words and sentences. But even with perfect diction, these words change their meaning based on context, relationship and facial expression. Sarcasm,

57

humor and intent are tricky to express. The most polite tenses and phrasing are only learned by a few. The definition of family in Latin American cultures is different, as are understandings of community and time. We Americans are famous for bringing our capitalistic, individualistic and efficient moral judgments out to the rest of the world and expecting them to be truths. Being an immigrant in another country teaches one, if nothing else, that all your assumptions are simply that: assumptions.

In my time here, I've seen a lot of people come and go. Most tell me they're here forever; most are not. Do you know what still amazes me? Folks from around the world move here to change who they are. I've seen folks move here to forget they have a bad marriage, or to forget they have a mental health issue. I've had the sad experience of working with a family who moved here to forget that their child had a serious learning disability. In all these cases, after the expected three- to four-month honeymoon period, each and every one looked in the mirror, and guess what? There they were, still and again, problems and all. Surprise!

I don't think I moved here to change; I moved here to be myself. We often talk about what our family would be like if we'd stayed in the United States. To be honest, I think we would be very much the same. I think we'd still be married, live in a nice home, our kid would be in college and we would have a tight community.

But I also think we would have missed out. We're healthier, more relaxed and less judgmental. I grew up in a Jewish middle-/upper-class home and lived and worked in the Bay Area. I could not have been more politically correct. My "bubble" consisted of people just like me. I think I was lying to myself when I said folks who had different lives were just fine. I didn't know these people, really; how would I have?

Here, I'm exposed in close quarters to people quite different from myself. Maybe they're not educated, maybe they barely work and maybe they speak a different language. But they're my friends. In a world without borders, we've raised a bilingual, bicultural son who feels comfortable in different settings and with different people. Taking yourself outside of your comfort zone helps you learn who you are as you can see which traits travel with you across those borders and which are simply left behind. Chances are the characteristics and traits that follow you in your travels are truly you. When you look in the mirror, there you are. There are certainly other ways to get out of your comfort zone and discover yourself besides relocating to another country. Whether it is for a year, a week, a day or a moment, try it out.

The other day I loaded up our three dogs and went to a nearby beach. It crossed my mind as I was pulling out of the driveway that I might have once thought twice about going to a quiet beach all by myself and feeling comfortable. Now, it's just something I do. When we got there, we were quickly joined by two other dogs who know us. With now five dogs in tow, I walked down the beach, cooled off in the water, chased birds (OK, that was them, not me) and finally plunked down under a tree to take advantage of the shade. I ate the sandwich I'd packed, gave the dogs some water and sat back to relax and read the book I'd brought.

About a half hour later, my dogs ran and barked at some folks walking toward me. I stood up to find out what was going on and a lovely Mexican man stood in front of my dogs and asked me if they were *brava*, or aggressive. I said no, but that the little one was a little nervous, my standard response. We started chatting and he said I had a lovely spot. I said, yes, it's lovely but it's not mine (referring to the house behind where I was sitting). He nodded and smiled, and then he and his family of about 30 joined me under the tree. Like all good multi-generational beach picnics, they had a cooler, fishing reel, a small BBQ and a speaker. I returned to my chair with my dogs as they set up camp. Some of the children came over to pet the dogs, ask their names and share their own pet stories. One of the young parents came over with his toddler and together we labeled dog parts for the little one: *cola, boca, naris* (tail, mouth, nose) … *quieres darles besos?* (Do you want to give them kisses?) After a bit, the kids were busy playing, the dad took his toddler in the water and the rest of the family started fishing, relaxing and socializing. My dogs were in the middle of all of them; nobody seemed bothered. I picked up my book and returned to my reading.

Once a practicing psychologist, Lina now lives with her family in Sayulita, Mexico and dedicates her time to random acts of volunteerism, whether they want her or not. Her passions include anything to do with the environment, good food and traveling. If she's not at home working, you can find her in town bothering people to get off their you-know-what and do something for the community, pretending she knows what she's doing in Pilates class or plotting some type of fundraiser. Lina loves taking her dogs to the beach, cooking for friends and spending time with her family. She is the proud founder of the local farmer's market, Mercado del Pueblo (http://mercadodelpueblo.org/) and Eco Sayulita, a community group focused on ecological projects in and around Sayulita.

6. "Bagels, Bats & Bikes"

Susie Morgan Lellero
Mazatlán, Sinaloa

In 1996 I was living what some would call the American Dream. I had a cushy job with seniority at the local hospital in Longview, Washington, a brand-new, custom-built home in the country on two acres, a new car and all of the material possessions a girl could ask for. And I had a very pleasant and handsome (albeit unbearably dull) husband. From the outside it appeared I had it all. And yet ... and yet ... something was stirring inside of me that made me feel like a caged animal. My perfect life was not a fit for me, and yet I didn't know what I wanted, either.

In September of 1996 my mother invited my sister and I on a two-week "girls' trip" to Mazatlán, Mexico. That trip was the beginning of the end; or better said, the beginning of the beginning. I felt alive there. I felt free there. I adored the beaches and the warmth and openness of the people. When the time came to get on the plane and go home I was inconsolable. I felt as if I'd left a huge part of myself behind. Once we arrived home my sister and I began to fantasize about moving there. It was obviously a pipe dream. (Or was it?). After all, what could a couple of non-Spanish speaking foreign women do to survive in Mexico? Hmmm ... what could we do? WHAT could we do?

I've always been very much in tune with my dreams and this occasion was no different. One night I woke up and realized that opening a bagel business was the key. Only God knows where that idea came from! Thinking back, it was just such a ridiculous and

61

random notion. But there it was. Bagels in Mexico in 1996? Yet instinctively I knew that was my "calling." I had no clue how to bake, but I bought a book titled "The Best Bagels Are Made At Home" and began to practice. I invoked the guidance of my late grandmother and asked her to sit on my shoulder while I kneaded and formed and boiled and baked. I baked like a madwoman and made my neighbors and co-workers be my guinea pigs.

Needless to say, most people thought I was nuts. I had it all, what the hell was I thinking? The only person who understood my restlessness was my psychologist. He told me that although leaving everything behind and moving to Mexico to start a bagel business was unorthodox at best for "normal" people, for me, living the life I was immersed in was what was unorthodox. I was born with wanderlust and had to follow my dream or die little by little every day.

Coincidentally, at the same time, the hospital where I worked was going through a "re-engineering" process and I was selected to be on the team. The task was to eliminate one position in each department in order to streamline work flows and save money. As luck would have it, the CEO of the hospital really liked me and we co-conspired a way for me to eliminate my own position. This came with a nice severance package that allowed me to chase this crazy dream of mine. Things were beginning to fall into place. I began working on a name for the business and the logo, and also started contacting the friends we'd made in Mazatlán to let them know we were on our way. When I shared with my very pleasant and handsome (albeit unbearably dull) husband what I wanted to do, he yawned and just said, "Okay." At that moment I knew I was choosing the right path for myself.

December 28, 1996. My sister and I arrived in Mazatlán armed with baking equipment, T-shirts with our logo and lots of enthusiasm. Things had fallen into place so quickly that I had no doubts what we were doing was going to work out. As luck (or synchronicity) would have it, while there on vacation we'd made a friend who was very influential and owned an entire block in the Golden Zone of the city. He gave us space to use free of charge and loaned us a wooden cart with wheels and an awning. The restaurant owner across the street from our apartment generously offered us the use of the big ovens in his bakery, as our apartment oven was way too small. I was baking 200+ bagels per day and needed an industrial oven. We were set!

Two Sisters Northwest Bagel Company officially opened for business on February 5, 1997. We enjoyed great success for a while, but the long hours of baking, shopping, working at the cart and passing out flyers in the evenings proved to be too much. The cart closed a few months later and I went into a partnership with a local restaurateur. A short time later my sister left and moved on to Cabo San Lucas, while I managed and worked in the restaurant. I was blessed with an amazing crew who trained me to be a decent waitress, and I hired a baker and taught him how to make bagels. My Spanish skills grew.

I felt like I'd finally found my niche. The bagel business grew and thrived and even the Mexicans started to order them. They pronounced them "beagles" and used them to make "*molletes*," a traditional Mexican dish of toasted bread with beans and cheese on top … but hey, they liked them!

Being a female business owner in a foreign country was tricky. I worked hard to prove to the employees and other business owners I was not the stereotypical *gringa* tourist in search of love and adventure. Some of the male employees found it difficult to have a female boss, especially a foreigner, but little by little we found our way and they became my family. To this day we remain friends, and they now own a successful restaurant in the tourist zone.

My partner and I made the decision to close the restaurant in 1999 because of a decline in tourism. I moved on to work for a woman who designed and sold clothing made from sarongs. I still sold my bagels on the side, but most days I was transporting clothing and models to the local hotels where we did poolside fashion shows. I was the "*animadora*" (Mistress of Ceremonies) and narrated the fashion shows in English and Spanish. When the show concluded I would help the tourist women stuff themselves into the designer dresses and wraps, assure them they looked amazing and that their fabulous frocks would be suitable north of the border as well. On the days there was a cruise ship, I worked in the boutique at the cruise ship terminal. I loved that job and actually saw many folks from my "other life" pass through as they disembarked the ships. It was surreal to have my old world and new world collide.

At the same time, I was worn out; worn out from being broke. I was worn out from feeling isolated (at this time there was no Facebook, internet phone service, nor a computer in every home.) Most summers I was one of very few foreigners remaining in Mazatlán and the neighbors in my all-Mexican barrio looked at me as if I had two heads. I was lonely down to my core and started to miss my "other life," if for no other reason than simply having enough money to buy groceries. One of the most valuable life lessons that's had a lasting impact on me is that there's zero correlation between what we need and what we want. Coming from a cushy life to being in a situation where many times I didn't even have two pesos for the bus was a leveler and deeply humbling. I hold these values near and dear to me to this day.

I often joked with the other shop owners at the cruise ship terminal that I was planning on returning to the United States soon, as I was going to get married. After they'd congratulate me, they'd ask me who the lucky man was. We always had a good laugh when I told them I had no idea. It was, after all, just a joke. What they didn't know is that I really was planning on packing up my cat and my few belongings and heading back to Washington State in the near future.

One fateful day, February 27, 2000, to be exact, an Italian crew member who worked aboard the Regal Princess cruise ship passed through the shop and asked me what frequency my cell phone was on. That still remains one of the oddest questions I've ever been asked. Ironically it was a very effective pick-up line as we got married six and a half months later. I returned to Washington State and once he'd finished his contract on the ship, we flew to Italy for an extended stay with his mother (That adventure could fill another book!) and our wedding. I was then able to travel with him aboard the ship for the first year of our marriage. He left the company a year later and we settled in Longview, Washington for a few months. A short time later we moved to Oceanside, California where I once again resumed the "normal" life of living the American Dream:

An expensive condo, new cars and a 9-to-5 job with a grueling commute. That familiar sense of wanderlust and restlessness started to return. It started as a faint feeling of uneasiness and finally grew into a relentless need to go home … home to Mazatlán, Mexico.

I don't believe in coincidences. I do believe in manifestation and synchronicity. My husband worked at Camp Pendleton Marine Base as an HVAC Technician. After seven years his entire team was laid off due to budget cuts. He unsuccessfully pounded the pavement and we grew behind on our condo payments. His unemployment checks and my job at an insurance agency were not enough to keep us afloat in Southern California. One evening I suggested he contact Princess Cruises to see if he could go back to work with them. He's a skilled technician and had been "Employee of the Month" on a few occasions, so they were delighted to have him back. In December of 2008 he flew to Italy to begin his training, return to the company and begin his six-month contract.

I remained in Oceanside, California. Alone. Bored. Restless. I found myself back in the rut of "go to work, come home, go to church. Go to work, come home, go to church." How did this happen? How did I manage to find myself at this point once again? Go to work, come home, go to church. I was miserable and lonely. My mother, sister and brother-in-law were living in Mazatlán and my husband was at sea. Well-meaning friends always promised to go out for a quick bite, catch a movie or hit the beach, but as is the life in California and most cities in the U.S.A., it never seemed to happen. People get busy and caught up in their own lives. I, too, was guilty of the same thing. There was nothing to bind me to Oceanside, so I made the decision to pack us up, lock, stock and barrel, and move us (and our two cats) to Mazatlán, Mexico. When I gave my notice at work my employer asked me if I would consider telecommuting and continue doing my job remotely. Needless to say, I said yes. It was March 1, 2009, when I arrived home. Home to my beloved city and adopted country. Once again, that was the beginning of the end; or again, the beginning of the beginning.

Unfortunately, our marriage didn't survive the long separations and we split up in 2010. We remain close friends to this day, but my ex-husband remains as closely tethered to Italy as I am to

Mexico. Moving there has never been an option for me, as moving to Mexico is not for him. *"Asi es la vida"* as we say here in Mexico. Such is the life.

Being a single foreign woman in Mexico has been an adventure, to put it mildly. There have been exhilarating highs and devastating lows, hysterical laughter and hysterical tears, proud triumphs and unbearable defeats. Although I continued to march forward in my day-to-day life in Mazatlán, I still felt a nagging disconnect for the first couple of years I was back. I didn't want to return to the U.S.A., and yet, I didn't feel truly at home here either. When I was here I missed the creature comforts of my "other life." When I had to travel to California for my job, I felt like a fish out of water. I felt lost and vaguely uncomfortable in my own skin. Where did I belong?

There are enormous challenges to living in a foreign country. For starters, the language barrier was, and still is at times, daunting at best. There's much to be said for being immersed in a sink-or-swim, do-or-die situation. The survival instinct eventually kicks in and we do find our way if we're persistent. Learning the language has been a double-edged sword. In my first few years of living here again I knew just enough to get me into trouble and not enough to extricate myself from it. I'll never forget one of the most embarrassing blunders I've ever made. I lived across the street from the Art Museum, where there were two large trees in the plaza in front that were home to an assortment of some birds, but mostly bats. Since I was on the third floor, the bats would occasionally fly into my apartment, but usually would do their business on my patio furniture. At that time I had no idea what the word in Spanish is for bat (it's *murcielago*) and asked a friend to help. He told me that bats are called *"vampiros"* ... "vampires" in English. That made perfect sense to me and I was excited that I'd learned a new word.

One morning I was cleaning bat poop off the cushions (*cojines* in Spanish) on my patio furniture. The precious old man who cleaned the plaza called up to me and asked me what I was doing. In my very best Spanish I proudly explained to him that *"Estoy limpiando mis cojones porque los vampiros cacaban sobre ellos."* In other words, I told him I was cleaning my testicles because the vampires pooped on them. I immediately realized my error, but it was too late. The expression on his face never changed and he continued to sweep while staring into space. He was cordial after that, but never overly friendly. I can't even imagine what was going through his mind.

Learning to speak the language fluently has been a priority for me. Although there are many English-speaking doctors, waiters, insurance agents and so on, it's empowering to know I can go anywhere and communicate effectively, even if I do continue to make epic blunders (and most of them are still of a sexual nature). Learning to speak Spanish has opened opportunities for me as a single woman that many single women in my age group don't have: The roller coaster world of dating Mexican men. Oh God.

Dating in Mexico requires skill, intelligence, above all patience, a thick skin and plenty of self-esteem. The Mexican men are handsome and charming and contrary to popular belief, are not all "womanizers." I've preferred dating Mexican men as opposed to age-appropriate *gringos* because my afore-mentioned fellow expats chase after the gorgeous younger Mexican women. Actually, much of the time it's vice-versa, but that's better left for another book. Ahhhh ... dating in Mexico. Ironically, the very attributes that a strong-willed, independent American woman needs to date a man from another country, culture and mentality is what makes it a challenge as well. The macho mentality is alive and well here. As much as many of the men like to think of themselves as progressive and open-minded, the macho mentality is in their DNA, bless their handsome, charming hearts. I've cried more tears and felt more joy than I ever did in my "other life," but continue to be open to the possibility that "Señor Right" will find me one day. In the meantime, I'm not looking, and I continue to enjoy my life to the fullest.

I've been blessed to have had the opportunity to work remotely. After living here for six years I was laid off from my insurance job in California and decided to try my hand at the restaurant business once again. Along with a romantic partner, we opened Casa Q, which sold "Bagels y Tacos y Mucho Mas!" (Life advice: Never go into business with your sweetheart. It's a relationship killer.) My house had a long driveway where we put the tables and chairs, and we rented one of the *locales* (storefronts) in front of the house as a kitchen. We had decent success for a few months, but the grueling hours and stress on the relationship forced us to close. Luckily, I've since found another job working remotely and most days I work in my pajamas. I wonder, how did I ever survive working in an office environment?

Living in Mexico has brought me many incredible opportunities I'd never had before. Since I live in a tourist town, there are always tourist activities to participate in. I can do as much or as little as I want. There are miles of beautiful beaches where I can sit under an umbrella and drink beer with my *compadres* or take a catamaran to one of the small islands to enjoy the day. I can zipline, parasail and hike. But the most life-altering thing I've done is buying and learning to ride a motorcycle ... a BIG motorcycle! I can't imagine my life without it. I laugh when I think that this 62-year-old woman belongs to a motorcycle club, complete with leather vests and patches (and a half-sleeve of tattoos on my right arm). I live to ride and ride as much as possible. It consumes me. Most weekends I ride with a group of friends out to some of the small outlying villages. We ride endless kilometers, have a bite to eat and come home again. As fun as it is to discover new *pueblos*, it's all about the ride. The feeling of the wind in your face and the exhilaration of taking curves is indescribable. The opportunity to ride with "the boys" is fantastic. They watch out for me yet demand that I keep up as well. They accept me as a fellow biker and don't view me as a middle-aged foreign woman who's old enough to be their mother. (Or grandmother!) I can't imagine I'd ever have had this opportunity in my "other life."

Although I'm blessed with many wonderful expat friends, the majority of my friends are Mexican. I was raised in central California in a family with no customs or traditions. My bloodline is a mixture of European and who knows what else; "Heinz 57 Variety" is how I've always described myself. We had no traditional Christmas dinner or holidays, no family recipes passed down from generation to generation. I guess one could say we had the typical American culture, which is no culture.

Here I've submerged myself in the lifestyle and attitude of my beautiful adopted country and made the traditions and culture my own. I joyfully participate in the Mexican celebration of Day of the Dead and paint myself as a *catrina* every year. I participate in the annual Carnaval (like Mardi Gras) and even had the honor of being on a float in the parade one year. Home; I'm home. I've always marched to the beat of a different drummer and was always the odd girl with the frizzy red hair that never quite fit in. Here in Mexico, although I'm still that odd girl with the frizzy red hair, I do fit in. I'm surrounded by the love and acceptance of the amazing people here.

Like everyone, my life is a struggle sometimes and I get overwhelmed with work, bills and drama, but as I always say, life here is so much better on every level. It's freer. It's more joyful. And it's so much more conducive to making friends. I have more friends here than I've had collectively in my entire life. It's amazing to me to be able to walk down the street and be greeted every few feet by friends and acquaintances. I do believe one must be a little "odd" to survive and thrive in another culture and country. My lifestyle is not a typical one of grandkids, mortgages, IRA funds, vacations and retirement. I was never a "soccer mom" with the white picket fence and mini-van. But this oddball quirky life of mine is a perfect fit for me, for who I know I am.

When I first came back in 2009 there were times when I asked myself where I belonged. It's been quite a process, but I know now without a shadow of a doubt in my heart and soul that here in Mexico is where I belong. I can't imagine living in the United States again. This is my home; my forever home.

Susie Morgan Lellero resides happily in her forever home of Mazatlán, Mexico. When not telecommuting she stays busy exploring the highways and byways on her motorcycle and keeping her hands in the bagel business. She continues to describe herself as that "odd girl with the frizzy red hair" and lives in terror of some day being forced to join a knitting club, talk about recipes and flash photos of her non-existent grandchildren. Although her life is a series of "Gee it seemed like a good idea at the time" moments all strung together, after all is said and done, those moments, albeit unconventional, have worked out pretty well after all.

7. "The Constructs We Construct: On Identity, Belonging & Home"

Emilia Rybak
México City, Distrito Federal

Our identity, and how we construct, shape and try to control it, has always fascinated me.

I appreciate that my identity has its fair share of idiosyncrasies. First off, I am a proud first-generation American. I'm not one of those sixth-generation, been-rooted-here-for-decades Americans. I was born and raised in New York City to a mother from Ukraine and a father from Poland. (But don't let them hear me say that, since their origins no longer primarily define them; after more than 40 years in the U.S. they're adamantly *American.*) Looking back, I feel significantly lucky to have multicultural roots, since I do believe they're one of the many factors that have shaped my ineluctable attraction to other cultures, countries and languages.

My upbringing was littered with family gatherings where various relatives spoke at just-bearably high volumes in Russian or Polish. My *babushka* (grandmother), or "Baba" as I called her, used to pick up my twin sister and me from school, feed us homemade *borscht* and speak to us in an eccentric Russian/English hybrid. While some of my childhood peers had arguably been raised with "purely American" family influences and a strongly U.S.-centric mentality, I felt that my upbringing had been characterized by opinions, behaviors, mindsets and values uniquely developed through the fusion of foreign origins with American perspectives and ways of thinking. My heritage, coupled with growing up in New York City, the epitome of diversity, not only nurtured my interest in other languages and cultures from an early age, but also helped shape a strong desire to seek out diversity of thought and experiences.

I studied psychology and marketing at Duke University, driven by a hunger to understand human behavior. Duke gifted me with the opportunity to experience Latin America for the first time through a program called DukeEngage in Guatemala. The program was funded largely by the Bill & Melinda Gates Foundation, and I worked with a microfinance organization for two months in both rural areas and the country's tourist capital, Antigua. The country and all the *Guatemaltecos* with whom I lived, worked and interacted on a daily basis, from homestay siblings to co-workers to field research survey participants, were so warm, welcoming and full of life—did I really have any other choice but to fall in cultural love? On that plane ride back to N.Y.C. in July 2011, I remember making a steadfast vow to myself: Someday I would be back in Latin America to work and live in the region, and it would be for much longer than two months.

However, upon graduating in 2013, I naturally slid right into the pursuit of the what-I-"should"-dos, working in various roles in marketing and advertising in the Northeast. Clearly this was the path that achieved the very delicate balance between what my parents and society seemingly wanted from me—to make money in a stable, flashy, corporate role—and what I could see myself managing to do in the short-term without losing my sanity, right? After four years of long commutes, high stress, daunting workloads, unreasonable bosses and even a few ethically questionable business experiences thrown in for good measure, I'd had enough. I applied to the Princeton in Latin America Fellowship, which connects recent college graduates to social impact-related projects across Latin America. Upon acceptance into the program I gave my two weeks' notice at my current job and started preparing for a role in Mexico City at Endeavor, a global non-profit that promotes high-impact entrepreneurship across both developed and developing regions worldwide.

Working at Endeavor Mexico was in several ways a much more enriching experience than my corporate roles back home. For the first time in my career I felt surrounded by people who were truly passionate about what they were dedicating themselves to, creating a communal sense of purpose I felt had been significantly lacking at the large bureaucratic firms at which I'd worked. Amongst the entrepreneurs I supported, I saw the level of success that could be achieved by devoting oneself entirely to something one believed in, not simply to something that pays the bills or attracts attention on a C.V. I also could see the tangible impact that my work, and our work as an organization, had on the entrepreneurs we constantly strove to serve.

I began to gradually question and shift my perception of what a job or a career should entail. How have we come to convince ourselves that the unhealthy, unreasonable and sometimes downright immoral practices and behaviors occurring in many companies are not only permissible, but also even worth sacrificing our well-being for? For the first time I didn't felt suffocated, constricted or dragged down by the unacceptable elements of corporate life that had been slowly chipping away at me prior to moving abroad.

Certain aspects of the transition to day-to-day life in Mexico City were relatively easy to adapt to, while others, well, not so much. As a born-and-raised New Yorker, the quick rhythm and chaos of the city made me feel at home from the start, yet at times also left me feeling exasperated. I appreciated the quick pulse of the city, with cars streaming down the streets at all hours of the day. Yet I wasn't as prepared for their daily bouts of relentless honking during rush hour. I liked the unpredictability of the city's symphony of sounds, from being serenaded by the saxophone player outside my apartment on Sunday mornings to enjoying the *cumbia* melodies flowing through my window from the taco stands out front. I even learned to love the omnipresent *tamales Oaxaqueños* street vendors. Yet at times the Mexico City orchestra sounded more like a cacophony and I longed for a small sliver of silence. As my roommate once pointed out, this is a city of countless realities colliding with surrealism, an endearing blend of contradictions that I just can't help but end up appreciating. It's tough love, but love nonetheless. And to be fair, not everything took getting used to; one thing I found immediate alignment on between me and my Mexican counterparts was our mutual loathing of Donald Trump. Initially I was lucky enough to find a job opportunity that brought me to this city, but I am now choosing to continue living here because all of these challenges ultimately provide me with that same diversity of thought and experiences I had craved from an early age.

As far as my personal life in Mexico City goes, my first year was filled with some extreme ups and downs. One particularly salient experience occurred on September 19, 2017, just four weeks into my transition to life in Mexico, when we were struck by the largest earthquake to hit the city in 32 years. It was a truly traumatizing yet also uplifting experience, a very difficult juxtaposition of emotions to handle all at once. After accepting the initial feelings of hopelessness and dejection from seeing the extensive damage to my neighborhood and watching one-too-many news segments announcing the rising death toll, I went out to volunteer. I was astonished to see how many people had not only felt but also acted upon a personal responsibility to help with the rescue and clean-up efforts. It truly felt as if almost every *chilango* had showed up to help their neighbor. Being a small part of this movement of strength and solidarity cemented a highly unique bond with the city I've called home over the last year, a connection I most likely will never experience again with any other city.

Once the city had rebounded and gone back to "normal"—more or less—I was lucky enough to take part in some of Mexico's most exhilarating events in 2018, like watching the Mexico/Germany World Cup game and the ensuing several-hour celebration my friends and I had upon Mexico's historic win, which we kicked off alongside the parade of loud and proud Mexicans dancing, singing, screaming and hugging at the Angel of Independence. Or Andrés Manuel López Obrador's historic win in the July presidential election, with hordes of people swarming into the Zócalo to hear his acceptance speech in which he affirmed that he would listen to, serve and respect indigenous communities. My roommate and I sat glued to the TV with tears silently rolling down our faces, utterly moved by the shift in tone of the leadership of the country and what it would mean for marginalized individuals.

Then when the holidays came, I was touched by the utter kindness of my roommate and his family when they offered to take me in for Christmas, opening their home to me while I was still in the process of trying to create mine in a new country. And when I had the chance to begin exploring beyond the bounds of the city, I began discovering just how multi-faceted Mexico's culture truly is; from eating *tlayudas* in Oaxaca and taking in Hierve el Agua at sunset, to eating homemade *pozole* on New Year's at a friend's house and celebrating with his family in Guadalajara, to touring the Lagos de Montebello in Chiapas with a local 15-year-old guide. My first year certainly hasn't been boring by any means, and I can confidently say the positives have outweighed the negatives.

I'm tremendously grateful to have had countless coworkers, friends and acquaintances who went out of their way to help me in times of need, who welcomed me into their circles and who gradually helped me begin to build a comfort zone and ultimately a life here. I'm so glad to have chosen this truly amazing and beautiful place to call home, and this equally fascinating city as part-microcosm, part-anomaly of the country as a whole. To friends, family and strangers alike, whether you're interested in coming to Mexico to visit for a few days or to settle down for good, please come and experience more than just a resort in Cancun. I promise there's a whole world waiting for you if you just open your mind and eyes to see it.

I've come to realize that making the transition to living abroad was such a colossal challenge at first because it meant not just leaving my comfort zone, but literally living outside it 24/7. Each day I completed entirely outside of my comfort zone was like overcoming a mini challenge. Each time I experienced a small personal or professional win, it was like taking one of the bricks in the walls of my original comfort zone and moving it to construct a much larger, much more diverse one. Creating a semblance of a new comfort zone in a foreign culture ultimately became one of the most rewarding and enriching aspects of my life abroad.

The new comfort zone is still not complete, and probably never truly will be. Yet seeing how much it has evolved and expanded over the last year shows me just how much personal growth I've achieved; a unique and intense level of personal development I'm convinced would be absolutely unattainable if I'd remained in my native country, with my native culture and language. It has been nerve-wracking, baffling and downright exasperating at times to try to embrace a new culture, language and political and economic climate, but successfully navigating this process has been equally invigorating. I feel like a ball of clay, taking a certain shape one day only to be molded into an entirely new one the next, professionally, personally, socially, mentally or culturally. I've grown thicker skin. I've become more empathetic and less judgmental of other lifestyles and viewpoints. What better experience to have when you're young, not yet settled down, not 20 years into a career and not yet overwhelmed by regrets and "what-if-I-hads?"

To live and work in Latin America was something I'd known for years I wanted to do, and I knew I would absolutely regret not seeking out the opportunity when I had the chance. But ultimately, making the decision to move abroad wasn't something that happened overnight. I can look back over the six years prior to that decision and pick out individual moments that, over time, accumulated to finally give me the courage to take the leap.

One such occasion was the vow I'd made on the plane ride back from Guatemala. Another moment of clarity came when talking to a friend about our mutual career-related uncertainty. I was discussing dissatisfaction in my job and mentioned how I'd always dreamed about working in Latin America, addressing it more as an afterthought than a real possibility. When I finished, she said she could see my whole demeanor shift when I talked about Latin America; my eyes lit up, the passion came through in my voice, and there was no doubt it was something I should pursue. I knew she was absolutely right. I'd known it all along, but time and again had brushed it off instead of truly accepting it and taking action to move towards it.

To all the young people aspiring to travel or live abroad yet hesitating due to fear, social pressure, career norms or any other reason, I urge you to fully listen to that yearning rather than ignore it. Acknowledge those moments of clarity each time they occur. I had made a vow to myself to come back to Latin America, yet in the subsequent years I saw myself getting sucked into the what-I-"should"-dos rather than prioritizing what I knew was right for me both personally and professionally.

There are so many excuses we can make for being unable to pursue a life abroad, but too often the sole roadblock is ourselves. If you're thinking about moving abroad but feel hindered by various factors, try to look at them objectively. Are these things directly blocking you from pursuing your goal and completely out of your control? Or are they circumstances that could be overcome in some way with a bit of effort? In my experience, it was almost always the latter.

I wholeheartedly acknowledge that my viewpoints come from a position of significant privilege. I'm grateful to have had the background, resources, education and health that enabled me to embark on this journey. Almost every day I try to remind myself this is not an opportunity available to everyone, and to therefore make the most of it. I also strive to remain highly conscious of the fact that my parents made a similar move more than 40 years ago out of necessity, whereas I'm lucky enough to pursue it as a lifestyle choice.

I do think that those who have the privilege and opportunity to live abroad, even for a short time, should absolutely take advantage of it. Really. Don't just seize the day, seize the world. And I'm beyond convinced that aside from being a fun adventure or unique learning experience, this journey has helped shape me, and countless other expats, into more informed, empathetic and empowered global citizens. Perhaps it may be too idealistic, but I think that living, working or just traveling abroad are some of the best ways to reduce ignorance, enhance empathy and spark action to combat some of the world's most important issues.

Born and raised in New York City as a first-generation American, Emilia developed an affinity towards foreign cultures and languages at an early age. After taking Spanish classes in high school and college, she discovered a deep appreciation for Latin American culture during summer jobs in Guatemala and Bolivia. Upon graduating from Duke University in 2013, Emilia held various roles in marketing and digital media in the U.S. before deciding to move to Mexico City to complete the Princeton in Latin America fellowship, working at the non-profit Endeavor to help provide mentorship and support to high-impact entrepreneurs across the country. She is now living and working in Mexico City indefinitely. In her spare time, Emilia enjoys (poorly) dancing cumbia, eating all kinds of Mexican cuisine, rock climbing, kickboxing, and embarking on adventure travel.

8. "The Long & Winding Road"

Kerry Watson
Lake Chapala, Jalisco &
San Blas, Nayarit

Living in a foreign culture is like holding a mirror up to your own culture. Each discovery in the new place also teaches you about yourself, about your old place. Each word you learn teaches you something about your native culture, too. Each event that happens to you is either better or worse than your old culture, and in the end everything adds up to create an experience that's either better or worse than the place you came from. It's like the goldfish that doesn't know it's in water because it has never been anywhere else; it must leap into the air to realize it has returned to water.

Today when I watch an American TV show—it can be nearly any show, really—I'm struck by the incredible number of unquestioned assumptions and waste depicted in each scene. Waste of money and time and energy, earning and maintaining and paying interest several times over on huge houses, with huge rooms to furnish and fill that you will rarely if ever use. Huge offices that need to generate huge money to stay in business, huge cars to transport yourself from the huge house to the huge office. And the assumptions that this over-production and waste is absolutely normal.

This over-consumption and over-production means that an average person "needs" a couple million dollars to retire in order to maintain this massive lifestyle. How many people are going to become millionaires in their lifetimes? Very few—and not very many of those who strive for this carrot-on-a-stick. But what happens if you strip away most of the over-consumption and over-production down to what's meaningful and actually necessary in your life? Why, then you can retire and lead a blissful life, perhaps even retire early. Especially in Mexico.

I, too, am guilty of over-consumption and over-production. But my mirror into another culture is the reason I'm aware of it. You can read, for example, studies that "heat map" homes and show only a small fraction of a house is actually used. But unless you've been elsewhere, lived where the assumption is not "bigger is always better," you have no way to apply this learning and quickly forget about it. How many people can live happily in a house? One? Two? A dozen? Eighteen happy people once lived in the Mexican home I now call my own. Do I have 18 times more happiness than they did? Hell, no!

The cultural mirror into another culture also teaches you to question the values you were brought up with. Is efficiency always an important value? Is standardization really important? Does business always come before pleasure, work before family? You learn that there are good points and also bad points to everything, depending on what values you hold dear. When Mexicans say family first, they're not parroting words, they actually mean it. They'll drop a ladder to bring something their child needs to their school. Family IS first.

It's been a very long process of acculturation for me, of accepting Mexican culture as my own preferred culture. Starting in my 40s I spent more than a decade going back and forth, spending anywhere from six months to two years here, before retiring "a little bit young" in Mexico. (I'm younger than most retirees.) Before that I spent most vacations and holidays exploring Mexico and dreaming of living there one day. Until I moved here though, I was always juggling my love of horses with my love of being in Mexico. Let me tell you how I got here.

I grew up in Minnesota, where the dreary grey winter skies can go on for weeks without a break in the clouds. I can say without much irony that all the food is white: white pasta casseroles, mashed potatoes, white bread, white rice, lutefisk. (I'm not exactly sure what that last one is, but being a Norwegian dish, it's surely white.) I've seen white snow in June and in August, and our suburb was overwhelmingly white folks, relentless conformity, and all I could think of in high school was how to get out of this white, white place.

One day in high school my casserole-making mom decided to try a new, exotic dish for our family; she told us it was called "tacos." Tacos. Living close to the Canadian border we'd not heard of this dish before. She bought McCormick seasoning packets and taco shells and painstakingly followed the instructions. Although I'm sure it was very mild, it was the pizazz-iest food our family had ever tried. My sisters crinkled their noses at the spicy dish, but for me, it was like a party in my mouth and it triggered dreams of living where everything wasn't either grey or white.

So picture little white-bread me: Signing up for high school Spanish class was the next-most exotic thing I had ever done. I remember naively thinking on my first day of class "Oh, so we just have to learn the Spanish alphabet and pronounce all the words 'their' way, *hola* instead of 'hello.' This is oh-so-easy!" Cringe. Day two I actually learned there are words beyond the cognates (words that are similar in both languages) and that it was going to be a bit trickier than I'd expected, but I was still hooked.

What I loved about my Spanish class—and what I still love today about speaking it—was that it was communication, language, puzzle-solving and pattern recognition, interpersonal skills and culture lessons all wrapped up into one daily class. My young teacher was married to a man from South America, which opened up vistas for me I'd never before considered in our small town. You can marry someone from another culture? I was so provincial I didn't even know that was possible.

Our senior high school class trip with my BFF, Jan, was our first taste of being treated like adults. We landed in Madrid under a brilliant flamenco sun. Two blondies going to the *discotecas*, young soldiers under the dictator Franco winking at us while holding machine guns, young love discovered and lost and discovered again at the next town. A home-stay in Segovia in an unheated, cold-water flat with a grandmotherly woman taught me that you can do laundry in an apartment with a washboard and be perfectly happy with life, even joyful. Returning home to be treated like a child again was an almost unbearable culture shock, and I'm sure I was miserable to be around. I debated "what is womanhood" with my mom. I had tasted freedom, adulthood, the excitement of being out on my own and making my own decisions. Hispanic culture was forever imprinted on my young brain.

When I learned that the University of Mexico in Mexico City offered free tuition, I was ready to fly down there immediately, despite not even having airfare to my name. But my ever-practical and well-read mom could only think of the student uprising of 1968 where police had shot into a crowd of unarmed student demonstrators, and she nixed that idea. My next idea was becoming a flight attendant so I could fly to all these places. I was so determined to get out and see the world. Mom again said nope, no flight attendants in the family. I went into the military, came out with the GI Bill, went to college and eventually married one of my former college professors.

In search of sun, in my 20s we migrated south on IH-35, the central highway that goes from the Canadian border to the Mexican border. It had been solid grey skies for 45 days and I pretty much snapped. The weather improved the farther south we went, and by the time we reached Austin to visit friends it was blue skies. Austin is about a third Hispanic, so I got to keep my Spanish in practice. Laredo was only a few hours away. It was a great blend of my dreams.

Throughout my adult life I was always in a hurry to get wherever I was going, and I learned pretty quickly you could get a lot more leverage using your brain rather than your body. For example, if you work with your muscles you're depreciating and using up your body. That's a 1:1 ratio, or perhaps even less since you may be destroying your body. But if you work with your brain, you're not using it up, you're just keeping it well-exercised. If you must work 40 hours a week, I reasoned, you should try to get as much money (leverage) for that time as you could. For example, at minimum wage it may take 50 years to save up enough to retire. At 10 times minimum wage, it may take just 10 years. This is also affected by your personal spending rate.

There are only a few ways to get maximum leverage of your time, mainly being in commission sales or running your own business. So for much of my life I ran my own business, polishing off my education with a master's in business to get as much leverage for my work hours as I could.

When my husband and I discovered the venerable "People's Guide to Mexico" it quickly became our Bible. The book talked about Mexican culture, "why" they do the things they do, not just where to stay for cheap grins. With vacation time and that guide in hand, we made the 25-hour journey in a land-shark mobile to San Blas, with three drivers driving around the clock dodging cattle in the road, drivers without headlights and of course, *topes*. This was in the days before the toll roads were built, so each segment of the highway wound from one plaza to another, like connecting a game of dot-to-dot. You wended your way into town following obscure or hidden or non-existent signs, drove around the town square, then back out of town. Repeat this snake pattern dozens of times, and then you're in San Blas.

As far as we were concerned, San Blas was the cultural center of the universe. It had a special energy. San Blas is a former shipping port whose glory days were more than 100 years ago. One hurricane after another has rearranged the town and coastline repeatedly. A hurricane caused the place to become famous for the longest wave in the world, and surfers flocked to the area for decades. A later hurricane changed the underwater topography, and those glorious surfing days are but another memory. Nevertheless, the town still has special energy to me, and it still draws many people from all over the world who feel it too. I knew this was my destiny—if not San Blas, certainly Mexico.

I remember meeting an elderly American woman living happily in a stick hut near the beach on a dirt road named Las Brisas. "What a magical life!" I remember thinking. I hoped I could be that woman someday.

While still in my 20s, my husband and I managed to save up enough money working for ourselves to "retire" to San Blas in an old Ford van that we converted to a rolling home. We had nearly worked ourselves to death with our own business. We sold everything we owned, including our horses, and recuperated in the San Blas sun for months. We met young folks from around the world who'd worked hard, bought four houses and used the income to perpetually travel the world. Others who worked their way around by teaching English. Since this was the old days when Mexican bathing suits were still knee-to-chin black lumps, I sewed and sold bikinis. If at the time I were wise beyond my years, this would be where my story ends with happily-ever-after. But of course, it's not.

It was in San Blas I first heard the Mexican parable of the fisherman. This is where an insufferably smug MBA on vacation meets a Mexican fisherman who is living a perfect life fishing a few hours a day, laying in his hammock, playing with his children and romancing his wife. The only problem is that it's a subsistence life. The MBA analyzes the situation and sketches out a plan, explaining to the fisherman exactly how he could work his ass off for 25 years building a massive fishing empire. The fisherman asks what all that hard work will get him. The MBA replies that the fisherman can retire and fish a few hours a day, laze in his hammock, play with his kids and romance his wife.

This tale always stuck with me, yet as much as I wanted to, I could never just let go and trust the universe enough to enjoy that subsistence life. This may sound strange, but life was too easy to be retired in one's 20s. I'd needed to relax, but I finally got saturated with relaxation and I felt like I was rotting and dying. I spent several months convincing my husband I needed to ADD some stress in my life. I had an unsatisfied need to "prove myself," to make it in the business world. I didn't want to just sit back and crow, "I could have made it if I tried! I just didn't try." This innate need to prove myself also became the undoing of our relationship much later on. At the same time my biological clock also started ticking, becoming an overwhelming alarm clock that wouldn't shut up. My husband didn't have a need to prove himself or have a child, but he understood my needs and kindly accommodated. We went back to Austin and sold the van.

I wanted to have my baby born in Mexico, but when the time came, I couldn't manage the logistics of traveling to the border to have my baby in a clinic on the other side. This was going to be my one and only. So we had her in Austin, at home with midwives. I went back to college, worked full-time, and we built a house with our own hands all at the same time. Stress, yes; I wanted stress and it's stress I got. I wanted it all! Life became complicated and it was all wonderful and stressful and fun at the same time.

I worked my way into high tech and ended up building a good life. I lived mostly in Austin but did a stint in Silicon Valley, where I was able to own a horse again. I was lucky enough to work for several startups including Netscape. Mexico became an annual pilgrimage, or a stop on a cruise. My daughter and I learned scuba and we became avid fans of Cozumel. Each time I returned to the U.S. the culture shock was a little more jarring. The endless variety in our huge, gleaming supermarkets was overwhelming for a few days until I adapted again to being back, when it would again seem normal.

I worked in web project management at a time when all websites were custom-programmed, and I started a consulting business, Pithy Productions, Inc., which I still run today. When the World Trade Center fell, I was watching it on TV as my major client called; their offices were a few blocks from the W.T.C. and they were closing down for a few months. I was far away from New York, but the collapse stranded me and my business.

My daughter was in college now and I needed a way to keep my income coming in, so I dusted off a primer I'd written for a client about an e-commerce program I'd installed for them called osCommerce, that allows a website to accept and process credit cards. My book was the only book on the topic, and it became a runaway success! I branched out to write about other e-commerce programs, and they too were bestsellers for the genre. It was a wild ride for a few years.

I'd been meandering my way through life, had earned and lost in the inevitable tech downturns and then earned again. I spent a lot in the good times, traveling the world and indulging in crazy hobbies like track cars (I worked my way up to be a Porsche Club instructor), scuba diving and endurance horseback racing, 25 or more miles. I don't regret a minute of it.

When I saw the real estate downturn coming in 2005, I put my house on the market expecting it to take a long time to sell. But it sold very suddenly, and I needed to find a place to live while I finished another book. Mexico finally seemed like the right place, but San Blas had become too hot and salty and jungle-y for me. Same problem with my favorite dive spot, Cozumel. So I asked my mailing list of women who love Mexico where I should move in Mexico, and Chapala, Jalisco was the overwhelming answer. Only 12 hours from Laredo, Texas, or a two-hour plane ride from Austin to Guadalajara International Airport. On faith I loaded up my Jeep and my dogs and headed that way. My horse, Pico de Gallo (I call him Pico for short), stayed in Texas while I scouted out the location. He's a spicy Paso Fino, a South American breed with a special smooth gait. "Paso Fino," loosely translated, means a "fine ride."

I still remember the first time I crested the mountain pass that towers over Lake Chapala: bougainvillea bursting in color around me, the white town of Chapala shimmering below next to the blue water. I cried because it was so beautiful. I was immediately bonded to the town as I made my way down the mountain and through the shaded, tree-lined main boulevard. I can't explain it except it felt like mine, like I was coming home.

I toured stables in the Chapala area, and when I found one after a few months I drove my Jeep back to Texas to get my horse. I loaded him into my horse trailer and brought him to the border. A customs broker imported him for me, verified he had all the necessary shots and paperwork, and gave him to me on the other side. We traveled slowly, stopping every couple of hours for a rest and a stretch. Luckily my horse loves to travel. When we stopped at a hotel for the night, I inquired about boarding my horse at the local vet but they happily indicated a place in their backyard that I could let my horse stretch out.

I lived in various places around Lake Chapala, including on the secluded south side where my horse lived happily next to me in a pen I had built on the beach. My horse and I went camping into the high mountains where we rode for days and days. I finished more than a dozen technical books, mostly while gazing at the lake from my laptop, as I am right now. I also wrote columns about my south shore discoveries for the local monthly paper.

But writing is often a labor of love. It's hard to support yourself solely by writing, and even harder to amass retirement amounts. Most people don't think about this part. You must juggle multiple books to keep their life cycles and sales current. As each book is waning, you must have a new one to promote. Only half the work is writing; the other half is promoting. I had a good life, but I needed more than I was making to sustain myself well into retirement. A quip about technical writing says that it's the form of writing where you actually get paid, and there's a lot of truth to that. But I'd have to work until my Social Security days or even longer if I were to continue that lifestyle.

I'd read financial books about a subject called "FIRE"—Financial Independence Retire Early—several times in my past. It finally hit home. Maybe I'd finally matured. The FIRE philosophy is very compatible with living in Mexico because the lower cost of living can let you retire much earlier. I knew I had to make a run for it if I was going to retire before my Social Security years. It would take some massive effort. I decided to take the plunge, ripping up credit cards, "paying myself first" and getting into investing as if my life depended on it. Because it did. The FIRE method got me focused on exactly what I needed to cut free. It also taught me how to live on a specific amount of money in advance, so that when I retired I knew for a fact that I could do it, because I'd tried it out already.

I was still living in Mexico when I was recruited to do technical writing exclusively for a tech startup. I didn't even have a resume ready. I assumed that while I was in Mexico everyone had gone digital like on LinkedIn, and paper resumes were passé. But I got the job anyway. I moved back to Austin with my horse and Mexican street dog, Chuy.

I wrote like a banshee for the startup and came home each night completely wrung out. Besides hacking my finances with FIRE, my hobby became hacking my health so I wouldn't end up with wealth but not health. Some estimates said being in optimal health is like having an extra $100k in your pocket, and I took that to heart. Losing weight is worth a certain amount. Exercising is worth another amount. It all adds up to money in your pocket.

I'm too embarrassed to tell you how much money I saved each

and every week, even every day. It was crazy. It was what kept me going. I updated my financial app each week with the new number. I subscribed to FIRE publications to inspire me and keep me on track. I was pretty obsessed.

While I was doing this I downsized to save even more. Like saving on health, money saved is money earned. First I moved from a wastefully big house to a two-bedroom apartment with a garage to hold years' worth of stuff from treasures to junk. After the first year I got rid of the junk and stopped renting the garage. The next year I moved to a one-bedroom apartment across the hallway to save another $500 a month—that's $6,000 a year, just for not having a guest room to use once or twice a year. My living room was piled with boxes for a few months until I got rid of most of that, too.

I kept traveling to Chapala, looking at houses to buy, trying to "time the market," waiting for signs that house prices had bottomed, and eventually bought a vintage fixer-upper house for cash. This was at the end of the buyers' market, and I may have gotten the last good deal in the area before prices started rising. The house had been on the market for more than half a year, and it looked like it might have some foundation problems that were scaring potential buyers off. But I bet that it didn't and put in an offer that was quickly accepted.

I painted the exterior walls a vivid orange and cobalt blue and hand-stenciled motifs above doorways and windows. Since it was high on a hill overlooking the lake, I named it *Casa Acantilado* or Cliff House, and painted a whimsical picture of the house that I then had made into a ceramic plaque with its name for the front door. My new home!

Just when I thought I'd saved enough to retire young and get Mexican residency, in 2017 the Mexican government moved the finish line by changing the value at which the minimum wage was calculated. Because retirement savings are a multiple of this number—something like 25,000 times the daily minimum wage—this meant I had to work longer to qualify for residency. I tightened my belt even more so I could get it done fast. Now I skipped Starbucks, opting for free company coffee. I made my lunches every day. I kept heating and cooling to a minimum, even in Texas, allowing my body to acclimate as much as possible. I didn't buy a lot of extra work clothes. I didn't go out to eat a lot, and no pedicures or massages. I kept telling myself that each sacrifice was a thing I'd reap later in Mexico.

I kept my eye on the prize so I could retire as quickly as humanly possible. My retirement account made a beeline straight up, and—ka-ching!—before I knew it, I'd made more than the minimum amount my financial advisor said I needed. I was walking a razor's edge with my health from all the stress, so I knew it was time to go before I developed any serious health problems. Working at the startup fulfilled a life dream of mine, and I'll always remember it fondly. Maybe it will even go public, and I'll make some money from my stock.

I arranged for my horse to be shipped again to the Mexico side of the border, got a shipper to move my stuff and headed south with my dog Chuy. I picked up my horse in Nuevo Laredo and had an uneventful drive to my home in Chapala.

It feels like I never left! Many of my health issues resolved once the stress melted away. This tells me I inflicted most of my health problems on myself; that love/hate relationship I had with stress. But I at last had proven myself; I'd succeeded at my own definition of success, and I was happy.

I am so lucky to live in a real Mexican *barrio*, a working-class neighborhood full of hard-working and hard-loving people where my neighbors all know me. And I have a Mexican family here; the family next door has adopted me as one of their own. While the married couple are my caretaker and housekeeper, they're so much more. They've taught me about Mexico and her ways. They've helped me with my Spanish. And I help them, of course. We're like family.

There are a lot of new expats in the Lake Chapala area now, and it seems there are a lot more planning to come here the minute they're able to. The newer expats seem less well-prepared than in the past. They seem more afraid to speak the language and assimilate. I do worry they're here for some of the wrong reasons, like purely political or purely financial. But coming here just to escape something is not a good reason to be here. The "escapees" quickly lose the dream and leave. If you're coming here because you're drawn by the energy, by the magic of Mexico, then this is your place.

So why did I leave America? At first I was in search of wild adventure, a break from the uniformity and conformity of expectations and from the sea of whiteness. Later it was my escape from adult responsibilities, my sanity check, an oasis of sun and fun and diving.

Today Mexico feels like my home; this is my normal. It feels right to me. I get culture shock when I go north now, rather than when I come south. I get stressed when I go north, but when I return my stress disappears at the border. I feel cradled in the hands of Mexico. The land where just greeting someone on the street results in an open smile without reservation, the real person shining through. Not the tepid smile of a fake polite social mask. That genuineness alone would be worth it to me.

I wish I'd had the courage to get here sooner, but life kept getting in the way. I enjoyed the heck out of my journey, though, so I have no regrets. I wake up every day in Paradise and have to pinch myself because my vacation never ends. I love Mexico for all her foibles and contradictions. She teaches me something about myself each day that humbles me.

Kerry Watson wanted to live in Mexico since her first trip when she was in her 20s and spent her whole adult life trying to get there. After growing up in Minnesota, she earned an MBA when that was unusual for women, and worked in high tech, which allowed her to travel the world and indulge in crazy hobbies like track cars, scuba diving and endurance horseback racing. "It seems I spent much of my adulthood checking boundaries," she says. Kerry began going to the Lake Chapala area, living in various towns including the secluded south shore, and writing technical books. It was love at first sight. Finally she made the break and retired for good.

9. "Finding Joy"

Lisa D. Lankins
Mazatlán & El Quelite, Sinaloa

The moment he asked me why I wasn't working for him in Mexico, I knew I was going.

I'd felt a little sorry for myself for a couple years before that. My parents had both passed away and I was divorced a few months later. I didn't have kids, and I was feeling lost. At one point, a friend at work looked at me while I was complaining and said, "You've got to be kidding me! I mean, don't get me wrong, I love my husband and my kids and my life, but YOU are free to do anything you want!" It didn't hit me until that point just how true that statement was, and shortly after, I stopped feeling sorry for myself. I was decidedly looking to make the best out of my life, but it had nothing to do with coming to Mexico—or so I thought.

My plan was to go back to school and became a naturopathic physician or a midwife. I was looking into schools and scholarships or grants for women of my age (44), when I ran into this guy who was a good friend of my father's. He owned a small hotel in Mazatlán, Sinaloa, Mexico, and after we'd talked for a bit, he invited me to come work for him as the public relations person at the hotel.

With two good jobs in the medical field, one at a hospital as a ward secretary for almost 15 years, the other as the doctor's nurse at an OB/GYN clinic for almost 10 years, plus working on the side as a certified doula for four years, it seems like it might have been a tough decision, but it wasn't. It was about following my gut instinct, which was yelling at me that I had to go.

I'd studied Spanish nearly my entire life and the idea of moving to Mexico just felt right. I had been to Mexico with my family many times since I was a little girl. I wanted to improve my Spanish, and since I try to listen to my premonitions, I knew it was right for me. It was July when I met the hotel owner, but not until December that I went with him and his family to Mazatlán to check out the hotel and decide if I wanted to work there.

Mazatlán was beautiful. Twenty miles of palm-lined beaches. The hotel left a lot to be desired, but the house I would live in was right on the beach, with a pool. The owner let me stay in the guest quarters of his house, next door to the hotel. I figured I'd be able to make some positive changes at the hotel and would love it.

I asked for two weeks to make up my mind after spending the week there, although I was already pretty sure. Once I decided that yes, I was definitely going to do this, I felt excited and couldn't wait to get down there. The doctor I worked for asked me if I was sure. I told her, well, the worst thing that can happen is I'm back in two months, homeless and jobless, right? Life is too short to NOT take some chances. I didn't want to arrive at the end of my life with regrets for not having done something I wished I had. That goes for telling people I love them as well. I make my share of mistakes, but I don't ever regret having tried.

I gave the doctor two months' notice, since she had a small office and I wanted her to have time to find a good replacement. I sold everything I owned for pennies on the dollar in garage sales on the weekends. The plan was I would drive to Mexico by myself in a van owned by the hotel. I packed what few possessions I had left and spent the night at my sister's house to say my goodbyes to her, my brother-in-law and my cherished nephews, who were eight and 17 at the time. I figured it would be a four- to six-day trip and planned to stop outside of Los Angeles to visit my older sister for a couple of days. I drove south from Portland to L.A., over to Phoenix and crossed the border at Nogales.

My younger nephews, my sister's boys, were the toughest thing for me to leave. I felt like their second mom. The night before I left, when I stayed at their house, the two boys sat on my lap and gave me lots of hugs, a little crowded but an appropriate goodbye, at least for the short-term. They had wonderful parents, and I knew they wouldn't have wanted me to not go. They could see I was excited and happy about going.

I guess I was nervous about driving in Mexico alone, something I hadn't really thought about. Once I crossed the border, I drove to Ciudad de Obregon and found a hotel. I parked the van and literally had to peel my fingers off the steering wheel—I had a total death grip on it. The next time I made this drive, I knew I was home, and I was never nervous again about driving in Mexico.

I had already travelled quite a bit in my life and in fact had worked as a travel agent for a big tour company when I was in my 20s. I travelled as much as I possibly could and had been to Mexico, Hawaii several times, many of the Caribbean Islands, and most of the East coast of the United States, visiting New York, Washington D.C., Miami and New Orleans. My parents gave all four of us the travel bug by driving from Portland into Mexico to Ensenada every winter, stopping at Palm Springs and Disneyland on the way. Then when I was 12 we started going to Hawaii every year, with a week in Victoria, B.C., Canada every summer. When I was 20, I tried to move to Victoria, but ran into a Catch-22 with finding a job and getting a visa; they really weren't keen on having a young, single, American moving into the country.

Even though I felt that I was good to go, nothing could have prepared me for the reality of life in another country. I was also going under a different pretext than most people; I would be getting my visa with permission to work and would have no income from the States at all, and only a very limited amount of savings.

The hotel job was a bit of a mess. The employees were stealing lots of cash from the owner, which he didn't tell me until I got there. So instead of being a well-liked person, I was considered the "enemy" and treated as such. The guilty employees worked in the office and made my life really difficult, lying about me, stealing from me and threatening me. Six months after I arrived my salary was cut to half of what I'd been promised (which is illegal in Mexico, but I didn't know that at the time). Not being someone that gives up easily, I found another part-time job as an editor for a local monthly English publication to make ends meet.

I had told my girlfriends that I was going to just work and volunteer and wasn't going to go out with anyone, ever. I was serious, but they all laughed. Well, that lasted only a few months, and soon I found myself falling for a professor from Mexico City I met at another small hotel nearby where he was the manager. I went there to use the internet and cheap phone service to call my family twice a week. After six months, he was hired to teach in one of Mazatlán's most prestigious universities and we decided to move in together. I desperately needed to get away from living at the hotel; it could be a 24-hour-a-day job if I let it, and now I had a second job, too.

We looked all over the city for a house or apartment to rent, but with our incomes, the places we could afford weren't in the best areas. We came up with the idea of looking in a small *pueblo* about 35 minutes from where I worked. El Quelite was a charming place to live, and we were there for almost two years. I became well-known as I was the only *gringa* to live there full-time, and our house was across the street from the church on the main street.

I loved our time there. It was an enchanted place, with cobblestone streets, wonderful people and—fireflies! El Quelite is one of Mexico's *Pueblos Magico*, a Magical Town. Every morning as I woke up, I could hear the streets and porches being swept; the sound of brooms on the cobblestones became one of my favorite things. However, eventually it became a little worrisome for me to drive the highway alone at night coming back from the hotel. There had been some carjackings. We decided to move back to Mazatlán. To this day I dream of having a vacation home in El Quelite.

Then, after two years of working at the hotel, I was let go. The owner was listening to the thieving employees, which made absolutely no sense to me. I agree that I wasn't very effective, because they had blocked me, but he should have let them go! He didn't offer to bring me back to the States, either. Over time I was able to forgive and kind of forget, because I felt a very special connection to Mazatlán. I felt I was on my correct path, and I still do.

Never in my life before—which I now call my "other" life— have I learned so much about myself, or about other people or about what's really important. I felt like I was actually making a difference. Not at the hotel so much, but in sharing my stories in the paper I was working for about what it takes to live in another country happily. I soon had a following of people on Facebook where I also wrote about my adventures. This was before blogging was a "thing." It sounds really corny, but I've always felt that since I couldn't have kids, the only thing I could leave in this world that would make a difference was my work and hopefully a job well-done.

Since moving to Mazatlán 12 years ago, I've worked various jobs, all for very low wages. In Mexico, at least in Mazatlán, people work for salaries—I've not really heard of any jobs paid hourly. That was a huge change of lifestyle for me; huge. I had a massage business, just myself; was an English and Spanish teacher, giving private classes; and worked as a hotel manager, concierge, tile salesman, writer and editor of a local English publication. Then I had the good fortune of being hired by the city, by the mayor's wife, who's traditionally appointed as president of DIF (Integral Development of the Family) Mazatlán, as the liaison for the foreign community. I did that for three years.

If your income drops by like 90%, how does your life change? It's true that things are cheaper here, so that helps, but things you used to think you had to have—expensive face treatments, make-up, specialty foods, your favorite perfume, brand of clothes and shoes—suddenly become optional. Every couple of months I had to find ways to cut spending even further. I never once thought of moving back, though. I loved it here too much.

I didn't have a car; the van I'd driven down belonged to the hotel. Taxis, *pulmonias* (Mazatlán's open-air "golf cart" taxis) and buses were the only way I could get around, because walking very far wasn't an option with my disability (two hips needing replacements, which I did eventually get).

At one point, I tried to open a tour company with a local Mexican friend and businessman. I worked with him for a year and a half without an income, using up all the cash I did have. The month we finally opened, all the cruise ships were cancelled due to a supposed increase in violence (which wasn't really happening). I did freak out a little. I had no other option but to find work—and fast. During that time, I sold everything I had, again, including all my gold jewelry, some of which was my mother's. It was a difficult thing to do, and I still have a mini-panic attack when I think of some of the things I used to have that I had to sell.

After six years of living in Mazatlán, I'd gotten used to cutting corners to lower my cost of living. By finding less luxurious places to live, my rent went from $5,000 or $6,000 pesos a month to $3,000 and $3,500. Even that was too high for me, actually. I should have gotten a roommate, but I preferred to live alone, so that was a sacrifice, a luxury. I dealt with it.

I had to keep internet access at my home, because I was always translating or working on the internet. Determined to cut my food costs, I started eating less expensive cuts of meat, simpler, common foods, and I only drank water and coffee and a little milk. I was intentionally avoiding processed foods, which for me worked well on a low budget. I used as little electricity as possible, opting for fans instead of air-conditioning, always turning off the lights. In the summer months, when the humidity was high and it was really hot, I would turn off the hot water tank completely, saving on gas.

I did go out with friends occasionally, but not often. It was just too expensive. It was a little humiliating, honestly, because people knew I was broke, but the benefits of being on the path I'd chosen in Mexico, helping foreigners feel like part of their new home by translating important info for them, or sharing things in English that were hard to find and teaching a little about the culture, made it worthwhile.

Most people would have opted out. I saw that happen many, many times. When they realized they couldn't live like they could in the U.S. or Canada while earning pesos, they would return to their own country where they had family or still had a home. I didn't have a home back in the States to return to, but decided I wasn't giving up. It wasn't, and still isn't, that common to find a foreigner working only for pesos without another income or savings.

So how can I say it's worth it? There are many reasons, actually, but first I love the fact that my life is so much simpler. Secondly, I came to realize who I really am. What I mean by that is when you ask most people who they are, usually they answer with the kind of car they drive, a picture of their family, what they do for a living, where they live or where they go on vacation. One day when I was feeling sorry for myself, it hit me that without having all of those things, I know I'm still the same person; a good person, an intelligent, creative, strong woman with a big heart. That's who I am. I don't think I would have been able to say that before. I leaned on too many external things to see myself clearly.

When a new mayor was elected, he wiped out the liaison program started by the previous administration, where I worked in the park, and my job. I went to work for another city department as liaison as well, this time for the local cultural center, which allowed me to keep my city employee health insurance. (Thank the Gods.) But this job was for less money and a lot more hours. It was a big blow to my ego and my pocketbook.

I absolutely adored the director, but in my particular department, the manager was really difficult to work with. I kept at it though, and tried to just ignore her, staying to the best of my ability on the "high road." Basically, she was racist. She had certain ideas about what an American woman was like, which was nothing like me at all. I felt accused all the time and she rejected most of my best ideas. She was angry and wouldn't accept that I had a disability. I needed the insurance the city position provided, so I just tried to do my job and hang in there.

I've seen very little racism in Mexico. It does exist, mostly in ideas they have of us, and just like most people around the world with racist ideas, these generalizations are unfounded. I think I've seen it more often than many people because I speak the language fluently, and dive into the culture as much as possible. I believe all negativity comes from fear, so instead of getting angry, I would try to show them the reality of who I was.

Finally, after a year and a half of looking for a second job or a different job, I found what seemed like a great opportunity. I think the angry department manager thought I couldn't just quit, but she was wrong. A new city department had opened, the Center for Attention and Protection to Tourists (CAPTA). Mazatlán is the fourth city in Mexico to open a CAPTA office. I quit right away and started the new job before I even knew how much I would be making because it just felt like the perfect job for me. Again, I had a really clear gut feeling, and just like when I was initially asked to work in Mexico, I knew I was going to do it. I'd already turned down three other jobs that year, knowing they weren't right. I'm so excited about this new position, as I know this is a place where I can help people and really make a difference.

One of the biggest and nicest surprises for me personally is that after working in the English-speaking media, then working as the only foreigner for the city as a liaison, I became very well-known to the local community, both Mexican and foreign. I have contacts, friends and new "family" all over town. I feel very loved and supported in my new life in Mexico.

Many people have asked me how I could take the chance to move to Mexico without a big bank account as back-up, and for a while I didn't know how to answer. Then a few years ago I read a quote I wish I could take credit for. It said life isn't about security, but about finding joy. That's my goal, and although I do believe being happy is a decision, sharing your gift with the world, making a difference, is pure joy.

The culture is definitely different here; not necessarily worse or better. To be happy in another place, you have to keep an open mind and open heart, be open to change and learning about new cultures. If you can't learn to relax and take things slower and accept that things happen at a slower place here, you just may go crazy and become a nervous wreck. I think the best thing to do is take deep breaths and keep saying, "*Mañana* doesn't mean tomorrow, it just means not today." Now I love the slower pace. I see people come down to Mexico to live for six months, and some don't adjust well to the culture shock at all.

I love shopping in the *mercado* and having fresh seafood at a beachfront *palapa*. I adore the fantastic music and cultural scene and enjoy helping to promote that. After 12 years, I can converse fluently in Spanish. I also help people translate when they need it: documents, medical info, whatever. Sometimes I also help local doctors and police translate to English by phone, when they need it.

Moving away from what your family thinks you should be doing and not doing and what society deems "normal" can be difficult. Sometimes family and friends take it negatively or get angry. I think these emotions come from fear; fear that your decisions leave you financially vulnerable or that you're putting yourself in harm's way. Sometimes people are jealous that you're following your dreams. I encourage you to follow your heart to the best of your ability; don't crack under pressure from family or friends or society. Take the chance.

I feel very passionate about helping our two cultures understand each other. I think the best way to achieve this is to accept differences with respect and understanding, dive into the daily routine, don't be afraid to get to know your neighbors, learn the language as much as possible, ask for help when you need it and smile.

My story might sound like an experience I could have had north of the border, a story about making little money, realizing your dreams, changing your life. But I couldn't be happier that it happened in Mazatlán, where the people, the language and the culture are so very beautiful. I am many times stronger and wiser than I was before. (And the beaches and sunshine certainly don't hurt!)

If you'd told me 13 years ago I'd be living in Mazatlán, doing what I'm doing, I would have asked you what you were smoking. But life is an adventure, and that isn't just a cliché. Life is short! Do what you think you need to do to be happy. You can do it alone. Take advantage of every situation and bloom where you're planted! Will you look back at life and say I wish I had—or I'm glad I did?

Lisa Lankins is an Oregonian, born and raised in the Portland area, but has lived in beautiful Mazatlán, Mexico since 2006. She has worked in Mexico as a writer and editor of local English media for about 11 years, but now works for the Mazatlán city government helping tourists. She has always enjoyed being a liaison for the foreign community. Lisa continues to write and loves sharing information that helps both locals and expats

10. "Wanderlust"

Joanna Karlinsky
Cozumel, Quintana Roo

I tell people I left because of the election. The disappointment was unsavory. It's easier than saying I was tired. But, honestly, I left the U.S. because I was tired. Tired of working too hard. Tired of struggling to restart what had been a successful career as a chef and restaurateur. Tired of the tears that came too quickly for every injustice that hadn't changed in my lifetime. Tired of the rising cost of living in San Francisco. Tired of dealing with cancer and chemo and surgery. Tired from caring for my dying mother. Tired of my 14-year relationship with Justine. Tired of the angry rhetoric being spewed during the 2016 election. I had perspective and was going to keep it. Dammit.

Cancer gives you perspective. You are forced to imagine the worst: pain and suffering, dying before you're ready, how others will feel about you dying. Probably more important for me was deciding if I'd be ready to go, unencumbered by regrets if I did die. Others' feelings have to be considered, but, ultimately, dying is something we all do alone. And I wasn't about to let anyone interfere with my decisions. I had been willing to fight my first cancer. And again for my second. But enough was enough. Fighting again wasn't/isn't looking appealing. Leaving was a good idea, but I didn't know how.

The problem with getting perspective is keeping it. It seems most people lose it as soon as their chemo-hair curls grow out. My first cancer was a rare sarcoma, in my forearm muscle. 50/50 to recover, but no stats on long-term. Most people would have had their entire arm amputated. I recovered, after intense, in-patient chemo, a nine-hour surgery, radiation and more chemo, with full movement of arm and hand. Why? Because science. Doctors. Western medicine, Eastern medicine and marijuana. It had nothing to do with faith, though I'll concede I had "faith" in my doctors! Overall it was exhausting and I was really tired.

The second cancer was Stage 3 uterine, which started less than three months after the last chemo for the sarcoma. Not a good sign. My first oncologist's office replied to my inquiry of the likelihood of another cancer by saying it was a billion-to-one shot. But yeah … that's me. Many months later, after the actual diagnosis and going on a treatment plan, I had gene testing done. It showed lynch syndrome, a gene disorder that makes many cancers more likely to grow. I suffered again through chemo, in order to make the 10-year survival rate increase. I left the U.S. because I wasn't going to spend the next 10 years working my ass off and struggling just to find myself with cancer … again.

In between my two adventures with cancer my mother died. Her companion dog had died in old age two years prior. She was almost distraught. It was of no matter how in touch with her three adult children she was, after her dog died, she'd given up. She was frustrated, having memory lapses and dementia-related episodes. I spent most of her last year with her. Burying a lot of hatchets. We admitted to not knowing how to talk to each other. We had some fun and made each other laugh. I made her ride on a carousel and chase sunsets. We told stories about my long-dead father, sister and brother. We looked at photos from her life, Face-Timed with her sister, niece and nephew and friends. And we let go of a lot of anger. She did the best she could and it was okay. It was time for her to go. I got more perspective.

Before the cancer and mother-dying adventures I had spent a not-so-good three years trying to jump-start my career, but being over 40 in my field sucks. I consulted with others and I applied for chef and restaurant management jobs. Unfortunately when you've been your own boss for many years you're not likely to be a good fit for someone else's restaurant. You'll always want things done your way. I was no exception. I blew through savings, wondered if I was cut out to do anything else. (I'm not.) Airbnb was very helpful. Justine, my soon-to-be ex, and I listed our guest room. People from around the world came to stay. A map with red dots showed all the places guests had come from. I loved it. The world came to me while I was going through chemo. Perhaps when I recovered, I thought, I would go see the world.

After the second cancer ordeal there was anger to let go of: Why did I survive? I'd already spent a lifetime battling mental illness and abusing drugs and living on empty. It had been a wild life, full of adventures and great loves and hard work and good deeds. I was over 50, without kids or a career, about to leave my girlfriend. It would've been okay for me to go. But no … I had to watch people half my age, with little kids, new careers and long bucket lists die too young. I'd never been good at self-care. Taking care of myself seemed a good first step to recovery. Moving on seemed a good second step. Trying to find a new purpose a third step.

Planning to travel seemed a good place to start. I'd never had a bucket list. I've done so many things, have experienced so many emotions that it seemed trite. So I made a list of some things I'd "like" to do.

- Bungee jumping wasn't on it.
- Whitewater rafting in Costa Rica was.
- Hiking the Appalachian Trail? Not with my arthritic knee, so all hiking was off the list.
- See the Louvre? Was there 30 years ago. Been there, done that.
- Travel to Japan? Not enough money.
- Actually learn Spanish? Yeah.
- See the countries my employees had come from. Why not?
- Learn to scuba dive? YES!
- Learn to play poker! Check!
- Take a road trip? Yep!
- With a new friend? Absolutely!

My neighbors rented their in-law apartment to a young couple: Eric, who I immediately clicked with while bonding over New

York City (where both of us were born and raised) and his Polish girlfriend, an over-achiever finishing at university. Most of my friends were busy with their lives while I was suffering through chemo, but Eric seemed to come and go at weird times. Eventually I invited him up and we talked. At 32 he told me stories of hitchhiking and camping his way through México, Central and South America. I told him about my limited travels. And about my high-maintenance lifestyle: To sleep I need my cervical pillow, my beanbag pillow for between my knees, fuzzy socks for the first hour of sleep and I can't sleep on sheets because I can feel every crease—only a soft fleece blanket spread tight will do. And a fleece blanket on top, but it must be the correct weight for the temperature. Eric laughed and told me to "get over myself." I told him I was trying!

Eventually he told me he was a professional poker player and I was hooked. My father had been a high roller in Las Vegas back in the day. As a child I'd spent many holidays in Vegas and knew how to play all the casino games. I'd watched Las Vegas grow and it had been a go-to place for many long weekends throughout my life.

Eric was going on a road trip to Las Vegas to play poker for a week and asked me if I wanted to go too. He had a small knapsack and I had my entire car packed with anything I could possibly need. It was an awesome trip. I remembered how much fun road trips were! I was post chemo/pre-surgery with no hair on my head and a giant tumor on my arm, mentally preparing myself for a surgery that could go wrong. In Las Vegas! On the road we talked about our lives, politics, goals and poker. We went to every good Spanish and Mexican restaurant in Las Vegas that he knew so he could show off his Spanish language skills and point out my utter lack of the language. Eric suggested I consider taking my travels by car! Light bulb moment! Two years later I left for Mexico on a road trip to ... I didn't really know where, in a packed SUV.

He did his seminar during the day and taught me how to play poker in the evenings. I swam and laid in the sun in the daytime and taught him to shoot craps and play blackjack at night. We stayed away an extra two days, something I could do because I had packed my car with anything and everything I could possibly have needed.

Justine and I had three dogs and a cat. In addition to leaving her I'd be leaving them. So I told everyone I was going to take this road trip with one of my little dogs. I chose the blind, deaf one. I'd adopted this old dog so my mother could have a dog during her last year of life. Angel is not affectionate, is clearly introverted and doesn't engage with other dogs or active people. She wouldn't be missed by the other dogs. She has few needs but is really curious and very brave. I aspire to be like her. She's also very pretty and I thought she'd be a good bridge to meeting people. (I was right, she's been super-popular.) We'd drive to Cozumel. On the way I'd see the Gulf Coast of Mexico, ex-employees who'd gone back home to the Yucatán, visit Mayan ruins, swim in *cenotes* and learn to scuba dive. I told everyone it would be a three-month road trip.

And then Trump was elected. So I left. I knew I wouldn't drive back. But better to not share that part. Let friends get used to my not being there. Let them stop worrying. I wasn't worried. I had little fear and a lot of courage. This lack of fear was not a good thing when I was young. But past middle-age it's awesome. I recommend it highly.

I did have to trade in my car for an SUV so I'd have enough room for everything I needed ... I mean wanted. I had a tent, many pillows, blankets and towels, my poker chip set, playing cards and three sets of dominos. I brought clothes for the beach, mountains, cities and farms. I had every medication, vitamin and supplement a human could ever want. And a tool box, zip ties, spray bottle of bleach and ropes (suggested by Justine). Apparently she thought I was going to become a serial killer! I outfitted the SUV with a single futon for me and three dog beds for Angel to choose from in case we needed to sleep in the truck. It was decorated with boas and beads and a Mardi Gras mask I'd picked up in New Orleans. I was ready.

And then I went. With very little Spanish. One of my old employees gave me some specific lessons. He wanted me to be prepared if I was stopped by police and asked for money. So he taught me to say, "*Podria su pinche madre.*" Loosely translated that means, "I could be your fucking mother." In 18 months I've only been stopped twice, for no reason. And it worked both times. They shook their heads, smirked, took the $200 pesos I offered and walked away.

I fell in love with scuba diving. For a person who didn't think she cared much for fish it was truly magnificent. On a whim I decided to return in the fall to settle in. My diving instructor and I hit it off and she suggested I try living on the island. Since I'd decided I wasn't going to go home any time soon, this was a great idea. Now I'd found a place to settle down. I would continue south for more adventures and then I'd return to make Cozumel my new home. I'd get my divemaster license, try to get some small restaurant consulting gigs, and learn to live on a very small amount of money. Looked like I finally had a goal. In the meantime we continued driving south.

In Belize we went camping. We explored Mayan ruins and caves, did some bird-watching, visited the Mennonite community in Spanish Lookout. We picked up German hitchhikers and drove to the sea, stopping at every waterfall and swimming hole we saw. I went scuba diving off Hopkins, met many locals, ate fried fish, listened to reggae, played dominos and drank too much rum.

In Honduras I met the family of my protege, Jerry. He came to the U.S. at 16 and I was his American mama. I met his actual mama and was welcomed with open arms by his family. They showed me how proud they are of San Pedro Sula—one of the most dangerous cities on the globe. Sure, if you get drunk, go to an ATM late at night to get cash for drugs and hookers, it's not safe. If you're joining a cartel or going to try your hand at selling or importing drugs without cartel cover, it's not safe. Otherwise it's like any suburban U.S. city with strip malls and fast food joints. Angel and I drove quickly to get to Costa Rica because I was told to fear Honduras and Nicaragua. On the way back I wouldn't make that mistake.

My sister and her wife treated us to the luxurious Four Seasons hotel in Costa Rica. Surrounded by screeching howler monkeys we enjoyed spa services, amazing restaurants, gorgeous beaches and a new jungle adventure every day. At the beach Angel had her own lounger and the staff made sure there was an ice cube in her water dish at all times. We were so spoiled. My sister expressed anxiety about my traveling alone. She said both she and my brother weren't thrilled about my wanting to stay away longer. Then I told her I wasn't going to return at all. She conceded that I seemed well and clearly wasn't lonely. My Spanish was improving, I'd seen amazing scenery, met many locals and other travelers. I was happy. I was even weaning myself off anti-depressants. Angel and I continued into Costa Rica.

I went diving with manta rays and floated next to white tip reef sharks, visited many animal rescues and learned about the unbelievable volume of wildlife in this country. We left the porch light on and went outside in the middle of the night to see hundreds of different insects and frogs, toads, lizards and snakes. We stayed on organic farms, met adventurous kids from around the world, sat on porches at sunset to see mated macaws returning to their nests after their day away. I played poker while in the chic city of Escazu. I experienced Easter's Holy Week in Guadeloupe in a way I'd never seen before! (It was scary.) I went rafting in La Fortuna and we slept in my truck high on the hills around Volcán Arenal. We went to hot springs, cold springs and drove through rivers on the Oso peninsula to meet a long-ago friend from culinary school who'd left the U.S. 25 years ago. In the rain, Ángel and I drove up unpaved mountain roads only to slide back down. In Puerto Viejo de Telemanca a flash flood resulted in my truck's passenger side sinking into mud high enough to cover the tires. We walked to our Airbnb. Our host called for a tow truck in the morning. In the morning the tow guys called for a construction crane in the afternoon! Note to self: Do not drive in the pouring rain on dirt roads in Costa Rica!

In San Juan del Sur, Nicaragua, we watched surfers and I rode a horse through the jungle. On Ometepe Island I stayed with Jose and his wife on their traditional family farm. I went to the school where he volunteers to teach kids skills to get them off the dirt-poor island. Sometimes to university in the hopes of adapting to the modern, global world we live in now. The kids are all adept with their smartphones; actually, everywhere on my travels they were. The sad part, however, is that phone plans come with Facebook, Messenger, WhatsApp and Instagram. No internet search apps. I found this after futilely suggesting a kid "look it up" for at least the twentieth time. I've since given up. It's been the most negative part of my travels. That this next generation has evolved away from clinging to the archaic churches of their ancestors is good. That they've fallen into the narcissism and self-absorbed behaviors of American kids is distressing.

I met a couple who were headed to Utila to dive. I was on my way to scuba dive on Roatan. In the dreaded Honduras. I twisted their arms into doing the driving and chipping in together so we could see more than we would have alone. We danced the night away in Tegucigalpa, tried to fish in Lake Yojoa, and stayed on an off-the-grid, sustainable, organic farm in Los Metallias. We never felt threatened or unsafe. The countryside is absolutely gorgeous.

On Roatan I practiced my scuba diving, held a sloth, played with monkeys and watched the sunset with altogether too-conservative expats. I was relieved I'd chosen Cozumel. Perhaps I'd find kindred spirits there.

Copan Ruinas is adorable. The ruins small but interesting, the locals happy and welcoming. Even crossing the border into Guatemala went smoothly. In Antigua I ate Texas-style BBQ and seriously considered moving there because of that, the beauty of the quaint city and the joy of seeing so many churches demolished by natural disasters. But an organic farm on Lake Atitlan called our names. The villages there are amazing. Textiles and coffee and chocolate made before your eyes. Water taxis to take you to visit other villages. Volcanoes and mountains more than 7,500 feet high surround a placid lake. We met the warmest indigenous peoples, most generous young travelers and the friendliest expats so far.

I thought I'd be homesick. I was wrong. There's so much to do, so much to see, so many people to observe. As I age I'm starting to get exhausted talking. Telling my story became tedious. Being told that I should write a book intolerable. (Still not sure why I'm writing this!) But when the people I met started telling me how much they admired me and aspired to be like me I had to sit up, take notice and look forward. Away from "take care of me only," and start, once again, to be an example to others. Thankfully I'm not so tired anymore.

Angel and I made our way to San Cristobal de las Casas, Chiapas.

I had met a couple in Tulum, Sergio and Carla, who lived there. They're Buddhist/Zapatistas and our conversations were slowly translated, one language to another. They were awesome. I adored them and looked forward to seeing them in their home state.

I always bought trinkets from children on my trip. How can you say no? In Guatemala the little girls would hold a rope across the mountain roads forcing you to stop driving, all in order to make you buy *plátanos* or mangos or trinkets from them. When I arrived in San Cristobal it was worse. Now my dashboard is home to many tiny toys and trinkets that I happily bought along my way.

Sergio and Carla woke me up to the truth. They pleaded with me to not buy things. To give the kids food instead. Not unlike many indigenous peoples around the world, the ability to process alcohol isn't common. Too many of these dark-skinned children are from traditional homes. They don't go to school; they work and give their cash to their fathers, who frequently drink it away. The middle-class in Mexico and Central America is thriving. But the poor are really poor and while never homeless, it's painfully obvious they're struggling.

On the summer solstice I visited Palenque. My truck was packed with all my belongings but I didn't hesitate to hand my keys over to the parking lot guys, who wash your car while you sightsee. They also agreed to watch out for Angel. If she seemed hot, they'd turn on the air conditioning and at least once they'd take her for a walk. It was an amazing tour with the solstice light glistening through the temple, pyramid and other buildings. I never once doubted my truck and dog would be well-cared for. And they were.

This is the best part of México. You and your things are safe if you do not make yourself a target. Tipping helps, but most people are honest. They're not constantly thinking about how to rip others off. Frequently they seem morally superior to most Americans, albeit less educated and less crammed full of propaganda; but also devoid of the self-help books and organized religions that seem to perpetuate the belief that we can't be good on our own.

Angel and I made our way back to Cozumel, where we've been for seven months now. The locals are lovely. I dive or snorkel some days. We go to a beach to swim and work on our tans the other days. I play poker online, and pen-pal with old and new friends. I'm working on my Spanish and keeping up with U.S. and world news. I host my landlord's Airbnb guests and I've decided to get my TEFL certificate to start teaching English online. Perhaps I'll find I do have another skill to share.

I'm often asked where my family is. But the longer I'm away the more satisfied I am being on my own. My landlord has become a close friend, one who frequently reminds me I need to look outward again. To go back out and be a part of the world, to continue to learn and to share.

It's about that time. I really loved being on the road. I'm ambivalent about being settled here. Cozumel is also hot; I may choose to leave; I may choose to be a nomad for the rest of my life. The amount of invitations from the single-serving friends I've made to visit their country is overwhelming. The only truly good part of Facebook is that they're all easily reached. I'm not sure I'll want to stay in one place for long ever again. And now I have places to go and people to see. It feels awesome.

The bottom line is that I have no interest in going back to America. I left so I could recover, get back my lost energy and find myself again. And I have.

Joanna Karlinsky grew up Jewish, intellectual and privileged in New York City in the late '70s-early '80s. In middle school she and her friends reveled in dressing up, eating out, ordering in and correctly pronouncing the names of the hottest French wines. In high school she babysat Anderson Cooper, had Truman Capote review her English homework, played basketball with James Taylor, smoked pot with Ben Stiller, danced with Billy Idol, snorted heroin with Jean-Michel Basquiat and snapped photos of graffiti-laden subways with Keith Haring. After a few years lost to sex, drugs, rock 'n' roll and community organizing, Joanna graduated from the Culinary Institute Of America. For 27 years she cooked hard, partied harder, worked ethically, supervised with love, served guests with compassion, taught with meaning and entertained with passion, playing for keeps and throwing parties where the good times rolled.

She also battled depression and manic depressive disorder, but failed at being a drug addict. Joanna owned five businesses in San Francisco and still keeps in touch with many past employees and customers. "Cancer sucked most everything away," says Joanna. "But I'm.back! With gratitude."

11. "Leap of Faith"

Nova Grahl
Guadalajara, Jalisco

In a weird way, Mexico saved me. It was 2008, and I was recently divorced. I'd been teaching middle school in Charleston, South Carolina to a pretty tough group of kids. I was burnt out, caught up in comparison and consumerism. I constantly compared myself to "the Joneses," and came up short every time. While I wasn't exactly looking for a life change, it was clear that I needed something new, some type of cosmic nudge to push me past my shallow and unfulfilling humdrum.

On a normal Friday night, I decided to go to a cook-out at a co-worker's home to blow off some stream from the stressful work week. An acquaintance who also taught middle school mentioned to the group that she'd recently interviewed with a school in Guadalajara and was planning on accepting a position for the following school year. She casually added that they had another available position, and if anyone was interested to get in touch with her by the following morning. Her formal Skype interview was at 10 a.m. I didn't think much about it at the time, but later that night I had insomnia, and my mind kept returning to the job possibility in Mexico. I kept turning over the idea of teaching outside of the U.S., but each time, I would convince myself it was a silly whim, and that it wasn't for a girl like me. A girl who'd lived in South Carolina her whole life.; a girl who wasn't brave enough to do such a thing.

The next morning, after little sleep and a lot of coffee, I phoned my friend and told her I was interested. I sent in my resume and cover letter and felt a tiny spark of hope begin to grow in my heart. I continued to tell myself that this wouldn't, couldn't work. However, when I spoke with my mom about the job in Guadalajara, I told her that if I got an offer, I was taking it, no matter what. In a way, I think I was giving myself an ultimatum. The following week I had a Skype interview and was offered a position.

My friends and family thought I was crazy. A few thought I was brave. Others thought it was all just "lip service" and that I wouldn't leave my near-decade-long job in Charleston for one in Mexico. My family was both worried and supportive. Deep down, I think they may have questioned my sanity a bit, too. But more than anything, I felt … free, and hopeful. I was excited, and nervous, and scared, and for the first time in a long time, I felt vibrantly alive. Saying goodbye to breathtaking Charleston, with its stately oaks, delicious food and fabulous friendships, was bittersweet. I knew that no matter what happened in Mexico, I would embrace this opportunity for growth and change.

In all honesty, it was a leap of faith. I'd never been to Guadalajara and had only traveled to resorts in Mexico for vacation. I'd only ever taken French and knew not even one lick of Spanish. I wasn't that adventurous of a person and never really considered myself brave. But that little spark of hope and excitement had grown into a flame that propelled me forward on this journey.

When I arrived in Guadalajara, I immediately called my mom in tears. The plane had been delayed in Mexico City and the taxi driver couldn't find my new apartment address. I missed my home. It was a real city, with graffiti everywhere, sirens and dogs barking and so many other new things. After finally arriving at my apartment, I remember lying in my bed that first night, listening to the sounds of the city and thinking, "What have I gotten myself into?"

The following weeks were some of the best in my life. It was like I'd been given the gift of new eyes. Everything was so loud, bright and colorful! I felt so alive, and for the first time in a long time, I felt strong enough to take on whatever life threw at me.

Since I didn't own a car, I walked everywhere, enjoying the golden Guadalajara sunshine. I hammered through conversations with my almost non-existent Spanish. (The locals were very patient.) I drank fresh-squeezed orange juice, visited my local taco stand, enjoyed the city view from my rooftop patio and bought a tiny Schnauzer puppy. I noticed that even though materially speaking I had very little—no car and a bare bones apartment—I was happier and far less anxious.

My teaching job was great, and absolutely different than my job teaching in the U.S. The students at my new school were happy and polite. They always said, "Good." The international community was warm and welcoming. On campus, birds were singing, fountains were gurgling and the students were laughing. I had a bit of culture shock because my job back in South Carolina was so incredibly different. I'd traded fist fights and school resource officers for blue skies and smiling students. When greeting students at my old school, I was often met with the rolling of eyes and negative body language. Here in Guadalajara, the students eagerly greeted me with, "Good morning, Miss!" It was definitely a different experience for me professionally.

One of the struggles I had when I moved here was how to process seeing so many impoverished people and children on the streets begging for money. Seeing little kids selling *chicle* or senior citizens washing car windows in the hot, squalid traffic broke my heart. More importantly, it also deeply humbled me. For the first time, I recognized the role consumerism and social class had played on my self-esteem, and how I had allowed it to brainwash me. I wondered why so many Americans were so angry that there are poor people, even while they rarely have to see these disenfranchised people. The U.S. has such strong safety nets, many for the very poorest of society. Yet Americans can't seem to get past "helping others." I think maybe the key to this is simply the old adage, "Out of sight, out of mind." It's much easier to demonize the poor, imagining they lead a life of leisure and begging, instead of "choosing" to work and support themselves. It's much more difficult to be angry when it's someone your grandmother's age, someone who should be taken care of in her old age, that you see begging on the streets.

One thing I realized only after moving to Guadalajara was this: Any happiness in my life would have to come from within me, and certainly not from any material thing I possessed.

Fast forward eight years. I absolutely love my simple little life here in Guadalajara. I'm a different person than I was when I first took a leap of faith and came to Mexico. I met an amazing *tapatio*, (meaning he was born in Guadalajara) and we hit it off. We now have a four-year-old son together. Raising a child here has been wonderful. There's so much less competition and judgment about parenting here. Kids are "allowed" to be kids, and not expected to be adults. Here in Mexico, we can afford to have a nanny that helps take care of our son and also helps around the house. It's so nice to have someone you trust that loves your child and enjoys spending time with him. We own a car, but I still walk almost everywhere in our neighborhood; to the *fruteria*, the grocery store, parks, taco stands, restaurants, coffee shops, popsicle stands, etc.

Our little family has traveled a good deal in Mexico and I've enjoyed seeing the beauty of this culturally vast and diverse country. My anxiety rarely rears its ugly head anymore. I eat freshly cubed mango from the corner fruit vendor for less than a dollar. I wake to the sound of the sweepers outside my window, and in the evening, I hear the screeching of green parrots flying overhead. Hummingbirds live in our garden year-round, and I've zeroed in on the best taco stand in my neighborhood.

Just this weekend, I went with a few girlfriends to a swanky spa at a lake in the mountains. On our way, while passing through a tiny town at the foot of the mountains, my friend's car broke down. Luckily, we were near an OXXO (like a 7-11). We pulled in and had the gas attendants take a look under the hood. They told us we likely needed a mechanic and directed us across the street. We found the mechanic, who was enjoying an evening meal with his family. He immediately got up to help us out. After looking at the car, he told us he'd need a part, and then hopped on his motorcycle to go get it. Ten minutes later, he returned with the part in hand. He replaced the leaky tubing and we were ready to go within half an hour. He was incredibly polite and professional the entire time. It cost $350 pesos, or about $17 dollars. As we headed back toward our fancy spa destination, we couldn't help but feel how fortunate we were to be living among such gentle and kind people here in Mexico.

Life isn't perfect, but it's pretty great most of the time. I'm a different person than I was when I left the U.S.A. I'm more grounded, humble, patient and open-minded. I don't care too much about having flashy things or "fitting in." The truth is, I likely wouldn't fit in here even if I tried, which has been quite a relief, actually. Here, away from my native country, I've found a way to just "be." To live simply. To slow down. Thank you, Mexico, for the second chance at authentic happiness!

Nova Grahl is a coffee connoisseur / Mama of Theo / International school teacher / Bibliophile / Lover of the slow life / Travel enthusiast.

12. "Falling in Love (Twice!) South of the Border"

Nancy Seeley
Mazatlán, Sinaloa &
Zihuatanejo, Guerrero

Three decades ago I got off a plane in Zihuatanejo and instantly fell in love. This unexpected event merged with a very strong dislike of cold Wisconsin winters to set the scene for my "temporary" move to Mexico in October 1995. I've since relocated to Mazatlán, but it's 23 years later and I've never once regretted my decision to pull up stakes and head south of the border. Barring an unforeseen catastrophe, I have no plans to move back to the U.S.

There's a quartet of reasons for my contentedness:

Weather: Some people scoff at the notion of seasonal affective disorder (SAD). Not me. As the temperature dropped below freezing and the sky turned gray and grim each year, my mood took a simultaneous dive. The first snowfall only worsened things. Sure, the picture-postcard perfection of the scene was great for a day or two. Then driving on slippery, ice-covered streets, getting off work in late afternoon darkness, seeing my breath the minute I went outdoors and piling on layers of clothes to ward off the frosty chill quickly diluted my appreciation of Mother Nature's idyllic landscape. By my late thirties I found myself cringing when turning the calendar over to November. Plus, I'm a worrywart and fretted about the harm I was doing to friendships and working relationships given my surly disposition. Time to do something about it, right? Mexico was—and is—the answer.

Pace of life: *Hijole!* ... as we say here in Mexico. Though I was thankful to be working for a state government agency where my job was generally fulfilling and the security and benefits meshed with my personal needs, endless meetings and rigid schedules began to feel uncomfortable ... REALLY uncomfortable. It seemed there was always a calamity brewing, something that meant I'd be taking my work home with me. Trying to fit in social outings with family and friends got to be more challenging. Coming back from vacations was angst-inducing because I knew my inbox would be overflowing. The relaxed state in which I returned would dissolve within hours. I realize that was partly due to my own personality, but still, I needed a change.

Cost of living: I was a white-collar worker, divorced with no kids. I had a lovely home nestled below an old stone quarry at the end of a cul-de-sac. My job paid the bills, but there wasn't a lot left over for the travel I craved, for the experiences I knew would broaden my horizons. Being my dad's daughter, I wasn't willing to go into debt to have the life I wanted. It only took one trip to Mexico to realize that here I could live at a fraction of the cost I was spending to be comfortable in Madison, Wisconsin—and there would be no snow, no ice and only infrequent gray skies.

Segueing to the present, here's a comparison I love: I recently vacationed in Washington, D.C. with my sister. We checked out the newly-renovated southwest waterfront area. Stopping for a late lunch, we each ordered a glass of wine. The price was $17 apiece before taxes and tip. A month later my *novio* (sweetheart) and I stayed in a squeaky clean, well-equipped hostal in Leon, Guanajuato for a little less per night than what I paid for that one glass of chardonnay. That's only one example of many. It's gotta get you thinking, right?

Finding love: I arrived in Zihuatanejo an unencumbered female. For the first three years I was truly finding my way, learning the culture, obsessing about whether my savings would be sufficient for my lifestyle, reveling in the freedom to do whatever I wanted to do whenever I wanted to do it. And then came the day when a friend said she'd met a Canadian named Nick she knew would be perfect for me. Yeah, right. I resisted. She persisted. I finally agreed to meet this fellow on the beach in a group setting. That way I could suss him out without a blind date at age 48. Smart, *si*?

I got there and saw a handsome man matching Nick's description sitting solo. I'd come this far, so I walked up and introduced myself. By the time the rest of the group arrived—profusely apologizing for a last-minute Friday meeting at the school where they taught English as a second language—Nick and I were deep in conversation. Within 10 days, we became a couple. Happily, we're still a couple. None of this would have happened had I not been in Zihuatanejo. I thank my lucky stars every day that I left my job in Wisconsin and found true love here.

Now let's go back to the beginning of my story. I said winter had become a big problem. In January 1988, my best friend from college and I took an impromptu trip to Ixtapa, Guerrero. We needed a break from the cold, and this package deal was incredibly cheap. We didn't have the faintest clue what—or where! —Ixtapa was when our travel agent suggested this spot on Mexico's southern Pacific coast, but it was warm and safe, we were told.

The plane landed on the outskirts of Zihuatanejo, a scant four miles from Ixtapa, at that time the newest jewel in tourism agency FONATUR's development crown. We disembarked by walking down a metal staircase, enveloped by soothing tropical air. No claustrophobic jetways back then. There was a large, elevated, open-air platform nearby where people awaiting friends hooted and hollered while sipping margaritas. If you turned your head, the ocean beckoned. I was enthralled, totally and completely enthralled. Ixtapa resembled a little Miami—sparkly at night with a great beach and top-notch accommodations, but Zihuatanejo to me was the "real" Mexico, a sleepy little fishing village, a throwback to life a couple generations ago.

After that marvelous week in paradise, I returned in November with another friend to stay in Zihua (as the locals call it). When it was time to go home, I was truly, utterly hooked. The friendly locals, the dependable bathing suit temperatures, the cheap and tasty food, the tropical breezes flitting under cerulean skies ... everything suited me to a T, particularly when teamed up with the more sedate pace of life and the lower price tags.

My goal became engineering a three-year sabbatical as soon as reasonably possible. I bought a timeshare in Ixtapa in 1989 and returned twice a year to make sure I really wanted to do what I thought I wanted to do. By 1992, the die was cast. I'm a planner by nature and put the wheels in motion to start my sabbatical in 1995.

My boss didn't believe I was serious, but I eventually convinced him. The turning point came when I got summoned for jury duty starting in June 1995. "You can't do that if you're leaving the next month," he said. "OK, I'll quit earlier," I replied. Negotiations ensued. End result: I became the jury foreperson, worked till July 27, 1995, and said my goodbyes to co-workers during a gala event at my favorite after-work haunt. Many well-wishers were envious of my plans, which somehow bolstered my confidence.

I must admit that during the period from 1992-1994, my cautious financial self obsessively wondered if my savings would be sufficient to support me. I had banked every raise for the past several years ... but still. Then another possibility presented itself: Isla Margarita, an island off the northern coast of Venezuela. I visited and loved the ambiance there too. On the down side, it was definitely more expensive to get there. The chance of friends and family visiting was less likely, but the cost of living was unbelievably low. What to do?

I constructed two collages—one for Zihua and one for Isla Margarita—and mounted them on opposite sides of a doorway in my favorite "at home" spot in Madison, the four-season room I'd built in 1993 thinking it might convince me to stay in the U.S. I looked at both collages daily seeking guidance.

Then the bottom fell out of Mexico's economy during my last "surveillance" trip to Zihua in December 1994. Three zeros were lopped off the peso exchange rate. Suddenly moving here was equally as do-able as relocating to Venezuela. The decision about where to start the next chapter of my life was pretty much made for me.

After my last Wisconsin work day, I spent three full months traversing the U.S. via plane, train, car, bus and bicycle, bidding *hasta luego* to family and friends. I rented out my home to a good

119

friend. On October 27, 1995, I flew to Zihua with only two suitcases, a backpack, a boombox and a bicycle—leaving most of my possessions behind.

The beginning of my odyssey seemed surreal. No one was demanding my presence at a meeting. My boss wasn't telling me I couldn't take an extra-long lunch hour to run 12 miles around Lake Monona (I was a dedicated marathoner back then), saying I belonged in the office supervising the dozen workers who reported to me.

Winter came ... and the skies were bright blue. The temperature occasionally dropped into the high 40s (causing the locals to wear fur-lined parkas they got from who-knows-where), but I was happy as a clam. I was the mistress of my destiny and loving every minute of it.

This isn't to say there weren't challenges. Back in 1995, life in Mexico was very different than today. My little apartment in a Third World neighborhood didn't have a telephone, a TV, hot water, laundry facilities or air conditioning. I neither had nor wanted a car, and there was no internet. Going for a couple of weeks without either the water or the electricity crapping out was a miracle. Rainy season was challenging given that drains perpetually overflowed. I'd hear a noise at my door, and it would be a pig grunting while slowly lumbering down my dusty, potholed road.

Zihuatanejo had no major grocery stores, no stoplights, very sketchy "snail mail" service and few of the snacks I'd become addicted to in Wisconsin (think Ranch-Style Doritos, aged Cheddar cheese, Johnsonville sausage and dry white wine). Doing business was a completely different ball game given that punctuality was not prized. One spent lots of time chit-chatting before broaching the real reason for a visit. Paying bills in person was challenging (sometimes still is!), especially since cutting in line seems to be a Mexican art form.

Looking back, some of my early experiences were quite comical—like when I bundled up all my dirty laundry and schlepped it to the nearest "*auto lavado.*" I knew the verb "*lavar*" meant "to wash" and intuited that "auto" meant I could do it myself. Wrong ... this was a car wash! It did give the employees something to chuckle about.

Then there was the time I took a local bus and listened while the driver told a woman she couldn't board carrying the live chicken she was holding in her arms. So she wrung its neck and paid her fare. That was OK since now the chicken—that night's dinner—was dead.

After the initial rush of settling down in Mexico wore off, not being able to see my family and friends was tough at times. I depended on letters from home for news. Getting them was challenging. I'd listen for the mailman's motorcycle and rush to the building's courtyard. He'd throw the envelopes over a 10-foot wall. If I didn't get there lickety-split, the resident dog would either chew them up or lift his leg and pee on them.

In the early days, I'd pen a three-page letter (no computer) four times a year and have nearly 100 copies made at a local *papeleria*. This task required patience because replacing ink or toner before you couldn't read anything on the duplicates was not a priority. I'd personalize each letter using the blank side of the second sheet and walk seven miles to the airport with my stamped and bundled envelopes. I'd search out American vacationers willing to mail my correspondence when they reached the U.S. There weren't the continual warnings back then about not accepting anything from strangers in an airport.

I walked nearly everywhere. Taxis weren't in my budget, and I liked the exercise. I'm gregarious by nature, so this gave me numerous opportunities to chat with the locals in my pidgin Spanish. Though I'd taken a few night classes before the move, the proper Spanish I learned wasn't cutting it here. I'd like to say I'm now totally fluent, but that would be a lie. I can certainly get by but am always grateful when the townsfolk slow their speech to accommodate my ability to comprehend. I highly recommend attempting to speak Spanish. It has reaped so many rewards for me. My experience is that one is often viewed as an "ugly American" if no effort is made to use Mexico's native tongue.

A recurring concern was money. I had socked funds away for my three years abroad, but time and again I wondered if it would be enough. From the get-go, I logged every single peso I spent every single day. More than two decades later, I still do. At the end of every month I tally up my cash outflow and project what I'll spend annually if current trends continue. My first year in Zihua cost me a grand total of $8,364 USD. That included shelling out $200 USD per month for U.S. health insurance, which in the past was picked up by my employer.

Troubling for the first few years was my dad's unhappiness with my decision. He was a dyed-in-the-wool family man. My living so far away in another country didn't set well. Thankfully, he did eventually come around, and he and my mother visited me in Zihua. When I pointed out it was really due to him I was here, given that he'd imbued his financial principles in me so thoroughly I could afford jettisoning my job (temporarily at least) at age 45, he became more accepting of me "living my dream" in Mexico.

Now about the three-year sabbatical idea. Well ... it took less than a year to realize returning to what I'd left behind would be very difficult. How could I go back to an environment which dictated fairly rigidly how I'd be spending all my working hours?

I put my thinking cap on and decided a crucial component was lowering my living expenses. By then I'd made many friends in Zihua, expats and locals alike. I got myself invited to myriad social events and spread the word that I was available for housesitting. Imagine my delight when a Canadian couple invited me to their splendid ocean-view penthouse high above a popular beach and asked me to take care of it during low season. I'd pay neither rent nor utilities; I'd be the troubleshooter and get problems fixed during their absence. That sweet situation carried on for six years starting mid-April and sometimes lasting until mid-December.

I clearly remember the first morning I blearily opened my eyes in the master suite of that two-level penthouse. It wasn't dawn yet, but I saw bright lights outside the condo. Drifting between sleep and semi-awareness, my first discombobulated thought was ... Is this heaven? Padding to the balcony, I saw a cruise ship festooned with strings of lights majestically making its way into Zihuatanejo Bay, looking like it was headed right for my bedroom. Bliss!

Despite all that, quitting my job for good was more difficult than I imagined. It meant I'd be sacrificing more than $25,000 in accrued sick leave benefits which would pay for increasingly expensive health insurance—if I stayed till normal retirement age. But could I hang on for another 17 years? (I was 48 at the time.) I nearly drove a coterie of friends crazy with my continual litany of indecision until finally one fellow snapped and said, "Look! You've gone over and over and over the pros and cons. Do it or don't do it—but PLEASE don't bring up the subject again. Enough is enough!"

So, I went away for a solo weekend in Wisconsin where I knew no one for the express purpose of returning with a final decision. (During those first three "sabbatical" years, I'd gone back to Madison every summer.) While taking long walks on a deserted hiking trail, I realized I really didn't want to be one of those people who postponed a dream so long that finally making it a reality became impossible. My resolve firmed up, and all my previous uncertainty simply fell away like magic. I would relocate to Mexico … no doubt about it!

I'd been renting out my home. I sold it during a propitious real estate market and pocketed $85,000. That money went immediately into investments to provide a nest egg without which my fiscally conservative self could not have comfortably managed. I made the crucial decision to leave my nicely-growing pension fund untouched till age 60 and vowed that if I had to dip into it before then, I'd move back to Wisconsin and go back to work.

I flew back to Zihuatanejo late in the summer of 1998, officially homeless and jobless, but debt-free and full of enthusiasm. Soon afterwards I met Nick.

When the housesitting ended because we wanted to travel more, together Nick and I sought out living opportunities where we'd troubleshoot in return for reduced rent. Neither of us wanted to work in Mexico and file all the required paperwork, pay monthly taxes, etc. Our solution involved handling routine maintenance and unexpected emergencies for "our" owners. Paying the bills with their money sweetened the deal! It's worked like a charm ever since, but it's vital to be reliable and resilient. For us, this equates quite smartly to employment without qualifying as such. Buying a place ourselves was a non-starter because we wanted the freedom to pull up stakes whenever we chose.

Though property ownership in Mexico comes with its own set of hassles, so does renting. When owners sell, you're out of a place to call home. We've moved frequently during our time south of the border, and it's really all been good. In 2012, when yet another Zihua landlord put her place on the market, we decided it was time to transplant ourselves elsewhere. Advancing age was making medical care more important, so we decided to try Mazatlán, 10 times bigger than Ixtapa/Zihuatanejo and considerably further up the Pacific coast. An ocean location was crucial to our happiness. Mazatlán appealed because we'd been coming here for a decade every December to experience the Gran Pacifico Marathon. Relaxing beach life was great, but here we have many more cultural opportunities as well.

Besides this "job," another way I found to keep mentally alert involved writing for a monthly English magazine in Zihuatanejo for a decade. Later, in Mazatlán, I began writing for a similar publication. I firmly believe the idea of sharing information with other potential expats on how we did what we've both done provides a useful service to a motivated audience.

With the advantage of hindsight, would I do anything differently? Hmmm … maybe some little details, but in the grand scheme of things, I'm happy to report a most emphatic NO!

In no particular order, here are some final thoughts:

If you're determined, it isn't that difficult to live on a very modest income in Mexico. What might be onerous is editing your "must haves" to a level that meshes handily with your budget.

Though some might disagree, approach a potential move with rationality and caution. Just because you love a place initially doesn't mean it's the right one for you. Check it out. Talk with other expats. I was fortunate enough to find that falling in love at first sight with Zihua was indeed the right course for me, but I gave the idea time to gel and did lots of research.

Reality check: If you can't handle noise with aplomb, then forget about moving here. Whether it's construction, music, traffic, loud parties or something else, noise is pretty much a constant.

Especially if you're not a property owner, handling your monetary concerns with a U.S. financial institution while living in Mexico is a piece of cake. I've been doing it since 1995. I have a bank account in Mazatlán but use it only in emergencies. (My confidence in the Mexican banking system is not that strong.) Relying on the ever-increasing possibilities offered by the internet has shrunk the distance between Wisconsin and Mexico considerably since my story started taking shape back in 1988.

Don't ever forget that doing business here doesn't employ the same guidelines as those you're familiar with north of the border.

To repeat: Punctuality is not prized here the same way as it is in the U.S., though things are changing as the 21st century advances.

So here's a corollary: Patience makes life a lot more pleasurable in Mexico. I keep working at it, still hoping I will eventually get the knack of realizing my natural tendency to want things done precisely when I want them done isn't ever going to work here.

Though I didn't dwell on it before, the food here is amazing! Ditto for the bus service—which can get you virtually anywhere you want to go. Plus, if you're at least 60 years old and hold a valid Mexican resident card (either permanent or temporary), you're eligible for a free government-issued INAPAM card that allows you to ride buses throughout the country at 50% of normal fares.

Safety warnings—to my way of thinking—are overdone. Yes, Homeland Security needs to be proactive, but I feel more secure here than if I were living in certain parts of Milwaukee, Chicago, Los Angeles, etc. The trick is to use common sense. Don't be stupid and wander into uncharted or sketchy territory alone, especially at night.

The changes in "my" areas of Mexico in the last two decades are mind-boggling. The internet has ushered in massive modifications, Amazon now delivers here, health care has made major strides, video phone calls are popular—but, alas, Ranch-Style Doritos are still not on most supermarket shelves!

Finally, keep in mind the much lower prices that probably figure heavily in your possible relocation. Here, within easy travel time from the U.S., you can often rent a nice-sized, ocean-view apartment for $700 or less per month. You can buy a hearty breakfast for two for under $7 … including a 15% tip (that percentage being perfectly fine). Phone service, including internet, costs as little as

$20 monthly in Mazatlán, where a first-class bus taking you eight hours down the coast to Puerto Vallarta will set you back about $35 if you buy it online. The comparisons go on and on.

The frosting on the cake for me was finally claiming my Social Security benefits at age 66. Adding this income to my annual budget has made me feel like I won the lottery.

Bottom line: America remains my homeland …. but Mexico is definitely my home.

Nancy Seeley moved to Mazatlán from Wisconsin in 1995 intending to stay for a three-year sabbatical, but she's still there. Traveling throughout Mexico has become a passion and avoiding Midwest winters has become a goal. So far, she claims a pretty high success rate on both fronts.

13. "Not Quite What I Expected"

Gwyn Higbee
San Felipe, Baja California

My story is one of losing control and learning to just go with the flow.

I was first introduced to San Felipe, Baja in 1997. My husband and I had just moved from Seattle, Washington to Tucson, Arizona. He had grown up in Southern California and spent a lot of time in Baja because he raced off-road. We made the seven-hour drive from Tucson to San Felipe that year.

My first time in Baja we stayed in a hotel and quickly learned that hotels in Mexico are not the same as in U.S. We had two rooms: one that had a heater but no hot water, and the other with hot water but no heat. (I've since learned that hot water is not always a guarantee at many hotels.) We explored the area, enjoyed the culture, met new people and overall were happy with our vacation and ready to do it again.

By 1999, we'd been coming to San Felipe frequently for a couple of years and were really starting to think about our future. We figured we usually spent a minimum of a few thousand dollars each year on vacations, and if instead we saved that money, in a few years we'd have enough to buy a small piece of property in Mexico and have our own place to go instead. Since my husband was in the construction business and very handy, we knew we could buy a fixer-upper and make it into whatever we wanted.

One day we were walking in the neighborhood and noticed a house for sale. We called the realtor and asked to look at it. He met us the next morning and told us the previous owner had been widowed, was overdue on her HOA fees and would probably negotiate. So we thought, let's make a ridiculously low offer and if she says no, so be it. We wrote up the contract, went to the beach and came back to our friend's house for dinner. We walked in the door and she threw us a huge pile of keys and said "Congratulations, you're a home owner!" The realtor had brought the keys to her to give to us. That was the beginning of our life in Baja.

The biggest thing that made San Felipe so affordable was the house. Our initial investment in our home was less than $10,000 USD. For that money we got a 480-square foot house with a 22-foot travel trailer, two solar panels, two batteries, a water tank and a septic tank, plus a year of HOA dues paid. We like to say that our house has been like a chia pet: We add money and it grows. Today we've grown from 480 sq. feet to 1,500 sq. feet, more than enough for a retirement home.

Our home is in a gated expat community that's considered the largest solar community in North America. Yep, our house is 100% off-the-grid. If you're not familiar with an off-grid solar system, in the simplest terms it means that your solar panels gather power from sunlight and store that power in batteries. Basically once you invest in your initial solar system you have very small utility bills. The batteries have to be replaced about every 5-7 years (newer technologies will make them last longer) so you do have that expense, but it's not a monthly expense like you're used to in the States. We have not just solar power, but wind power as well. Our water is trucked in from the city and stored in a cistern. We have both a wood stove and propane for heat. That's what we do for utilities.

In those beginning years we spent every holiday and school vacation at our house. We developed friendships with people that were snowbirds. Through those friendships we could see how people were having a great life and living on modest incomes.

My husband had a very physical job as a union sheet metal worker and he always knew he wanted to retire young. He loved Baja when he was in his teens so even before we were married he knew that San Felipe was where he wanted to live. It offers him the off-road racing and laid-back lifestyle he loves, plus easy fishing and biking nearby. When Mike turned 50 he decided he was going to leave Tucson and go and work in Seattle to finish his working career. The pay and benefits in Seattle were way better than in Tucson, so he figured he could go and work, and bank some money for early retirement. We figured if we could swing it we'd be able to retire when he turned 55.

That left me alone in Tucson. My daughter by this time was married with a child and had moved to California. My employer had an opportunity for someone to travel once a month for a week at a time, so I thought I'd give it a try. The owner of our company had started working remotely and I thought if I could figure out how to continue to do my job while traveling maybe I could approach them about telecommuting and working from Mexico, at least part-time for a while.

As retirement approached and I started looking through my rose-colored glasses, I pictured a life of Mike enjoying his hobbies while I telecommuted for a few more years. We would have no house payment, minimal monthly expenses and a new, relaxed and improved quality of life. When he turned 55 he started planning when his last day of work would be. We filed all the papers necessary to start drawing his pension. Then confusion set in as we got the figures back from the trust funds about his pension amount. If we chose to take monies out at age 55, it would be reduced; the alternate option was to wait and work a few more years until he was 62. Add to that if you want your spouse to get your pension when you pass, and there's another reduction.

There were lots of hard choices and decisions to be made for our future, and we really had to consider what was best for us. That was the moment we decided we still wanted to retire early and live in Baja, but that we'd have to supplement our income for a few years before we'd be able to draw our Social Security benefits.

Mike decided that if he was going to have to work, he'd rather do something he likes and knows—which solar was. We started a business selling and servicing complete solar systems, batteries, solar panels, wind generators, etc. I don't know who he talked to originally about setting up the business in Mexico, but I can tell you that it was way different than starting a business in the U.S. We ended up becoming a Mexican corporation. Neither Mike nor I speak fluent Spanish (me hardly any) and what Spanish Mike does know was not enough to understand all the legal terminology. We were lucky to find an accountant and other mentors along the way to help us get our business launched.

One year later and I'm still trying to understand and accept the way business is done in Mexico. Cash is king here, whereas in the U.S. credit cards prevail. We've had to be interviewed and observed by bank officials to make sure that we're a legitimate business and not a drug front. Banking is very complicated, especially since we only have one bank in our town. Simple tasks like asking a general question, having a password reset or getting a bank statement require sitting at the bank for a minimum of two hours waiting for one of the only two bank reps that can assist you. I find that accountability and lack of deadlines is a major problem here; I don't know if it's just in San Felipe or if it's the way the whole country works, but the best way to describe doing business in Mexico is FRUSTRATION.

I'm still finding my way trying to develop new friendships and hobbies. As a working woman, I find it a bit challenging in our community since the majority of people are retired. With economics the way they are in the U.S. though, I definitely see more people moving here who are in their 50s and choosing, just like us, to leave the U.S. at a younger age.

The question I'm always asked is, "Are you happy with your decision to move?" My answer is always yes. It's very comforting knowing that I have a roof over my head that's paid for, as well as being pretty much self-sufficient with our power supply. Moneywise our dollar goes a lot farther here, and we can enjoy our life in a much more stress-free environment with other like-minded friends. Living a more minimal life and enjoying the beauty of my environment is very fulfilling.

Some of my family thinks it's great that we live in such a beautiful place but can't comprehend making the leap. I think the language barrier is one of the major drawbacks for most people. Unless someone comes down and experiences the lure of Baja I think it's hard to explain. My daughter grew up spending time here so she loves it like we do. Now my five-year-old grandson has the Baja bug and wants to come down whenever he can.

Reflect on your life and decide what's best for you, but this girl definitely prefers to live here in the little fishing village of San Felipe!

Gwyn Higbee is a full-time resident of San Felipe, Baja California, Mexico. While living in the U.S. she was a corporate travel agent for 20 years and then changed careers at age 40. Her last 16 years have been spent with one company as student services/accounting manager. Married for 32 years, she is now ready for the next phase of her life. When not working she enjoys traveling, exploring the outdoors and spending time with family and friends.

14. "Rebirth"
(A series of blog posts)

D'ana Baptiste
Puerto Vallarta, Jalisco

I feel helpless. Gutted. No phone conversation or in-person exchange could ever, ever, get to the root of how I feel. Processing this abandonment will have to be done alone.

For the first time since I started my working life, I'm not running a business and have no clue what job I'll have next. I'm in a tunnel, the space between, a space created by default. On my fiftieth birthday, my business, my livelihood—what and who I was in the world—was ripped violently and suddenly away from me by people I loved and trusted.

The wave of nauseating social media filled with lies and misrepresentations and hatred began to truly crush me. The vapid emojis, hollow one-liners and patronizing well-intentioned memes didn't really help me feel any better. In fact, I felt guilty about not feeling better. I realized that moving through this "space" will have to be done outside of the realms of social media.

Life has stopped. I am swallowed whole. I've disappeared into the belly of the whale. No breath, no light, no air, no reprieve. While I was busy cleaning up the mess of what had happened, I mistakenly thought my pain was just boxed up all neat and tidy; something I could store in my attic and forget about.

But that's not how this works. Contrary to popular belief and a culture that perpetuates numbness—I can't move it or shake it or drink it or chase it or throw it or bury it. The only way out is through.

I chose to retreat to Yelapa, Mexico to move through it. To feel and write and cry and sleep and walk and swim myself, breath by breath, out of the well of grief in which I was submerged, out of the public eye.

These are my musings, the lessons I slowly learned from the people and the place that is Yelapa. These are how I renegotiated my relationship with yoga. These entries are my way of coming back to myself.

Water Taxi

The only way to get to Yelapa is on a water taxi, after flying into Puerto Vallarta. You can also travel around the small bay by water taxi, if you decide you don't want to walk through the *pueblo*. (There are no cars and no roads in Yelapa.)

Water taxis are not only a great way to travel, they also provide entertainment value. Especially when full of tourists. Part of my daily routine at the beach is to watch the travelers disembark the boat after it pulls up on the beach. One thing you can count on is that at least one person will fall into the surf, get wet, lose their flip-flops, soak their beach towel, watch their sunglasses drift away or get stuck in a spontaneous yoga pose halfway in the water.

What's amazing about this process is that everyone is smiling, laughing and even posing as they attempt to get out of this boat "safely." Back in the U.S.A., if we fell while trying to exit a boat, we'd be furiously blaming and taking legal action, vowing to get even with the company who dared to get our feet wet. We'd demand safety measures, outfit everyone with a life jacket and helmet, hire people to escort everyone safely off the boat and petition for new laws against allowing companies to put people in such danger.

Here in Mexico though, getting out of the water taxi becomes a part of the adventure. An immersion into a culture that does not provide safety rails. Here, we fall from the boat on our asses, in front of a beach full of people. Here, rather than getting embarrassed, we laugh along with the spectators and actually ... have fun. We have fun falling. We laugh as we watch our flip-flops washing down the shore. We wave at the people on the beach laughing with us. We acknowledge our klutziness as we realize we're entirely okay.

Maybe we're all craving a respite from surety. A rest from our guardrails and safety rules. Maybe we crave an opportunity to fall, even to be seen falling. Maybe we need a reminder that even when (or if) we scrape a knee or bruise a butt cheek, we're alive. We're living. We're falling and we love it.

Thoughts Upon Waking

So here I am, crushed and annihilated and heartbroken. Alone in Mexico. I wish I could hire a doctor to surgically remove the heaviness. I wish I could lift it or hold it or throw it into the sea. I wish there were a shortcut to send these feelings off into the stars where I never have to see them or feel them again. But I can't get rid of any of it.

I wake up to the memory of the 13 people who, a year ago, began planning to steal my business from me. In a series of secret meetings and with a lot of pressure and monetary reward promised, the instigator of this devious plan convinced two-thirds of my staff, men and women I felt were my family, to stab me in the back. They agreed, because if they didn't all do it then no one would get the financial reward to help her steal my yoga studio right out from under me. My life's work.

They staged a "lock out" on my fiftieth birthday so they could spread the lie that a beloved studio that had served the community for 12 years had closed for good. They believed I would go under within a few days, without enough teachers and support staff. They encouraged the community to stop supporting not only me but all of the instructors who chose to stay. They systematically spread egregious lies, telling students I'd gambled the payroll away, or didn't pay them or that I was losing my mind. They defended their very non-yogic actions by claiming they were doing this for me because they loved me.

I was publicly humiliated. My integrity was impugned; my reputation slandered. It was particularly unfathomable and shocking because the people who set out to destroy everything I'd invested in for the last 12 years of my life were the very same people I thought of as family. People who'd celebrated my birthday with me a week before the planned walkout.

I wake up every morning wondering how they spent time with me, hugging and dancing and laughing with me, without giving away what they were about to do. Long-time students/friends/colleagues I'd gone out of my way to support and accept. I never saw it coming.

I wake up every morning wondering what I did to warrant this level of betrayal. And then I move from wondering to intense waves of self-doubt. I doubt my ability to be in this world. I feel stupid. I feel worthless. I feel expendable; wadded up and thrown away.

All of this remembering occurs before I open my eyes. I force myself to notice where I'm at today. The ocean is there for me. She's constant, she's real and she's inviting me into her warm embrace. A quick swim will do me good, so I run down the stairs to the water, and dive in.

Doors

I spent the day in Puerto Vallarta today. Started to notice the way every door seems to have its own personality. Lack of uniformity here leads to quiet expressions of singularity. The buildings themselves seem to exude an interesting history; an invitation to step through the door and find out what awaits me.

People leave their doors open more often than not, and tend to hang out in their doorways, beckoning my gaze toward their open door, welcoming a glimpse into their transparent lives. I notice how people here aren't putting on an act. Their smiles are real and their laughter, genuine. Their willingness to include me makes me want to know them better, each of them in their own unique way.

As I walk through the neighborhoods it dawns on me that it's not complex understanding I crave, it's simple connection. I love being in the presence of someone who isn't trying to sort me out, define me or best me. I love experiencing the shy wave from the old man smoking his cigar, the playful *hola* from the little girl on the sidewalk, the quick story from the shopkeeper selling me a fan. The interest they show me makes me feel like I matter to them. People here seem simple only because they lack pretense.

I believe a lot of Americans see this culture in a one-dimensional way; dismissing it as "too simplistic," as if there's nothing to learn here. As if we're still missionaries out to bring all of our knowledge and superiority to them, these "simple" people.

But here, even the doors prove that theory wrong.

Sounding Time

Water taxis bounce over the sea this morning to wake me. I realize it's 7:30; the first taxi of the day is headed out from the pier. The sky is still dark. Every day there's difference in where and when the sun shows herself. A natural, non-fabricated change that introduces difference softly, reassuringly, not harshly.

I roll over to wake and feel the thick, salty air move through the mosquito net. With no TV and spotty internet, the sunrise becomes a major attraction, one I don't want to miss.

Wrapped in my warm blanket, coffee in hand, I watch, I listen, I feel and begin writing. It's cold today. My hands keep cramping up. Small snails have appeared on the rocks along the shore. Jellyfish are visible in the gray sea; billowy clouds cover the sky. The rhythm of the horses, mules and donkeys carrying their workloads is the perfect backdrop for my musings.

It's 8:30 a.m. now, and I know this because the water taxi is stopping to pick up passengers from Playa Isabel, a small beach just steps away from my *casa*. People bound for Puerto Vallarta jump in, braving the surf, because everyone gets their feet wet getting into and out of the water taxi. It's an adventure I've loved from the first time I had to do it.

I can now differentiate other sounds. I can tell when a water taxi bounces past, or when a fishing boat slowly floats by. The sound of the surf on the rocks changes at low or high tide. The intensity of the crashing of high tide is easy to hear.

The ocean doesn't drown out the songs of the parakeets, the arguments of the crows and the remarks of the jays but by this time of the morning the birds are quiet. The seagulls, however, squawk all day long. A heavenly sound; one I've grown to embrace. The turkey vultures, perched on top of black rocks, have full conversations.

My mind is full of wonderings now. I wonder if pelicans make any sound. I don't want to Google the answer. It's not about knowing the answer. It's about letting myself stay in wonder. Curiosity feels good to me, so I let it lead me for a while. Having no answers empowers me somehow. When people ask me what I do, who I am, where I'm going next, I feel the pressure to offer an appropriate answer. The answer of a 50-year-old. A responsible adult.

So I say, "I don't know." And my soul smiles. This is a time when I sound like a mess.

The 9:30 a.m. water taxi has just pulled up to Playa Isabel. This marks my day in the way the alarm at 5 a.m. used to. There's no clock here, so I keep time by water taxi. Which means it's time to walk to town for breakfast. I still want to know if pelicans make noise.

The Path

The path through town, although literally set in stone, is cobbled and uneven. The width varies, sometimes only wide enough for one person and then opening up again. The path is impeded daily by various elements.

Dogs and cats, sunning themselves, stretch out for me to step over. Piles of wet cement often greet me as I get to the edge of the *pueblo*. A delivery of eggs or bottled water or cases of beer may show up to block my path. The four-wheelers, the mules, the horse shit and the dog shit (although it gets cleaned up daily) are also present to keep it interesting. The obstacles keep me alert and give me the opportunity to actively engage with my surroundings.

There are natural and daily obstacles here that feel benign, and yet when looked at from our antiseptic, totally measured and manicured lifestyles can seem threatening. Back in the U.S., it's easy to check out. We've uniformed everything. We demand smooth highways, even sidewalks, level floors. We value consistency above all else, confusing this for integrity. We end up ossifying and become hardened in our need for uniformity. We get rigid and set in our ways. We celebrate those who are the best at being rigidly who they've defined themselves to be because it feels reassuring to go to bed and wake up with exactly the same person.

What is much truer is that we all wake up different. I wake up as a different person than who I was the night before. Last night I finished a book that opened my mind in a way it had never been

137

opened before. Last night no coatimundi woke me. Last night the earth rotated to give me a new and unique relationship with the sun and the moon this morning. The sky shyly offers another glimpse of herself to me.

This morning the tide is low; there are new snails covering the rocks along the shoreline. The current is flowing in a decidedly different direction than it was yesterday. Today awaits. The cobbled and obstacle-strewn path through the *pueblo* invites me to walk with both eyes open, blinders off, guard rails missing, safety measures non-existent.

Sleep

Tonight, there's a palpable sense of peace and security I feel as I prepare to sleep alone in my open *palapa*. I feel "safe," even in the knowledge my heart is truly broken; sometimes I feel the sharp edges in my dreams. While the initial splintering occurred in an instant (followed by a spectacular and very public free fall) I spent six months scrambling for footing that continued to crumble like sand. I lost my foundation. I lost peace of mind. I lost my name. And I lost a lot of sleep. When it first happened, I would wake myself crying every night for months, becoming so accustomed to my eyes leaking that eventually I slept through it, only to wake to the evidence of dried salt on damp pillows.

Here in Mexico though, I've noticed that I'm sleeping through most nights. My nightly ritual is to say goodnight to the moon and the stars, put the extra blanket on my bed and climb under the covers. There's not one good strong light bulb in any lamp next to the bed—and they still attract bugs—so I rely on a headlamp for the minutes I can actually stay awake to read under the relative protection of my mosquito netting.

The waves lull me to sleep as soon as I settle in with my book. The sound of the ocean roars into the open space, washing away any potential "review" of the past. My mind settles into silence, and in that space right before sleep, I find my name. My perfect and true remembrance of me is allowed here. As I sleep, rolling over into another shattered piece of my soul, I am comforted by the salty, thick, night air and the Mexican blanket that I've come to believe has love woven into it.

No Walls

A *palapa* is what people live in here in Yelapa. Open-air *casas* without walls. The ocean crashes right at the foot of this palapa. The ocean breeze keeps the mosquitoes from congregating. The sun wakes me up eventually and gradually. It's cold every morning, refreshing as I face another day of heat, so I wrap myself up in my beach blanket, snuggle up to my coffee cup, stare out into the abyss that is mama ocean, and an hour goes by.

This is my new way of practicing presence. I keep my eyes open to watch the pelicans dive, the magnificent frigates (and they are magnificent) hovering, the shimmering sardines jumping out of the sea to paint the surface silver. I wait for whales and dolphins to surface and play. To see a whale breach, to hear the sound of a huge tailfin slapping the sea's surface. To witness the grace of dolphins as they traverse the bay. To feel completely connected.

You can't miss experiencing the world when there are no walls to block it.

Pie Lady

I've started to consistently live in this different mentality of "You don't know if you'll ever get to experience this again." It's why I dive into the waterfall rather than simply observe its majesty. Why I kayak by myself even though it scares me. Why I don't mind living with lizards. And it's why I eat pie on the beach.

Yes, pie on the beach. Warm, freshly baked, lovingly offered, pie from the famous pie lady of Yelapa. She and her family walk with Tupperware containers full of warm pie offering it to us tourists in our chaise lounges; those of us who come to Yelapa to eat fish and guacamole and drink tequila shots, but who return again and again for the pie.

And since she sells eight flavors (apple, banana, cheese, chocolate, chocolate coconut, coconut, pecan and lemon meringue), I of course indulge every day. I can't say I didn't gain any weight, only that the weight I did gain was well worth it.

She's not going to be around forever and I may never make it back to Yelapa, so I'm going to keep enjoying these tastes of heaven for the present moment.

Stairs

Here in Mexico stairs have their own personality. The stairs I walk daily to and from the beach (*a la playa*) require my full attention. I've started to get to know each step and have even named a few of them. One is tall and wide, another only half covered with cement so one side is higher than the other. The next step is so short your toes hang off it, and the next step shallow enough to have me teetering precariously for a moment. The next step feels deep in comparison. As though I'm stepping into an abyss. Then the stair seems to rise up and meet my bare foot, reassuring my body that it was there all along.

Each stair offers itself up to me to be known and seen and understood. Each step requires my full presence. The stairwell, a mish-mash of personalities, the very opposite of "formula," keeps my mind checked in. This to me is the perfect walking meditation. Perfectly manicured Zen gardens, fabricated labyrinths, smooth sidewalks pale in comparison.

Self-Help

I know that when I go back to the States I will unwittingly fall into that dangerous game of either/or. I'll allow myself to be pigeon-holed, sorted and labeled. I'll feel guilty and ashamed for feeling "negative" emotions like grief, depression, sadness, anger or horror.

Here, it feels entirely possible that we as humans are capable of feeling all the feelings. Here I witness my capacity to hold a myriad of emotions quite gracefully, all at once. And I want to cultivate that part of me that can hold it all and feel it all. I'm afraid of losing this feeling when I return. It makes me not want to return. Because feeling happy and sad at the same time, peaceful and wild at the same time, makes sense when I'm here. I need this to keep making sense.

The culture here is a whole new world in some ways. I've learned so much from the people of this village. People here do not spend any time trying to define who they are. They aren't trying to be "better" or "more" or "spiritual." They're complex in their simplicity. There's no guile here; no need to pretend they're someone else. No need to put oneself in a box to be just one small part of the amazing humans they are.

I spent most of my life believing I needed to better myself. Change myself. Improve myself. Then I started paying attention to when I feel the most at ease in my body and the people I'm the most relaxed around. I'm drawn to people who are easy on themselves and others. Who don't question their worthiness, have nothing to do with the yoga industrial complex, have never bought one self-help book. I'm not super-comfy around yoga people, or self-help crowds or people who are self-proclaimed healers, gurus and light-bearers.

I'd rather be on the beach with a good book and a nice shot of tequila, a cigar and some good music, than attend another superiority seminar masked as "help." I'm good. You're good. I don't need help being myself. I am myself. And I love the energy surrounding people who are themselves.

Rebirth

I cried all day yesterday. For so many reasons, I cried, grieved, felt broken in two. I've been through the ringer. Especially in the past nine months. Yesterday was the nine-month mark since my fiftieth birthday and the events that led to why I left. Today I know the tears were a sort of rebirth—preceded by a nine-month gestation—and that this person I am today is not at all the person I was nine months ago. The fact that it was Easter isn't lost on me. All this to say that today is a new day. I'm 50 and I'm just barely becoming me again.

I believe we all become who we are until the very day we die. I feel more carefree and child-like than I did when I was 20. I feel less certain and more raw than I've ever felt. This is me today.

I'm still broken. I don't know how long it will take to feel whole again. But because of Yelapa I have the courage to stay broken open. To stay alive and awake and aware and tender in the face of this tremendous, beyond-ability-to-comprehend life.

I believe in myself again. I believe in my dignity. I believe that I'm going to have an exciting, bittersweet, joyful adventure and, for those of you who've witnessed a little taste of this chapter of my life, I feel honored and humbled and astonished and thankful you've been willing to join me.

D'ana Baptiste is a yoga teacher born in Utah, raised in Oakland, California, whose philosophy is to embrace all that life has to offer, using all the senses to do so. She graduated from U.C. Berkeley with a double B.A .in international relations and French, and then promptly moved to Mexico to teach aerobics. D'ana has been a part of the fitness/ wellness movement for 23+ years. Her down-to-earth approach to business as well as her authenticity and confident personality have made her a natural leader in the mind/ body industry. She has developed a superior teacher training program in Utah and also manages and organizes workshops and retreats. Her nonprofit, Yogis in Service, is a grassroots volunteer "yoga army" which offers yoga to those in need, or who cannot afford it. When she's not spreading her message, she learns much about life from hanging out with her three boys, who help her keep it real.

15. "I Call Oaxaca, Mexico, Home"

Norma Schafer
Teotitlán del Valle, Oaxaca

"How did you get there?" people ask. I ended up living in Oaxaca, Mexico, by accident, I reply. Life has a way of happening in surprising ways. Many of the best things that happen to us are a combination of serendipity and determination. Choices are presented to us in this journey we call "life" that we either recognize or not. When we do recognize them and take risk and action, they become life-changing events that can open us up to more than who we thought we were, creating opportunities for growth and creativity. It was this way for me.

It all began with a 2005 Christmas vacation.

Where I live is not in the colonial heart of Oaxaca de Juarez, the city founded in 1532 by Spanish conquistador Hernán Cortés. My part of Mexico is based about 30 minutes away in a small Zapotec village called Teotitlán del Valle. You may have heard about it. It is famed for wool tapestry rugs that very talented weavers create on fixed frame pedal looms. Some even use ancient natural dye techniques developed by their ancestors. I live on land owned by a weaving family who invited me to build a *casita* there. I do not legally own it, though I paid to build it. There is no written contract, only a verbal agreement based on honor and trust.

Zapotecs have lived in the central valleys of Oaxaca for 8,000 years. Back then, they hybridized a plant kernel we call *maize* (corn) that is an important food source worldwide on land about five miles up the road from my *casita*. Monte Alban, their social, political and economic center, is featured by the Field Museum of Natural History as the most important civilization in Mesoamerica.

The textiles and the history called to me like the blast of an ancient Zapotec flute, pitched, piercing and deep.

It was winter. The sun was warming though we wore light sweaters; temperatures in the high-60s to mid-70s during the day, dropping to mid-40s at night; a perfect climate for walking, hiking and sleeping, I thought. I was with my "wasband" Stephen on vacation, invited to visit by our North Carolina neighbor Annie, who'd made the village her permanent home two years before.

Annie would come twice a year to North Carolina to visit and she always brought rugs to sell, usually made by young, up-and-coming artisans who needed a leg-up and some money in their pockets. When she laid the rugs out on the floor of my North Carolina home, I fell in love and wanted to know that place.

Many years before as a young woman living in San Francisco, I learned to weave and use natural dyes. I've always collected textiles and have been a maker—a knitter, quilter, sewer of home goods and dresses. Cloth is my calling, though I crafted my professional career in university administration, marketing, communications and development, and retired from the University of North Carolina at Chapel Hill in 2011.

It was only natural then, that Annie's invitation came at exactly the right time. I hadn't been back to Mexico since the early 1970s, though I'd traveled in Asia, Central America and Europe. I was thinking about retirement but avoiding the question. Going to a small rug-weaving village on vacation was about as far as I got.

At that time, Annie had taken two widows under her wing. The mother-in-law and daughter-in-law had both lost their husbands in recent months. Their grief was fresh. The men, both weavers, were the family's only income source. The daughter-in-law, age 36, had three young children.

Magdalena and Josefina were (and still are) excellent cooks. Annie was helping them imagine what it would be like to start and operate a bed and breakfast. Stephen and I were the guinea pigs, the first guests. I can do this, I said to myself. I've been to rural China, forewarned about the basic living conditions.

Their sleeping, living and altar rooms surrounded an earthen courtyard where life centered: the cooking fire, dish and laundry tubs, playground, empty looms. We moved into the mother's humble adobe bedroom adorned with her late husband's hunting tools and machete. We strung a clothesline for our closet. Today, this is a beautiful and thriving B&B, complete with modern kitchen, plumbed bathrooms and four generations of family underfoot. We became a part of seeing the possibilities, and part of the support system.

On the day my life changed, I went in the opposite direction and took a different path. I always wonder what would have happened if it had been otherwise.

It was our daily practice to go to the internet café. (This was years before Wi-Fi reached the village). I was with my "wasband." We usually turned left to return to the house, walking past the church and the market. This day was different. I turned right to meander through the rug market, doubtful I would find anything of interest.

A voice called out to me in perfect English: "Would you like to see my rugs?" It sounded so perfect that I was taken aback and instantly said no. No one here could speak English so perfectly and I suspected a scam, encountering someone who had practiced this one line so well as a tactic to lure in unsuspecting visitors. Funny, how we make up stories.

As a textile lover and collector, I had made it a point to research weavers and natural dye techniques in Teotitlán del Valle before the trip. I was, and still am, interested in sustainability and public health in addition to the innate beauty of a piece made completely by hand. I knew that fumes from chemical dyes were dangerous and the residue ended up in the ground water, resulting in undocumented health issues.

Not much came up in my research. I wanted to buy and take home a rug, and I wanted to find an excellent maker who had not been "discovered" and whose prices were affordable. I wanted to buy direct and know the family. I made it my mission to go around town, talk to people, meet makers and learn about their weaving and dyeing processes.

Then, after the call-out in English, as an afterthought I looked up into the small space where a young man was standing. I could see the tapestries were extraordinary, of the finest quality, and I stepped in. Within moments, the "wasband" lost interest and left.

Eric Chávez Santiago and his sister Janet, curled in the corner studying, were college students, ages 20 and 18 then. Eric planned to graduate the following year and work in a bank. Janet set her sights on becoming an elementary school teacher. They were the first in their family to go to college. This is an important note, because education in this family was a key value, rare then when most their age completed middle school and went to work at the loom. They took me to their parents' home to see the complete rug selection and I fell in love.

I remember being there for several hours, getting down on my hands and knees to touch the warp and weft that were joined together in traditional designs derived from the Mitla archeological site where Zapotecs lived in the late Classical period. I fell in love with the colors and the imaginative ways they were combined. I picked out favorites, laid them on the floor, and then rolled around on them to see how I felt. I especially fell in love with the *caracol* pattern, the ancient Maya symbol of communication, adopted by Zapotecs on the trade routes passing through the Isthmus of Tehuantepec. Oaxaca was coming alive for me. I didn't want to go home.

When I did get home, after buying several rugs and hearing Chávez Santiago family stories about the decline in tourism and economic opportunity, I wondered what I could do to help. I also wondered what I could do that would get me back to Oaxaca and this small textile-making village. I was smitten.

I approached the Arts Center in Carrboro, North Carolina with a proposal to bring Eric and his dad Federico Chávez Sosa to the U.S.A. to teach and demonstrate and sell rugs. My premise was that it would benefit Mexican immigrants in North Carolina to understand and have pride in their rich cultural heritage, and for Americans to better appreciate the art and culture of Mexico. We joined in writing a grant to the North Carolina Arts Council that was funded. With letters of invitation and support, and with a call and help from Congressman David Price, Eric was awarded a 10-

year visitor's visa and Federico got a six-month visa. They came in spring 2006, and for the next three years, the family members regularly traveled to the U.S.A. to teach, exhibit and sell their work at galleries, universities, art centers and museums.

In 2007, they invited me to live on their land. Then, in 2008, with my coaching help, Eric Chávez Santiago became the founding director of education at the Museo Textil de Oaxaca, a position he held until the end of 2017. In 2018, he was hired by the Alfred Harp Helu family to open and operate the independent folk-art gallery Andares del Arte Popular in Oaxaca's historic Center.

Janet finished college and became a linguistics educator, working with university faculty directors and students from the U.S.A. to preserve Zapotec indigenous language and culture.

Their youngest brother, Omar, has just completed an industrial engineering university degree and is instrumental in taking the family rug-weaving and design business to the next level. I helped him get a 10-year visitor visa to the U.S.A. and arrange for gallery and museum shows.

While the *casita* was being built, I lived with the Chávez Santiago family in their home, and began to bring small groups of visitors to study tapestry weaving and natural dyeing with them. Living with the family gave me an intimate perspective on daily life, religious practices, negotiating family relationships and interrelationships, and a chance to delve deeper into village life. My friendship circles grew to include extended family members and their children. I learned that the longer I lived here, the more layers of complexity were revealed. I learned that cultural competency depends on observation, acceptance, listening, understanding and suspending judgment. My host Federico urged me to stay calm and tranquil, remain patient: "*Calma, tranquila, paciencia,*" he would remind me if I became frustrated when things didn't move along as rapidly as I expected. There is definitely a different pace here, family-centric, focused on the now with no need for urgency. This is a culture that has thrived for 8,000 years. I figured I had a lot to learn—and still do.

In 2007, I began writing a blog, too, that talks about Oaxaca life, culture, textiles, food and a lot more. My program offerings grew to include arts and textile workshops, and study expeditions. I spent all my vacation time in Mexico, stretching the long holiday weekends, yearning for the day when it would become my full-time home.

You will notice that I write this from the point of view that I have not left the United States of America, but that Mexico has beckoned me and I have chosen her.

Mexico offers me a world beyond the one I grew up in. I was raised to be fearful and cautious, to make personal and family decisions based on what would guarantee security, to put my own adventurous spirit aside in favor of the practical. As a college graduate, I never went to Europe for the summer but went to work instead. I continued to work for a lifetime, taking two vacation weeks each year to visit family on the west coast. In my 40s, I realized I needed to start building a retirement fund and work for Social Security benefits. I dreamt of being a Peace Corps volunteer and became a mother, transitioned to becoming a single mother needing to provide health care and contribute to the college fund. I learned to be responsible and dedicated. I never had the full self-confidence to break away from the expected, although during my professional working years I always pursued modest creative arts endeavors, finding ways to sell my work.

Oaxaca is full of life, food, color, opportunity and infinite exploration of the physical world. This environment for me is stimulating and encouraging. It's a place that's also grounded in tradition and family, where local families have lived in the same town for generations. Roots here are deep. One cannot be here without feeling grounded. There is assurance in this, a comfort and security that most of us do not know in the U.S.A. Tradition is to be celebrated and families come together frequently to celebrate each other and their communities—birthdays, baptisms, *quinceaneras*, engagements, weddings and yes, even funerals. Community service is honored and supported. I am in awe of how people resolve disputes and conflicts, how mutual support—emotionally and economically—makes up the fiber of closely-knit-together indigenous people.

This is one reason I choose to live in an indigenous village rather than in the city, although I have many expat friends with whom I visit when I do go to town.

My choice to live in Mexico is more about social/cultural lifestyle and what I value than anything else. In the U.S.A. we live in a diaspora, dispersed, far from our sons and daughters, brothers and sisters, mothers and fathers. How often do we see them? How well do we know our aunts, uncles and cousins? Why do we do this? Because we go where we have employment. In Mexico, we stay because we have deep connections to family.

I never chose first and foremost to live in Mexico because my retirement dollar would go farther, although that has certainly helped. I chose to live here because I admire the culture, history, art, the work ethic of the people, their ability to innovate and adapt, to make use of things we might normally discard, and to endure despite deprivation and political pressure from El Norte.

I admire the ancient indigenous spirituality of paying attention to the earth, the cycles of life and death, planting and reaping, reverence for the natural world. The political and economic movements to preserve the original strains of corn from being contaminated by Monsanto, to preserve the varieties of peppers, tomatoes and squash—the gifts Mexico gave to the world—are sophisticated endeavors that few from El Norte appreciate or understand.

I love where I live, in a high desert valley surrounded by 12,000-foot mountain peaks, fertile because of rain and irrigation systems, with clear skies. My *casita* has no need for air conditioning or a heating system. When I walk my adopted street dogs out into the *campo*, I breathe deep. These are the first pets I have ever owned. I took them in out of their need and I stretched to embrace a new experience.

Here, the air is clean. I can see for miles. I'm healthier and stronger here. I walk trails shared by sheep, goats, cattle and herdsmen, along a path marked by stone pillars that delineate boundaries between villages. From the rise on the land, I see the Pan-American Highway MEX 190, once a footpath and trade route between Central and North America. Here, I feel a deep sense of connection to time and place.

And, yet, it is very important not to idealize or romanticize Mexico and living here. Many of us know it's easy to fall in love. And, those of us with tendencies to fall hard and fast can make impulsive decisions. We can get in trouble. Did I anticipate the pitfalls? No. Would I have done anything differently if I had? Still, no.

Things That Have Tripped Me Up
- Adjusting to a different pace, lifestyle and culture, i.e., the longer I live here the less I know
- Overcoming nuanced language barriers that limit understanding
- Overcoming subtle, unspoken, nonverbal signals
- Assuming, out of arrogance, that because we come from the U.S.A. or Canada we know better
- Keeping to ourselves, staying safe in the "Expat Enclave"
- Dealing with bureaucracies that grind slowly, make no sense
- Unknowingly assuming an attitude of entitlement, especially in restaurants and shops
- Expecting that we don't need to wait in line like everyone else
- Expecting that people will keep appointments and be on time
- Disinfecting everything we eat, especially fresh fruit and vegetables, without exception
- Not eating on the street
- Using receptacles for toilet paper
- Using bottled water for drinking, without exception
- The everyday inconveniences we don't encounter in the U.S.A.

We have an ongoing debate where I live among those of us who have relocated to Mexico: Are we expats or immigrants? The definition of "immigrant" is one that brings us on par with our Mexican sisters and brothers who seek a better and permanent life in another country.

Some say the word "expat" has the connotation of being "apart from" and "better than." I've read that "expat" is often interpreted as one who has no interest in learning about the country or culture where they live and see their place as being temporary. Expats are often snowbirds who come for the winter to escape the harsh climates of El Norte.

An immigrant, on the other hand, fully embraces where they live and intends to live in their new country indefinitely. These are subtle differences yet very meaningful. The term "immigrant" integrates me into my Mexican life. I come from a family of immigrants who left Eastern Europe for America in the early 1900s, wanting to escape oppression, discrimination and limited opportunity.

At the end of 2016, after the last presidential election in the U.S., I bought a condominium in downtown Durham, North Carolina, after living exclusively in Oaxaca for many years. This gives me a legal base from which to vote and advocate for change. While I'm only there for short visits, I feel this keeps me engaged in the effort to support the social and political values that are important to me. This gives me comfort and I try to stay hopeful.

The difference that living in Mexico has made in the quality of my life is enormous. Since I first visited Oaxaca in 2005, I began to independently study the textile culture of the state out of interest and curiosity. I visited and became friends with many artisans. Over time, I developed knowledge about Oaxaca, and by extension Mexico's, weaving and natural dye techniques. This practice added to the knowledge I'd already gleaned about indigenous textile-making from travels in China, Malaysia, Europe and Central America. I decided it was time to go deep and not wide. I took it upon myself to visit regions in Mexico where the textile culture was strong and thriving, often to mountain and coastal villages hours away from Oaxaca City where people speak native languages other than Spanish. Sometimes I went on my own and sometimes I went with guides.

"Life begins at the end of your comfort zone." This is a sticker on my sewing stand. Fear is natural. Will I be safe? This question has often kept me from experimentation and discovery. I've had to put this aside as I explored new places in Mexico. I'm aware and cautious; I weigh the consequences. I advise others how to navigate their journeys. With each step into unknown territory, my fear dissipates and it becomes easier to embark on something new.

Since 2007, after I began to offer weaving and natural dye workshops in Teotitlán del Valle taught by my host family, I expanded offerings to include photography, filmmaking, creative writing, textile-making and mixed media arts workshops. Then people asked to come with me on discovery trips I was making in Mexico, so I began offering longer, multi-day textile study expeditions. For Oaxaca visitors with only a limited amount of time, I created one-day natural dye and textile study expeditions.

By the time I retired in 2011, I had my transition plan in place. Today, I continue to seek out new locations to study, explore and navigate, doing my part to identify and give artisans the recognition and income they deserve.

This Mexico life has given me the gift of unlimited freedom to create and to manifest my dreams. I've learned key life skills by living in an indigenous community, among an ancient people who know more than I do about family and relationships. I am happy, content and satisfied to call Oaxaca, Mexico home.

Norma Schafer has offered arts education travel workshops and study expeditions in Mexico since 2006, based on her curiosity and love for Mexico and respect for indigenous people. Her Oaxaca Cultural Navigator programs include travel throughout Mexico; topics include art history, weaving, natural dyeing, creative writing, photography, mixed media art and general study tours.

Norma retired from the University of North Carolina at Chapel Hill after a 30-year career there and at several other colleges. She currently works with organizations developing customized programs for alumni, donors and friends that can also be fundraising opportunities. Norma is a contributing writer to the travel guide, "Textile Fiestas of Mexico," and has been featured in The New York Times and Mexico News Daily. She's also a published photographer and writer, and blogs at http://oaxacaculture.com. Contact her at norma.schafer@icloud. com and: Instagram: @oaxacaculturemexico, Facebook: https://www. facebook.com/normalee.schafer and YouTube: https://www.youtube. com/user/normahawthorne.

16. "In Search of Connection"

Jan I. Davis
San Miguel de Allende, Guanajuato

I think I pissed off the first expat I ever met. He was an ex-Peace Corp volunteer in Ecuador who had written a few books. I tagged along with a fellow student who wanted to interview him about his decision to live abroad. He served us tepid cups of chamomile tea and grumbled answers to our questions. When I tripped and broke the frayed cord of his space heater, he scowled. The expats I met after that were mostly barflies.

But that was the late '70s and I was young, and because of these encounters I couldn't see myself as an expat. Yet I've wanted to live in another country since I was a child. I had a few opportunities, but they weren't meant to be until I found myself in my 50s, divorced and with no children or extended family.

I felt alone, and the U.S. is not an easy place to feel alone. Here's what I mean. One day after my then-husband had just moved from Morocco to the U.S., we walked to a neighborhood café. He asked, "Where is everyone?" I understood what he meant. The streets were completely empty of people. My neighbors were in their homes, in their offices, in their cars, and now more than ever, on their electronic devices. I've always felt life in the U.S. was centered around work, making money, getting ahead, shopping and being productive. It wasn't a life I related to, nor wanted to relate to. And my travels overseas showed me that life could be different.

Nevertheless, it wasn't a simple decision to leave the U.S. I was worried that I was thinking "the grass is always greener on the other side of the fence," and I was afraid of leaving the comfort of my home, my nest, in Portland, Oregon. But it was time. A comment made by a good friend helped me gain clarity about my decision.

"You go to San Miguel de Allende to disconnect," she said at a dinner gathering.

"No," I mused. "I go to connect."

I realized then that I just felt happier, more myself, in a country where the people—and the climate—were warmer. And my curious and empathetic nature yearned for relationships with people unlike me.

I spent many hours as a child reading the obituaries. Not all of them, just those of people with foreign-sounding names, marveling that someone born in Portugal or Armenia had left their countries to live in California's San Joaquin Valley. I remember my disappointment when I learned that my last name, Davis, was the seventh most common surname in the U.S. But I was delighted that my Scottish ancestors had their own tartans: Innes and Ayers.

I don't know if I can attribute this odd pastime to my inquiring nature, or to my parents' tendencies to point out people who weren't like us: WASPS. My mom refused to go to Kmart because that's where Mexicans shopped. My parents would remark that our neighbors, the Echeverrias, were Basques, and the Asadoorians were Armenians. It didn't matter that they were born in the U.S., they were foreign. I was too young to understand some of the comments were racist, but I did register that many of their remarks were unfair.

In the early '70s, when I saw the yellow school bus full of Mexicans and Blacks arrive for the first time at my elementary school, my heart ached because I thought they must feel angry or scared or embarrassed. So naturally, I made an effort to be friends, developed a crush on Jesse, and invited Teresita over for peanut butter and crackers. When Josie invited Shanna and me to attend her birthday party, my dad told us to "lock the doors" when we crossed the tracks.

I relished school. My third-grade teacher, Mrs. Tomajan, showed us slides of her native Armenia, and Mrs. Nance taught us to play bingo in Spanish. While my mom taught piano in our living room,

I'd spend the afternoons in my bedroom, spinning the globe to see what country landed on my index finger. Or I'd type stories on my dad's Olivetti typewriter about kids in other countries. I sent letters to postmasters in Scotland and Canada and asked for pen pals.

I had a happy childhood until my mom found Jesus, and a different man. She was the organist at the church and he was the choir director. I don't remember any Brady Bunch-style talks with my parents about the divorce and about how "everything was going to be OK." I do remember my dad's barely furnished apartment across town, and my brother graduating early so he could leave the house and bolt to the coast.

Within six months the new husband moved in, and my mom told me, "We won't be happy with you living with us" and said I should get an apartment with my friend Stacy, whose parents had also just divorced. I was 15 years old. Later on, I realized my mom was very depressed at that time, but her emotional outbursts created in me a lifelong battle with low self-esteem and a deep yearning for connection.

I didn't move in with Stacy; instead, an American Field Service (AFS) summer abroad scholarship landed me in Seville, Spain after my senior year in high school. I was too unworldly to understand the significance of my host family being pro-Franco (the dictator had died the year before) and felt slightly intimidated by their wealth and sophistication. My host mother was an elegant woman who gathered her reddish hair with an ornate tortoiseshell clip. She'd smile as she indicated which plate to use for each dish during the daily two-hour lunch. My host father was aloof and would smoke a cigar in the salon and take a quick snooze before returning to work. I'd tiptoe past him to my room, while the three eldest daughters would get ready for their beaus to take them to the swim club. I spent most days exploring the city alone.

While I didn't bond with my host family, I connected with Seville—the language, the kissing-on-both-cheeks greetings, the Islamic architecture, the *tortilla Española* and *jamón serrano*, even the men's catcalls. And, I made a friend that summer: Barbara, a British woman in her 40s who lived upstairs. As I was alienated from my mother, she was estranged from her daughter. Barbara taught me how to drive a stick shift, and also took me shopping, to discotheques, and to my first flamenco show, performed by drag queens. I've never forgotten her.

I had always excelled in school, but after my parent's divorce I felt unmoored and didn't want to go to college. Yet with a hefty dose of financial aid and my dad's practical insistence I went to a small college in Portland. While I felt out of place among the children of Rockefellers, Weyerhaeusers and Saudi royalty, the liberal arts education rocked my world. My dad is a staunch Republican, and if he'd known where I'd focus my interests during those four years, he might have thought twice about paying for my education. I favored classes that focused on anything alternative to my status quo, such as Labor Literature, Pedagogy of the Oppressed, and Politics in Latin America. In my dorm room hung posters with slogans like "It Will Be A Great Day When Our Schools Get All The Money They Need & The Air Force Has To Hold A Bake Sale To Buy A Bomber." I wrote a letter to Pinochet in Chile protesting the disappearances and torture of thousands of citizens, joined Amnesty International and draped "Stop U.S. Intervention In El Salvador!" banners over freeway overpasses in Portland.

Perhaps the best part of college were the two semesters I spent in Ecuador and Costa Rica. I designed two independent studies that put me on buses far into the Andes, ranches on the coast, in the company of warm and generous locals. I remember calling my dad from a phone booth in Liberia, a town in Northern Costa Rica where I lived with a family. A sweetie, a bike and a healthy diet of rice and beans made me one happy camper. I told my dad I wanted to stay longer. He said, "I understand, but if you don't come home now and finish your last semester in college, you never will." He was right. I went back.

Fast forward 10 years, through random jobs and enjoying my 20s. Then I settled down. I married a lovely man and got a Masters in Library and Information Studies at UC Berkeley. Working in academic and corporate libraries stifled my entrepreneurial spirit, so I started my own research company. Because we were both self-employed, I had hopes we would move somewhere in the Caribbean. I subscribed to "International Living" magazine and looked into work options. But that dream, along with plans of having a child and a happy marriage, ended after 14 years. It took me many years to understand how discounted I felt by his change of heart over having a baby. It was lonely and often gut-wrenching to go to one baby shower after another, listen to endless book club discussions over choices of schools and have to answer the question "When are you having a baby?"

Towards the end of my marriage, I received a grant to teach in Argentina for three weeks. I was excited to see if I actually could work from anywhere. In Buenos Aires I made a good friend, Roxana, who invited me to visit as often as I'd like, and I did.

After my divorce, when Roxana wrote, "Come on down," I thought it was the perfect chance to move overseas. I packed my bags. But the time and place weren't right. Excited when I arrived, it didn't take long for the pain from my recent divorce to surface. I was depressed, felt very alone and didn't have the energy to deal with a bustling city of 13 million people. Plus, Roxana preferred staying home over going out, and when I asked her to introduce me to some men, she said all her male friends were gay. Deflated, I returned home.

Back in Portland, one rainy November evening I made the unusual decision to take an *American Photographer* mentor workshop in Morocco. Unusual because I wasn't into group travel, especially with tourists with big cameras around their necks. But the street life in Marrakech's streets, the colors, smells and smiles (and the handsome men), had charmed me into going back many times. I found an internet shop in a hotel, where I spent several hours a day working on my research projects. I liked this particular shop because it was lively with tourists and locals, and its manager, Abdel, was friendly and funny. He would often place a glass of mint tea over my shoulder while I was working, and we'd chat while I was waiting for web pages to load. Little did I know at the time that we would end up marrying two years later.

It was difficult to date Abdel in Marrakech because he was an observant Muslim and it was inappropriate for him to visit me at my bed and breakfast. We decided it was easier and more economical if I moved in with his mother (and nine other family members, but that's a novel in itself). So, at the age of 44, I found myself with something I'd always wanted—a large, extended family who embraced me. I wanted so badly to fit in. I bathed at the communal bath down the street, learned to make balls of hot couscous with my hand, and endured excruciatingly long visits with his friends and siblings. Living "like a Moroccan" with his mother wasn't easy, and I couldn't afford to have a home in Marrakech without selling my house in Portland, which I wasn't ready to do.

So, Abdel came to the States. As it was challenging for me to live in Marrakech, it was hard for him to live in the U.S. Inter-cultural marriages can be challenging, as ours was. We divorced after six years, and it was heartbreaking because we so wanted it to work. We remain good friends, and Abdel always reminds me if I ever find myself alone and in need of a family to take care of me, there's one waiting in Marrakech. I believe him.

One day I received a phone call from my brother. "Let's go to San Miguel de Allende and write a book about a brother and sister thinking about buying a house there." This was a strange request from a brother I'd never traveled with, and while we get along, we weren't exactly close. But we were both curious about the expat community in San Miguel, so I said, "Why not?"

We never wrote the book, but we did both fall in love with this colonial city in Central Mexico. He bought a lot and built a small house, and I returned many times over the following five years to house- and pet-sit. With each visit I'd stay a week longer, then two weeks, then three, to test if I was ready to leave the U.S. I never was.

Back in the States, friends and colleagues would comment on how happy and relaxed I was. But within a month I'd be irritable again. The rain, the isolation, the traffic. Don't get me wrong—I loved Portland, my friends, my house and my neighbors. But it was a solitary life, and I wanted the contentment I felt when I was in Mexico. When I was housesitting in San Miguel, my life was reduced to what I had in my suitcase. No fussing over stuff, and since I didn't have a car, no fretting over traffic. My daily routine changed. Buying groceries was easy because fruit and vegetable stands and colorful markets were easily reached on foot. I "worked smarter" to get work done in fewer hours so I could get together with the interesting people I was meeting. Life seemed so much easier.

But I had doubts about moving. Why couldn't I recreate the life I experienced in San Miguel back in Portland? I thought of that scene in the movie "My Dinner with Andre" when Wally says to Andre, "Why do we require a trip to Mt. Everest in order to be able to perceive reality? Is Mt. Everest more real than New York? Isn't New York real?" Was I simply running away from an unfulfilling life in Portland? Wouldn't "my reality" be the same in San Miguel? The answer was no. Life in Mexico is just different because the culture is different.

It took five years of going back and forth to Mexico before I sold just about all of my possessions. A hot real estate market in Portland and the perfect, furnished house I found waiting for me in San Miguel made the decision feel "just right." It wasn't easy, but I've never looked back.

My life in Mexico has forced me to change, all for the better. Who knew I had control issues?! I've become more patient, I'm calmer and more spontaneous and creative. And more importantly, I've found my "tribe" of kindred spirits, people who make time for each other, people who check in when they haven't heard from or seen me in a few days. And I do the same with them. This leads me to say that my expat experience wouldn't be the same if I'd moved to some random town in Mexico or Morocco or Argentina. For me, it's important to be in an expat community because of its tendency to attract out-of-the ordinary people. San Miguel de Allende draws a lot of mild eccentrics, like me. I love that.

But, as Jon Kabat-Zinn titled his book, "Wherever You Go, There You Are," I have the same personal issues I've struggled with throughout my life. Moving to Mexico didn't magically make those disappear. But the lifestyle here is providing the space and lots of opportunities to grow.

San Miguel isn't perfect. Like in a relationship, the reasons for falling in love with the city often irritate me. Part of the joy felt in San Miguel is because its inhabitants love to celebrate. A wedding, a birth, a funeral or a particular Saint's Day will warrant dozens of cherry bombs, or shall I say watermelon bombs, all day long. I love the fact that almost all my shopping is done within a few blocks from my house, at family-owned businesses. But show up at any given hour and the shop might be closed. I admire and learn from the laid-back manner of most locals, but that attitude can be frustrating when tasks take longer to accomplish. And I *do* miss the lush Pacific Northwest environment and grocery store aisles filled with chocolate.

But for the moment, San Miguel de Allende is where I'm supposed to be. I feel lucky to live here. And if I move on one day, I doubt it will be back to the U.S. because now I know how it feels to be connected.

Jan Davis hails from the U.S. West Coast and now lives in San Miguel de Allende, Mexico. She loves to hang out in her home reading, painting and rummaging through her bins of fabric. Meeting up with good friends in cafés and rooftop bars ranks high on her list of favorite things to do. For more than 20 years, Jan has made a living by providing research and writing services to business professionals in the U.S. She admits to being a crazy cat lady and is devoted to a group of eight street cats near her home.

17. "You're Moving WHERE?!"

Gayla Jones
Jocotepec, Lake Chapala, Jalisco

It all really started in March of 2017. I was working a temporary job as an executive administrative assistant at a major university hospital.

After my retirement from the Air Force as a jet engine mechanic in 1996, I did many things for employment. I wound up as secretary at lots of different types of businesses, including a district attorney's office, a tribal council and for the director at a Veteran's Administration hospital.

But let's back up a little to get some history. In 2015, my husband decided we needed to open our own business. Long story short: The business failed. I lost all of my savings, money that I'd carefully put away for more than 25 years. In the latter half of 2016 and early 2017, I was alone, divorced and without the money I'd counted on for my senior years. I felt desperate.

I was without a job and needed to get back into the job market to survive. I worked several temporary positions for about a year and a half. During this time, I was in my early 60s, and even with all my experience, I couldn't get an interview anywhere. No one wanted to hire an older woman. I was finally hired by the University of Kentucky working for the vice president of the hospital. It was only a short-term position, but they ended up keeping me on longer than was originally planned to help me out.

I'd researched becoming an expat a year earlier but knew my husband at the time would not go for it. Now, in March of 2017, my husband was gone and I was looking at losing my temp job. I was single with three dogs, a house and a car, and nothing in the future to keep me working.

A magazine I'd found in February talked about becoming an expat. The bug bit me again and I started doing more research on locations and housing. I narrowed down the places I was looking at to Mexico, Costa Rica and Belize. I ordered books from Amazon about these places and the expat life in those areas. I subscribed to YouTube videos that had a lot of practical, on-the-ground information about shopping, housing, etc. And some of the videos were interviews with single women who had made the move on their own.

And so it began. I'd already contacted a realtor about selling my house, and the housing market in the Lexington, Kentucky area was exploding. I upgraded some things in my home and put it on the market the first week of May. By this time, I already had all my plans laid out. I would fly down to Guadalajara and visit the Ajijic/ Lakeside area to find a place to live, and then come back, sell the house and anything I couldn't move with me, pack my car and be on my way around the first of July.

In May, I decided to go to an expat conference in Atlanta that answered a lot of my questions about moving outside of the U.S. and it got me even more excited. There were speakers that talked about medical coverage, visas and just a lot of information about becoming an expat in multiple South American countries. I then spoke with the gentleman that put on the conference, who at the time was residing in Ajijic, Mexico. I was able to get some great information about that area from him, and my decision was made. I was moving to the Ajijic area, or Lakeside as we call it.

My decision was based on several factors, including that it had a great base of expats which would make it a good place to begin my new life and become familiar with the language and lifestyle. I figured I could always change my mind after I got my feet wet. I was receiving a retirement check from the Air Force and knew that since I would turn 62 in May, I could go ahead and apply for my Social Security retirement, too. Between these two checks, I could live comfortably in Mexico, according to what I'd learned.

Everything went as planned. I flew down in June and found a rental casita in Jocotepec that would accept my three dogs. The landlords were from Kentucky also, so we had a lot in common. I signed a lease and told them I'd be back by the middle of July. I returned home and found that my house had sold. We closed on the house on June 30 and I stayed with a friend for a couple of days getting everything packed into my small Kia Soul. On Wednesday, the Fourth of July, I loaded my three little dogs in the car and we headed for the border. Happy Independence Day for me!

The drive through the States wasn't too bad. I'd researched pet-friendly hotels and made reservations before I left. The trip from Kentucky to the border took two days. The dogs had never ridden in a car for this long of a trip, but they settled down after the first day. We made it to Laredo on Thursday evening, and on Friday morning we were at the Colombia Bridge border crossing. I was scared to death! I'd been overseas before during my military service, but they had taken care of everything then. Here, I was on my own.

It was July and it was hot. At the border crossing, I had to leave my car running with the air-conditioning on for the dogs. (At least the area they told me to park in was covered.) I had no idea how long it would take me to get through customs and get all my paperwork. I was coming in on a tourist permit that was good for 180 days. They took a look at the contents of my car through the windows and said OK. Sometimes they'll make you unload everything to search through your items. I was lucky. I think it was because I had three dogs in the car.

I went inside with my stack of papers. No one else was there at 8 a.m. I highly recommend the Columbia Bridge crossing if you're coming across at the Laredo area. It's hardly ever busy except on holidays. I went to the first window, which turned out to be for my vehicle. With no Spanish language experience, I was nervous. We were able to understand each other enough so that they could direct me to the visa office. It took just minutes to finish there, then back to the vehicle window. Over a course of about 20-30 minutes, we got everything done. I had my Mexico paperwork in hand, and the dogs and I began our drive to Jocotepec.

By posting on various Facebook pages, I'd found a pet-friendly hotel and we spent our first night at Las Palmas Hotel in Matehuala. Of course, the dogs needed stops along the way. There weren't any rest stops as we know them in the States. I just stopped at gas stations and tried to find a grassy area. They were few and far between.

We made it to our new home on Saturday, July 7. I will tell you that during the drive down, I was "gringoed," as I call it. When you stop for gas, always check the gas pump to see that it's zeroed out. I wound up paying $1,500 pesos ($80 U.S.) for a tank of gas that should have cost no more than $700 pesos. Oh, and be ready for driving rules that are nothing like the States! You just have to keep your eyes on the roads and the other vehicles, especially motorcycles.

I've been living in Mexico now for more than a year, and I'm very happy here. I've made new friends, gotten involved with horses (since I'd owned my own in Kentucky) and taken several classes for different types of creative artwork. I'm an avid karaoke singer and I even found a place to do that. I've taken some Spanish classes, but I find it easier to just pick up words as I go along. I'm still working on it.

After being an executive secretary and military retiree, I was used to being on-the-go most of the time. Life here takes a little getting used to; it's at a very slow, laid-back pace. You can just sit and relax on the patio, enjoy the wonderful weather, see historic sites or meet up with other people who've made the move and exchange war stories about your experiences. Really ... you're allowed to slow down! My friends and family thought I was being foolish to make this type of move alone. No one has come to visit yet. Some of them say that they won't come to a Third World country, others just say, yeah, we'll make it down sometime. They still doubt that I'm really happy and enjoying myself and that it's safe here.

But I'm here to say that you can do it with all the right planning and preparation. You have to do your research! There are many Facebook groups and YouTube videos that you can check out and get questions answered about living in Mexico. I did it all in just a matter of months and I wouldn't change a thing.

Why did I leave the United States? After working since I was

14, I wouldn't have enough money between my Social Security and Air Force retirement to live in the States. I'd always dreamed of somewhere semi-tropical like Lakeside, and now here I am!

Gayla was born in Hamilton, Ohio and raised in nearby Middletown, where she lived for 17 years. After high school, she moved around the Ohio, Kentucky and Tennessee area before joining the Air Force in 1979 as a single parent. Gayla had learned auto mechanics during her teen years and signed up as a jet engine technician. There were not many women in the maintenance field at that time. Her duty stations included Travis AFB, California; Kadena AB, Okinawa, Japan; Kunsan AB, South Korea and Hill AFB, Utah, where she worked on F-15s, F-16s, C-5s and C-141s. She stayed in Utah for 10 years until her retirement from the military as a Master Sergeant (E-7). Gayla then moved across the country to North Carolina to attend college for equine technology. In 1997, she and her husband purchased a 28-acre farm in Lawrenceburg, Kentucky and raised horses for several years. Gayla has three children, six grandchildren and now lives on her own in San Antonio, Jalisco, Mexico.

18. "We're Not in Kansas Anymore"

Dianne Hofner Saphiere
Mazatlán, Sinaloa

Growing up in northern Arizona among the Hopi and Diné instilled in me a passion for justice and a disdain for the abuse of power. Most of my native friends spoke three languages but were forced to live in BIA (Bureau of Indian Affairs) dormitories away from their families on the reservation during the week, and as students they found it really tough to get a part-time job due to prejudice. The situation infuriated and baffled me.

As a teenager, I was fortunate to spend summers in Mexico City with a homestay family. This instilled in me a desire to work internationally and a commitment to helping people understand and respect one another. After living and working in Japan and Spain, in the mid-2000s I was married with a son and living in Kansas. I'd begun to feel the U.S.A. was becoming more insular and protectionist, less humane, more rule-driven and authoritarian. I didn't want our son taking on such mindsets, and I especially didn't want him growing up blind to the privilege he had been born into as a middle-class white kid in a world superpower. Most of his elementary school friends didn't think farther than K-State or KU; I wanted Danny to be a citizen of the world. I began dreaming of living overseas again, so our son could experience life as a minority and develop the skillset to succeed in that dynamic, and so he could be raised with a second language and culture.

My partner, Greg, had a wonderful job that paid great. He worked hard, very long hours, but there were incredible benefits;

he loved the job and they loved him. Moving would mean giving all that up. My career, in contrast, was more portable; as a consultant, as long as I was near an airport and had internet, I could work. After heartfelt discussions and lots of soul searching, we made the decision to move. It was one of the most difficult decisions we've ever had to make and involved us listening deeply to one another's hopes and fears, clarifying our values individually and as a family and exploring various strategies for achieving our goal.

Where to move, on the other hand, was an easy decision for us. We owned a vacation home in Mazatlán and had good friends there as well—locals that Greg had worked with decades ago. We loved that it's a real city with a diversified economy, not just a tourist town. We loved that it has a vibrant arts and culture scene and numerous universities. Greg was all for the move, but he was uncomfortable leaving without having a base in the U.S. as well. We weren't sure where it would be, but we agreed we'd buy a condo somewhere in the U.S., "just in case." Since I'd inherited a bunch of my Mom's antique furniture and wasn't yet ready to get rid of it, that base would become a glorified storage unit.

We made our decision a year prior to our move, because we wanted to give ourselves time to clean out and downsize our huge home, and we wanted to give our son (and ourselves) time to learn Spanish and get used to the idea. He was in fifth grade and vehemently opposed to leaving his friends. We hired a young woman to come in twice a week to tutor him in Spanish. Learning was slow and at times painful. He wasn't motivated. The tutor was great and has become a lifelong friend.

We worked that full year to strategically clean out our home, as we'd be living in a condo one-third its size. We gave furniture away to family members, had several garage sales and made monthly donations to charities. We looked at possible sites for our U.S. base, and settled on getting a condo close to my birthplace in Wisconsin. Since Danny is an only child and we'd always lived far from family, we thought it might give us a chance to get him more connected to his extended family. I studied Spanish with a tutor also, another woman that I became dear friends with. We looked into visa requirements, finding a new home for our beloved dog (we didn't want to subject her to life in a condo after she'd grown used to running free) and banking.

We spent loads of time and a trip to Mazatlán to visit and assess schools—at the time there were several bilingual but no international schools, and we looked at a couple of public schools, too. We wanted to be sure Danny picked up the language and culture, but we wanted to ease his transition as much as we could, and a bilingual environment would help with that. We got his school transcripts and apostille documents prior to leaving Kansas, as we knew we'd need them to enroll in school in Mexico.

Nine months prior to our planned move, Greg gave notice at work. He wanted to give them plenty of time to find a replacement. Leaving a terrific job at the height of one's career struck everyone as foolhardy. "You've worked your whole life to reach this point; enjoy it a while. Put in just another five or 10 years and your nest egg will be that much bigger," we were told repeatedly. "Most people would kill for your job. You'll never find another fit that's so very perfect. Be grateful and enjoy it."

We were very grateful. And we knew that moving was the best choice. Greg worked weekends, evenings and holidays; family time was a rare event. Moving would change that. He'd take a six-month sabbatical, and then look for a job that would allow him more time with us as a family. The decision appeared foolish to many, but over the previous four years we had both lost our parents, my sister and her son, and a couple of good friends. We knew life was short, and we should seize the day. We knew it was time.

Several weeks after Greg gave notice, I was diagnosed with cancer. Everything happened fast, as you can imagine: two surgeries, advice to get our affairs in order, lots of tears and angst. His employer very kindly offered to rescind his resignation. They knew we wouldn't have health insurance once he quit, and with a cancer diagnosis we surely needed health insurance. We appreciated the offer, we discussed it, but we had faith. We knew in our hearts we were doing the right thing, and we hoped and trusted that things would work out.

Fortunately Greg was still working, so our health insurance covered the surgeries and treatment. By the time we left five months later I had a clean bill of health. Though of course with a history of cancer, no insurance provider wanted to enroll us. We subscribed to IMSS (affordable Mexican public healthcare) in case of a major cancer relapse, and finally found an insurance provider based in France that would accept us for the non-catastrophic medical bills. The premiums were higher than we'd have liked, but we could swing it. We dropped IMSS after two years once we were fully covered by the new provider.

Our actual move was pretty complicated, at least for my brain. Greg and a friend packed up a shipment of antique furniture and any extra housewares we had and took it up to our new condo in Wisconsin. We arranged for an estate sale company to sell the remainder of our furniture and household items in Kansas City. We packed what we'd need for the first month of work and life in Mazatlán into our Honda Civic hybrid, and on June 14, 2008, we picked our son up from scout camp and commenced the big drive south! That same day I also wrote the first entry in our blog, VidaMaz.com, which we started in order to keep family and friends up to speed on our new life. The movers had already packed up the remainder of our things—one chair we just couldn't part with was the only furniture we'd move, and the truck was heading south ahead of us. The moving truck, which held several other household's worth of stuff, too, was due to arrive in Mazatlán in three weeks, customs permitting.

The three of us will never forget driving south and seeing the ocean for the first time, a couple of hours' north of Mazatlán! Every time we pass that spot now we reminisce about the joy and excitement we felt that day. We moved in our clothes and computers and were very fortunate to already have furniture and the basics in what for the past three years had been our vacation home.

We look back on our first year in Mazatlán as a blur. We spent loads of time running errands and dealing with vendors those first few months. So many people were very helpful, yet we all remember the "curtain lady from hell," from whom we bought shutters and blinds that never quite functioned correctly. It was hard to get work done as we were so busy running around getting our life set up; most things in Mexico are done live and in person, not virtually, and much more so in 2008 than today. Our work required reliable, robust internet—which really didn't exist in Mazatlán in 2008 and for years after. So, we paid for two different internet providers, hoping at least one would work on any given day; the cost of doing business in Mexico.

Our first big shock after our move was when the moving truck arrived. They were missing something like four boxes from our load, and a few very expensive items had mysteriously disappeared between our homes in Kansas and Mazatlán. Greg's effective negotiating ended up getting us the move for almost no cost, but we were sadly out some family heirlooms.

Danny studied with a tutor several nights a week after school. He worked with a teacher and an outside tutor. He turned 13 shortly after our move—I'll never forget the young girls hanging on the young boys during his birthday pool party, another shock. We moved at an age when Mom and Dad knew nothing, at least in his eyes. Helping Danny with homework brought tears and frustration, so the tutors were a godsend. We all clearly remember one day about six months into living in Mazatlán, when Danny woke up and "suddenly" understood his homework. From then on out it was smooth sailing. At university he was commended by a professor for being one of the "career-best" bilinguals she'd worked with. Reading her comments sure did my heart good!

School brought a lot of cultural adjustment—we moved because we wanted a minority experience, and we were repeatedly reminded to watch what you ask for! Creative casting had Danny starring in the school play as the "ugly gringo boss" of a tall skinny white boy in the role of a poor *campesino* named Jesús, and we were often unaware of soccer practice and games until the very last minute, occasionally not at all. We also remember leaving town for summer vacation with plans to return on a certain date, only to learn three weeks later the school district had moved up the start of school by a week! We couldn't imagine that happening in the U.S., and quickly and expensively had to change our return flight reservations.

The parents of Danny's friends at school were one of the most difficult adjustments for me. I remember the mothers pushing and shoving to purchase books for their kids that first year, so much so that I left school crying and shaking. We had quite a few parents of Danny's friends shame us for having moved here: "Why in the world would you take your son out of a good quality school in a safe neighborhood in the U.S. and bring him to Mazatlán?! It's irresponsible parenting!"

It was disheartening to me that they could feel so negatively about their hometown. We experienced a very high quality of education in Mazatlán, but their comments naturally caused us to doubt our parenting. Our families and friends didn't understand it, either. Barely anyone visited us the first few years after our move, convinced that Mexico was too dangerous. I think I finally felt redeemed when Danny was accepted to all but one of the universities he applied for and received four or five scholarships of U.S. $80,000 or more. It seems both U.S. and Mexican colleges look for multicultural, multilingual kids with life experience.

As with any move, it took us a while to find friends we really resonated with, but fortunately we now have a good core group of both locals and expats. We'd host parties at our house, and quickly found that we couldn't mix upper- and working-class local friends; neither set would be comfortable with the other present. We still find it challenging to invite mixed groups of locals and expats to the same shindig, as many of our local friends don't speak English, and sadly quite a few expats aren't comfortable for an entire evening of Spanish. I still don't like how during parties women gravitate to one room and men to another, and I've learned that local women stay in touch much more frequently and effusively than what I was used to, with WhatsApp and phone calls being the preferred methods.

Greg, Danny and I developed new traditions, like "*palapa* Friday:" fresh seafood lunch on the beach with our toes in the sand, designed to help us decompress after a hard week in a foreign culture, to remind us why we moved here in the first place. I did not imagine the career implications our move would have. Many of my colleagues insisted on believing we had retired. Even though they were international consultants, trainers and educators, many of them remained convinced that you didn't move to Mexico to continue working.

So, what changed with our move to Mexico? We began eating a lot healthier. I'd always prided myself on daily home-cooked meals made from scratch. But here it was much easier to get fresher produce, fish, seafood and meat; there are far fewer processed food options, which is a blessing to one's health. And the big meal of the day is eaten in the afternoon, with more of a snack in the evening, which has been great for our weight. We keep *agua fresca* in the refrigerator—water flavored with fresh fruit or vegetables and sweetened with stevia. In addition to the carrot and celery sticks we always have on hand for snacking, we've added jicama, which we all love.

Our son was very upset when we first told him we were moving to Mexico. Now he loves Mazatlán: the warm weather and the beach, the view of the ocean and the mountains from our condo. But he didn't want to leave his friends. On the one-year anniversary of our move, Greg woke him up for school and told him what day it was. "One year since the best decision of our lives," the 13-year-old proclaimed. And, indeed, it was. In Kansas I'd always put time limits on Danny's screen time, but he loved video games and television. Once we'd moved to Mazatlán he didn't have much time for either. He played soccer, did school-required social service (walking dogs, cleaning trash, helping teach English), and he was very active in Scouts, which here are co-ed and intergenerational. Scouts were a godsend. There Danny perfected his Spanish and formed friendships I know he'll have for a lifetime. He learned to look out for and teach the younger kids. He developed skills that we dearly miss now that he's not living with us anymore. He also had a lot of parties. Both middle- and high-school brought multiple parties every week: birthdays, friends' families' events, group and club events. He was too busy for television, and if he played video games it was now with a group of friends playing Guitar Hero or some such; life became much more communal and convivial.

The move greatly strengthened our nuclear family. After his six-month sabbatical, Greg ended up joining me in my consulting business. Working with him has been a godsend and allowed us freedom to spend time with Danny. In Kansas he had to battle to leave work, wearing his suit, to watch Danny play soccer or basketball. Here he was able to be around most of the time, help with meal planning and cooking, and be available when the teenager needed advice or correction.

Ironically, moving to Mexico reconnected us to family. After the loss of our parents and my sister and nephew, we sort of felt like we didn't have anyone left. Once we moved to Mazatlán, we made the commitment to go north to visit extended family over the very short summer break from school. I never would have imagined what a blessing this would become! Each year our stay got a bit longer, as Danny got to know and enjoy his cousins more, and I reconnected with my long-lost beloved cousin-sisters and aunts.

That blog we started to connect with family and friends hit a sweet spot with lots of people thinking about moving to Mexico. Over the years we've helped dozens of families choose schools, find a neighborhood to live in and settle into their new lives in Mazatlán. I've consulted friends on raising multilingual, multicultural children, or coping with culture shock and coming out the other end stronger and more resilient. VidaMaz.com was honored by the Sinaloa State Secretary of Tourism for its contributions, and we've received recognition from quite a few other sources as well. What's been fabulous is the variety of incredible people we've gotten to know through our curiosity and the blog, people we are privileged to now call friends. When I wrote that first entry I never would have dreamed what a blessing that blog would become.

Finally, the change of scenery and friendships gave me the push I needed to devote more time to developing my photography. I've always loved taking pictures, but being surrounded by creative friends in Mexico motivated me to take a class and dedicate a day a week to learning new techniques. Photography quickly became a passion, and last fall and this spring I was blessed with four exhibits in a row. Two were in Europe—Paris and Vienna—on the Mayo-Yoreme (natives of northern Sinaloa and southern Sonora) *Konti* (Lenten festival). Europeans were delighted to learn how the Yoreme have used ritual and tradition to keep kids off drugs and the streets and connected to community, and the Yoreme were in turn psyched to have Parisians and Viennese learning from them. The third and fourth exhibitions were in Mazatlán, one breaking attendance records for a gallery opening by our municipal CULTURA office, and another exhibit forming the entrance to our Mexican international tourism fair, where even the President stopped to have his photo taken.

The move to Mazatlán has most definitely been a major success for our family on so very many fronts. Our son sees himself as a world citizen; he defines himself as multilingual and multicultural. His employers value that in him, and repeatedly note on performance appraisals that one of his most helpful skills is his ability to facilitate teamwork and decision-making, especially when there are diverse opinions. To me, that in itself is priceless, and I doubt seriously it would have been a skill Danny would have developed growing up in Kansas City.

Greg and I are much healthier than we were up north. We've both lost weight and exercise daily. He's returned to running, a sport he did when he was younger and is very much enjoying again in middle age. He reads widely and is always keeping me up-to-date on the latest inventions, oddities and pop culture in our world. I believe we've all developed emotional resilience living in Mexico, flexibility, the value of a positive outlook and constructive problem-solving, and we're much better able to go with the flow and enjoy life.

We told our son from a young age that it's not the party that's good or bad, it's you and the people present who make the party. These are our lives to live, and our lives will be what we make of them. We are very happy to have seized the day and hope to continue doing that for a long time. Our path is no doubt very different than yours, and we hope our experience might provide some food for thought or inspiration for your journey.

Dianne Hofner Saphiere was born the middle of five children to a German-American family in southeastern Wisconsin. They relocated to northern Arizona when she entered middle school; there she began a lifelong fascination with indigenous cultures. Dianne graduated with a master's degree from colleges in northern California and lived and worked for more than a decade in Japan. She's married to an incredibly talented and supportive partner, Greg, and very proud of her Third

Culture Kid (TCK), Danny, who is an economic geographer.

Professionally Dianne wears several hats. She's an intercultural organization development consultant who has worked with people from more than120 nations and traveled to over 85, living for 10+ years in Japan and for a shorter time in Spain. She's the creator of Cultural Detective, an online series of intercultural competence development materials co-created with 160 international professionals.

Dianne is an avid photographer at Thru Di's Eyes (https://www. thrudiseyes.com), and has had exhibitions in Paris, Vienna and throughout Mexico. Follow her family's personal journeys at VidaMaz. com (https://vidamaz.com).

19. "Seeking Paradise"

PC Nordhoff
Chuburná Puerto, Yucatán

Our retirement in Mexico began as more of a necessity than a spur-of-the-moment life choice. In fact, I investigated Costa Rica and Panama before making Mexico our final decision. Otherwise I knew my husband and I would have to continue working until we were 70-plus just to get by had we decided to stay in America. At that time, our "lifestyle" was nothing more than working steadily just to pay the bills and worrying constantly about making ends meet every single month. In other words, no real quality of life as we grew older. I felt depressed and desperate every time I thought about the future.

We chose Mexico because of the lower cost of living, the proximity to the U.S. and the beauty of the beaches I'd only previously seen on internet travel sites. I was simply unaware of the incredible beauty that truly exists in Mexico until my flight landed in Mérida and I began my quest for a beach house where my husband and I could happily retire and make our own personal Paradise.

The day I arrived in Mexico and walked out of the airport it was as bright and shimmering as a watercolor painting. The brilliant sunlight not only heightened the colors of everything, but also intensified the smells and scents of the flowers and trees. I was astounded and amazed at the sheer beauty of the place! I'd landed in Mérida and took a taxi to my hotel. On the way there I saw the backwoods Third World country I'd read about, but when we pulled up in front of the hotel I was pleasantly surprised by the stately beauty of the old colonial inn, with its captivating design and structure and gardens full of all manner of glorious fragrant flowers I'd never seen before. I was soon to discover that this magnificent capital city of the Yucatán had a marvelous way of bringing its past and present together.

I stayed in Mérida for a week, wandering around the city. I fell in love with the surroundings, especially the Gulf beaches of the *puerto* (port) towns of Progreso, Chelem and Chuburná. The latter two are sleepy little fishing villages which are exceptionally charming, full of the traditional flavors and culture of the Maya people.

I was thrilled and ready for my adventure and had a few days before an appointment with a realtor. I filled my time with getting to know the area: touring the Mayan archaeological sites, ruins and relics; viewing the famous *cenotes* (natural pools or sinkholes filled with crystal clear groundwater found only in the Yucatán), exploring the city of Merida, buying Mayan handicrafts, visiting the local museums and sampling the Yucatán cuisine. I was simply astonished at the creativity and artistry of the local Maya culture.

The day of my appointment was another beautiful day. I traveled 40 minutes north of Mérida to the Gulf Coast and once again I found myself astounded at the stunning, intense light that brought out every minute detail of the palm trees and the sea. Gentle breezes carried the sweet aromas of colorful tropical flowers and flowering trees. I fell in love with it all, especially the small villages, which I found exceptionally charming. They were enchanting and magical, and I felt incredibly fortunate that I'd found exactly the location my husband and I were seeking.

This area is known as the Emerald Coast, and to this day I'm not sure if the name comes from the gorgeous emerald green water of the Gulf or the emerald green/gold of *henequen*, a local plant grown commercially that's native to southern Mexico. During the nineteenth century it was used to make a durable fibrous material which made the Yucatán wealthy and famous.

With my husband's agreement I purchased a small beach house in Chuburná Puerto (one of those quaint fishing villages on the northwest side of the Yucatán, on the Gulf of Mexico). When I returned to the States I sold our house, and within four months we sold all of our furniture and personal possessions. We literally packed nothing but what fit in three suitcases and flew to our new home.

"Crazy!" "Stupid!" "Ridiculous!" "Weird!" "How could you?!" "They'll shoot you because of Trump!" Oh yes, we heard all of these negative comments and more, but nothing deterred us. Sometimes one has to do what the heart tells you to.

And so we slowly settled and adjusted to the sometimes-primitive conditions of our quaint little beach house; we brought so little with us our cottage was almost bare. No furniture, no flowers, plants or trees, no air conditioning, 110 wiring, no car, no friends or relatives, incredible *nortes*—fierce wind storms that came down from the north—unimaginable sun and heat, huge multitudes of mosquitoes carrying all sorts of diseases, and just the sand and the sea ... endless sand and sea. We've endured two-inch-long, ink-black scorpions on the walls and floors—oftentimes females carrying as many as 30 babies on their backs—immense flying cockroaches so big you need a large sturdy shoe to kill just one of them, huge, scary, hairy spiders, iguanas of every size and Mexican street dogs that are wild, aggressive and so starving you have to look away to prevent yourself from sobbing. (We now own four.)

A move to Mexico is definitely not for the faint of heart, and one has to gradually become accustomed to the abject poverty that exists in the small villages. It's not uncommon for local families in these small villages to live in one-room houses with dirt floors, with sleeping hammocks hanging in so many places it's difficult to enter the home. Chickens and clotheslines and skinny horses are crowded into already cramped and small front yards, and starving dogs slink around the corners into the street. I've learned not to pity these folks, though, as this is all a part of their way of life. Their neighbors live the same way and as a whole they are very happy people. Total acceptance is the key to residing in the Yucatán, and it's important to remember that one is living in their country.

I've found the children of these villages to be very well-behaved and extremely clean and tidy. I teach an English class offered completely free of charge for the primary and secondary grades in the village and I couldn't ask for better pupils; they're so polite, eager and willing to learn. These classes are offered through a program implemented by the Canadians and Americans living here and is strictly voluntary; no former teaching experience is required, just an earnest desire to commit your best to the children.

Despite all these challenges—or maybe because of them—this is definitely our Paradise and has become, without a doubt, our home. My heart will always be in our cottage by the sea. The whole atmosphere and the pleasant, friendly native Yucatán people encourage the eccentric in one to emerge and spread its wings. It's as if Merlin himself touched this entire peninsula with his magic wand!

PC Nordhoff is an ex-TWA flight attendant and as a result has visited and lived in many cities and states in the U.S. She was born and raised on her grandfather's farm in the hills of West Virginia and is now happily living on the Gulf of Mexico in the Yucatán Peninsula with her husband and four delightful adopted dogs. She absolutely loves Mexico, the local people, their art and culture, and also enjoys volunteering to teach English classes for the children in the quaint little fishing village where she lives. Her future goal is to author a book relating to her experiences and life as an expatriate in this remarkable and beautiful country.

20. "Choosing Happiness"

Janet Blaser
Lo de Marcos, Nayarit
& Mazatlán, Sinaloa

I guess the simple reason I left is because I wanted to be happy. Was my life so bad? Not really, at least from the outside. I had a job (although it was tenuous); a big community of long-time friends and a vibrant, beautiful place to live in Santa Cruz, California. My three children were wonderful young adults and as a single mother, that alone made my life worthwhile.

But something was terribly missing, because, as I said, I wasn't happy. I tried to fill my life with all the things that are supposed to make you happy, but inside I knew I wasn't. More mornings than I'd like to admit I woke and cried my way through coffee, breakfast and getting ready for work. My journals from that time are filled with sadness and confusion. I constantly felt like I wasn't "enough" and didn't have "enough." When I looked around I saw people buying million-dollar homes and expensive cars and the latest fashions and the whole thing exhausted me. Did all of that really matter so much? It didn't to me. I'd studied the Bhagavad Gita and other Eastern spiritual traditions when I was younger, and more and more it seemed like I was a bird in a gilded cage, slowly dying while no one noticed.

I watched friends buy homes they couldn't afford—taking out giant mortgages with no down payment on nondescript houses that weren't worth that much at all— thinking what a literal house

180

of cards the real estate market in California seemed to be. No one wanted to hear that though, until a few years later when it all fell apart. But whatever the case, I couldn't afford to buy anything anyway.

At about the same time my mother was in the last stage of many years of debilitating illness. I was the only one of her four children who would talk to her about death; what happens to the body, what is the soul. And she told me about her life—her joys, yes, but also her regrets, of which she had many. She hadn't done so many things she'd wanted to, deferring her desires and dreams for those of my father's. "Don't wait," she said to me. "Do what makes you happy."

My kids got older; my mom passed away; I was still single. Nothing really changed, except that it became more and more expensive to live in California. The internet had upended my career as a journalist and I was worried about how I could keep making a living. What dreams I had were constantly pushed aside in favor of just paying the bills and staying afloat. I'd just turned 50 and I was looking at my life: where I'd been, what I'd done, what I wanted to do with the next half. I knew I had to start thinking outside the proverbial box but didn't know exactly what that meant. I read the book "Who Moved My Cheese?" (again) and saw the maze ahead of me as the best option, although that complete unknown was definitely scary. The writing on the wall was clear though—change was a'coming.

In 2006 I was on a long-planned vacation in Mazatlán, Mexico, where I'd never been. From my oceanfront suite, I could hear the calming sound of the waves below, and I spent a lot of time walking along the beach, swimming in the ocean and reading by the pool. I wasn't thinking at all about moving to Mexico; the thought had never crossed my mind. I had thought about moving away from Santa Cruz—where I'd lived for 18 years—to somewhere inland where the cost of living would be less, but I was hard-pressed to let go of that lifestyle, my friends and community, and the beauty of the coast. Without a steady and bigger income, though, I knew I wouldn't be able to afford living there much longer.

The hotel was in the busy tourist zone, but from researching online I'd seen that there was a Centro Histórico with beautiful old buildings and a main plaza with restaurants and a theater, musicians playing on the street and a very different ambiance than the part of town where I was staying. On the third day I took a *pulmonía*—Mazatlán's signature golf-cart taxis—south along the beachfront boardwalk, or *malecon*, to the Plaza Machado.

From the moment I stepped out on the corner of the plaza I was enchanted. There's no other way to explain it; there was just some sort of energy that spoke to my heart. Somehow it felt like home. I walked block after block, taking tons of photos, smiling the whole time. I had lunch and coffee and bought post cards and a colorful coconut shell mask. I saw lots of *gringos* and lots of locals, too. I ended up watching a gorgeous sunset in Olas Altas, the beachfront section of Centro Histórico. I knew this was where I would end up; I knew I could be happy here.

For the rest of my vacation, I spent as much time as I could in Centro, people-watching in the plaza, asking lots of questions and imagining what my life would look like if this was my home. I had many dinners at Pedro y Lola, a popular restaurant in the Plaza Machado, so much so that I became friends with the owner, whose family had been in Mazatlán for generations. One night he introduced me to another friend of his who asked if he could join me at my table. Unbeknownst to me, his father had been governor of the state and he, too, was involved in politics; this became obvious as person after person came over to say hello and the waiters became ever-so-deferential. Although Antonio was a big man, tall and imposing, he had a quick smile, an easy laugh and an amiable demeanor that made everyone feel comfortable around him. He also spoke perfect English.

After telling him my story—and all the reasons I loved Mazatlán and how it seemed like the right decision to move there—I ended with, "But I'm still not sure." He asked, "Why, Janet? It sounds like the perfect thing for you, all the pieces make sense. Why not?" Without thinking, I blurted out, "I'm not sure it's OK to do something just because it makes you happy."

Antonio looked at me and smiled. He stood up, cleared his throat and paused dramatically. Everyone in the crowded plaza turned and looked. Then he extended his arms and declared several times, in a loud, booming voice, "SOY FELIZ!" ("I'm happy!") People applauded and cheered. They stood up and cried, "Bravo!"

I cringed, wanting to crawl under the table. Antonio looked down, then motioned that I, too, could—or should—stand up beside him and make the same declaration to the world. But I couldn't. Now, I'm kind of a shy person in public so that may have been part of my hesitation. But his point was well made. Of course it's OK to be happy. In fact, that's kind of the point of life, wouldn't you say?

That happened almost 15 years ago and I still remember it like it was yesterday. It's one of my most important life lessons: It's OK to be happy.

I made a plan to take a month-long leave of absence from work in the fall, when Mazatlán's annual Cultural Festival took place and the majority of the snowbirds returned. I wanted to see if I could be really comfortable living in this new and different culture, if I could have the lifestyle I was used to, and, most importantly, what it would take for a foreigner to start a business. I had the idea that I could start an English monthly magazine to share information about the town to all the *gringos*—expats, snowbirds and tourists— I saw around me. In preparation for my next trip, I looked at rental options in the Centro Histórico, which felt like where I wanted to be. I went back to the U.S. enlivened and excited.

Before I knew it, I was back in Mazatlán. I explored stores to see what was available and what wasn't. (Good coffee? *Si.* 100% cotton sheets or towels? No. Tofu, Basmati rice, organic body products? No.) I looked at phone and internet service, checked out some rentals and met with an insurance agent about my car. I wandered through neighborhoods and spent a lot of time at the main plaza, imagining this as home.

Everything seemed to fall into place and the month passed quickly. I made lists of concerns, questions, challenges and fears, but also of all the positive aspects about the move. Ultimately it was the feeling in my heart that Mazatlán was "home" that gave me the courage to just do it. And the fact that the Mexican government made it so easy for foreigners to live in their country.

My three kids were supportive of the idea and encouraged me

to follow what had become my dream. The youngest was barely 18, and we had lived together happily and contentedly in the same house where they'd all been raised, adding roommates to cover the rent. I still cry when I think about leaving him and our life together. He was (and still is) very independent and self-sufficient and said this was all OK. We put the utilities in his name and I started packing in earnest, planning for a departure after Christmas and New Year's. One of the housemates was a massage practitioner who worked with a good friend of mine, a man in his late 30s whom I trusted, and that made me feel a little better about leaving my son in charge of the house.

The kids all said I'd given so many years to them, and that now it was time for me to do something for myself. Buoyed by enthusiasm and the thrill of change, I didn't realize until I was actually driving away how much I would miss them. I can't tell you how many times I called each of them from the side of the road sobbing, wanting to go back home, that it was all a big mistake. I remember when I got to Los Angeles there was a sign on the freeway that said "San Francisco" and my heart leapt at the thought that maybe I'd gone the wrong way and could just go home. Instead, I checked into a hotel and cried myself to sleep, missing my children and the life I was leaving. It felt like I'd ripped an arm off.

My little Toyota Echo was packed to the roof with boxes and random things, including a big carved wooden angel that I kept in the back window of the car; my guardian angel, if you will. (I still have it and can see it out the window in the garden.) I'd tested how many empty banker's boxes would fit in the trunk and the backseat and had packed accordingly; that's all the space there was, so that's all I could take. In hindsight, I wish I'd kept more things I was sentimentally attached to; in the months and years that followed, those reminders of my family, my children and our history would become more precious as we ceased to make as many new ones—except for the few weeks a year when I visited them.

I arrived in Mazatlán after what I could only describe as a harrowing four-day drive down through California, over the border at Nogales, and through the Sonora desert to, finally, Sinaloa and Mazatlán. Harrowing not because anything really happened;

harrowing because I was so emotionally overwrought and as I drove, alone, I was finally really realizing what I was doing. OMG! What WAS I doing?! Was I nuts?!

I had two cell phones, both of which were supposed to work in Mexico; neither of them did. My year of intensive Spanish classes was useless as I realized I couldn't even read the highway signs (We didn't learn those words!) and didn't know how to convert kilometers to miles to figure out how fast I was going or how far from the next town I was. Coffee—which always helps me ground and focus—was nowhere to be found once I crossed the border, and I'm embarrassed to say when I saw the golden arches of MacDonald's in Hermosillo I almost cried for joy to find coffee—albeit terrible and in a Styrofoam cup with powdered creamer.

Looking back, I can see these things were just the tip of the iceberg of the culture shock to come. So much was just, well, "foreign." Despite all my preparation, this was completely unexpected and I was thrown way off-balance. I would say it took me at least a year to really feel settled. I moved so many times it became a joke with my friends, like the children's book "Where's Waldo?"—"Where's Janet?" My life in Mazatlán was so different than anything I'd ever experienced, and also, for the first time in 24 years I was living by myself—no kids. What kind of home did I need, just me? I had no idea.

At this time in Mexico phone service was unreliable and international calls were very expensive. VOIP systems were just starting (like Vonage) and WhatsApp didn't exist. So, communication with family and friends in the U.S. was really difficult. That made the alone-ness feel worse and more empty. I did a lot of crying in private while maintaining a cheerful facade on the outside and trying to stay focused on a bigger picture and the knowledge that it would get better; things would become familiar, I'd learn more Spanish, even that someday I might have internet in my house.

The fact that everything was in a different, often incomprehensible language was a huge adjustment. I knew some Spanish but took more classes and practiced, practiced, practiced. Everyone jokes about *mañana* not meaning tomorrow, it just means "not right now"—but it's not funny when you're waiting for a phone or cable line, electric service, the plumber or locksmith to show up. It could literally take weeks to accomplish basic things like that, endless hours spent sitting at home and waiting, waiting, waiting; all of it a colossal test in patience for my super-efficient Western way of being.

Eventually though, my life did settle down. I found a place to live that seemed "right," bought some furniture and began to really explore my new community and the people living there. Mazatlán has a big expat community spread along the coast and there are lots of activities, events and places where *gringos* gather. There are also many expat-owned businesses—restaurants, beauty salons, stores, coffee shops—making it perhaps too easy to not speak Spanish or get to know the locals. I think that's both a blessing and a curse, but it does make Mazatlán a great place to ease into living in Mexico.

One of my dreams had been to start a real, direct-from-the-farmers' market in Mazatlán; I'd worked as manager and assistant manager for two big farmers' market associations in Santa Cruz and that culture was important to me. Sinaloa was such a big agricultural state, and I believed there had to be organic growers somewhere. So, using the bylaws of markets I'd worked for in the U.S. as a template, I assembled a committee of locals and expats, mostly growers but also a few chosen for their skills or their position in Mazatlán's very status-conscious society.

I get teary-eyed now looking at photos from the first few markets, remembering how we worked to make it successful, how challenging it was to bring this new concept to Mazatlán and how the local press supported us in our efforts to bring locally grown, pesticide-free produce and products to the local population. I watched each week as our initial half-dozen small farmers blossomed, as customers returned, more and more enthusiastic about the fabulous, flavorful fresh things they'd bought the week before. We hosted farm tours and cooking demos with local chefs and organized the city's first Farm To Table event at one of our member's farms. We held side-by-side "Taste Tests" of heirloom and commercially grown tomatoes; raw and boxed milk; pure, uncooked honey and corn-syrup-added commercial honey. Today, the Mercado Organico de Mazatlán (MOM) is still going strong, run now by a committee of farmers and vendors in Zaragoza Plaza on Saturday mornings from November to April.

The first year I lived off my savings and what I made from one editing job I'd kept that I could do online. (Living in Mexico is cheap!) I spent so many hours on the beach it's embarrassing to me now, but it's what I needed at the time: the sun, the quiet, the healing ocean. I needed that emptiness, that free time, to get my bearings, "re-create" myself and figure out what I was doing. And then I started that business I'd dreamed of: I published an English magazine for nine years, modeled after the arts and entertainment weeklies in the States. It not only supported me but became an integral and beloved part of the community.

A few years later I began bodyboarding, taking lessons from a local guy; that turned into surfing, something I'd always wanted to do but never had the time or money for. I was 55 when I started surfing on a surfboard, and it has filled my life with a delirious joy that's unmatched by anything else.

Then, suddenly, I saw more writing on the wall: change, big change, was coming again. My Social Security could start and I wouldn't have to work anymore. I put my magazine up for sale and within six months it was bought by a Canadian expat who's excited to take it into the future. It felt like I was done with Mazatlán.

About a year ago, I moved to a tiny *pueblo* six hours south, on the coast in Nayarit, north of Puerto Vallarta. They say the population is around 3,000; most of the locals are related to one another in some way. There's a small year-round group of expats, and maybe a couple hundred snowbirds that come for only four months or so, mostly French Canadians who drive big RVs here to escape the cold winters.

It's a much different life than how I'd lived for the past 11 years in Mazatlán and I often feel like I'm a "newbie" once again. I've had to learn anew where and how to register my car, get a phone line, pay my electric bill and register with this state's immigration office. I knew two people when I moved here; one a long-term friend for 20+ years from California, who spends five months a year in nearby Sayulita; the other, his girlfriend, is a local woman who, thankfully, has taken me somewhat under her wing.

I'm 62 now, and it's awkward, at this age, to realize you don't know basic things about how to conduct your life. Where can I get keys made? Which is the best mechanic? Is there a vet in town? Where's the nearest bank? Is there dependable mail service—or mail delivery at all?!

After more than a decade of living in Mexico, I've become a little cynical. I don't rush to watch the sunset every night anymore, or think everything is great here, because it's not. There are issues in this country too, not just in my everyday life, but in the systems, the culture, the politics, the deep-rooted dynamics between men and women, between rich and poor. And like that old saying, "Wherever you go, there you are," well, here I am, still and again, with my own personal set of challenges to deal with. I find I have less patience with "newbies" who come here and think "everything Mexican" is wonderful; again, it's not. I've also come to realize that all sorts of people come to Mexico, for all sorts of reasons, from all sorts of places. And just because we speak the same language doesn't mean we'll necessarily be friends, or even relate to each other. That was hard for me in the beginning, maybe because I'd come from a relatively small, close-knit community of like-minded people. Now I don't expect to connect with everyone, and the friends I do make are precious. Quality over quantity, I guess.

I still can't find underwear here (tops or bottoms) that will do what it's supposed to, or is made from the fabric it's labeled to be, and have found most clothing that's "*Hecho en Mexico*" is really low quality, as are many other products: kitchen utensils, pots and pans, towels, sheets, vitamins, shoes. I don't buy into the way of thinking that there's "more fresh produce here;" my experience as a food writer and with farmers' markets taught me otherwise, that Mexico uses some of the highest levels of pesticides and hormones in the world, and in vastly unregulated amounts. All those pretty piles of tomatoes, onions and peppers? Commercially grown, full of chemicals. Unless you're buying from a farmer who says it's organic—and many of the smaller ones can't afford to grow any other way—it's not. I'm fortunate in that the area where I live has lots of small, organic farms and a thriving culture of conscious eating, and that's one of the reasons I like it here.

Yet for all the challenges, I can't imagine living in the U.S. any more, despite the heartstring pull of grandkids (Three so far!) and the deep comfort of being around my adult children. When I visit, it doesn't feel like home anymore; I am indeed a visitor. My kids laugh at my "Mexican accent," whatever that means. I know I've changed—I see it in so many ways—and hope that it's mostly for the better. I'm more calm, more accepting, more patient. I'm not as attached to material things (although I still get excited about Target, Ikea and Trader Joe's) and am more open to plans changing or having to wait. When I think about who I would be if I'd lived the last 12 years in the U.S., I'm so grateful and so glad I didn't, and that I'm not that person.

Living in Mexico has also made me humble. I don't see how else you can survive here, without a healthy dose of humility each day, in almost every exchange. You learn to expect that you're going to make mistakes, and the only way to learn and move forward is to do exactly that: Learn and move forward. After all, I'm the foreigner here; the clueless one struggling to use the correct pronoun in a simple sentence.

This past spring I visited my grandchildren for a month; it's the longest I've stayed in the U.S. since I moved. The youngest, not yet two, loves the Disney animated film "Moana," that's based on a Hawaiian creation myth about the island of Maui and is more sophisticated than you'd think. Often we'd snuggle on the couch and watch it together, and one afternoon, I realized suddenly the lyrics to one song: "You may hear a voice inside ... And if that voice starts to whisper, to follow the farthest star, remember that voice inside is who you are."

That song had always pulled at me, and I never really understood why. Once I heard the lyrics, though, I got it: That's what drew me to Mexico; that's what I'd heard: That voice inside I'd somehow, thankfully, had the courage —and the *chutzpah*—to listen to.

Janet Blaser has been working as a writer, editor and publisher for almost 30 years, at daily, weekly and monthly newspapers and assorted other publications and projects in and around Santa Cruz, California. She moved to Mexico 12 years ago and has never looked back.

From her current home in rural Nayarit, Janet is learning how to be retired and a grandmother, surfing whenever she can, tending a wild garden and doing a bit of freelance writing here and there. The idea for this anthology came from the peaceful luxury of finally having time to contemplate, create and just "be."

21. "Poco a Poco"

Cat Calhoun
San Miguel de Allende, Guanajuato

The kid from next door was over at my house and we were playing at top-speed like kids in their single-digit years do. We were tearing through the house when an image on the television my father was watching stopped me in my tracks. Neil Armstrong was saying, "One small step for man, one giant leap for mankind." Neighbor kid was unimpressed, but I was mesmerized and felt like I was glued to the living room floor. My dad took me by the hand and I sat on his lap, watching with him as history opened before us.

After that, we never missed a launch, a splashdown or a televised transmission from Earth's tiny pocket of outer space. Even as a child, I was constantly amazed at the expenditure of energy it took to break out of this planet's gravity well, followed by the relative ease of movement that came after the escape. This has been my experience of moving to Mexico as well.

Though my wife and I had talked about moving out of Austin, Texas for several years, we'd never mustered the energy to get it going until the U.S. election of 2016. We watched in horror as the map turned ever more red. Though we had both obviously lived through Republican administrations and congresses in the past, this was different: the rhetoric of intolerance and hatred fueled this election and it was frightening. This became the rocket fuel we needed to break out of our gravity well of comfort in the United States.

The morning following the election our planning began in

191

earnest. The bones of the plan included selling our house and our "stuff," saving as much money as possible in the meantime and then leaving the country. Though there were many places in the world we could have gone, I'd had a long-time love affair with Mexico. I'd majored in history in college with a special emphasis on Mexico, and I'd followed it up with multiple trips across the Texas/Mexico border, mostly to the town of Guanajuato. Two months after the election my wife and I made our way there and she fell in love with it, too. We came back home after a 10-day stay and began to put our plan into motion.

"*Poco a poco.*" We've heard this over and over again since we've been in Mexico; "little by little." Over the course of the 15 months it took us to complete the move, this is how we progressed: *poco a poco*. We updated our house for a better selling price and donated or sold our combined century's worth of acquisitions. We learned all we could about emigrating to Mexico, read expat blogs and researched where we wanted to land upon our arrival. While the original fear served as a powerful booster rocket to launch us out of "someday" and into "let's get this done," it became clear early in the process that fear was not a sustainable fuel source for the day-to-day tasks needed to move out of the country. We deliberately shifted our focus from "running away" to "moving toward." We became excited about learning Spanish, immersing ourselves into a new culture, living on less and having more time to enjoy each other's company, create art and travel.

Before a rocket leaves earth, aeronautical engineers work hard to make the craft as light as possible so that it can leave the ground and reach orbit. Like those engineers, our task before leaving was to seriously lighten our personal payloads. While we could have simply put our stuff in storage, rented the house out and walked away, we were looking for a total lifestyle change which included living with less in order to have a more mobile lifestyle.

It took a tremendous amount of personal effort, a few squabbles, many doubts and reassurances, a lot of planning and an increase in our respective spiritual practices to complete the move. To further complicate matters, my mother-in-law segued from independent living to assisted living during this time. Because my wife is an only child, care-giving and arranging care fell to us. We not only moved ourselves, but my mother-in-law too, which meant we had to sell her stuff, acquire her *visa permanente*, and find assisted living in Mexico that would accommodate her physical and emotional needs. This meant changing our target location from Guanajuato City to San Miguel de Allende, as there is no assisted living facility in Guanajuato.

Even after all our efforts, the paperwork we needed for my mother-in-law and the cats wasn't ready by the time we closed on the house sale. We lived in two temporary houses in Austin before the paperwork was done. We finally drove away from Austin, owning only what was packed in the car, about six weeks after the final sales and donations were finished.

So now I sit here at my kitchen table in San Miguel de Allende on a cool, rainy morning while my old friends in Austin are enduring the usual scorching summer heat and drought. While life here definitely isn't Disneyland and not what I imagined it to be, it is nevertheless amazing. Since coming to Mexico I find that I have more free time to enjoy my life and to create. I have rediscovered art, after many years of denying myself time to sketch and create because so much needed to be done all the time in order to sustain a small business and an income that paid the Austin bills. I walk more. The city I now live in is more compact than most in Texas. I can walk to Centro (downtown) in 20 minutes, or I can take a bus for seven pesos (currently about $33 cents). If the weather is bad or I have a lot to carry, I can hop in a taxi for $50 pesos (about $2.50).

I eat better, too. I relied on a lot of processed foods in the U.S. because they were easy and faster and that worked better for our hectic lifestyle. Now I walk to the *mercado* a few times a week and load up on an incredible amount of fresh foods for just a few dollars. Because life is more relaxed here, I have the time to cook delicious meals made from fresh produce. I can feel the difference in my body. I have less pain, more energy and better digestion now than I have in decades. I've rediscovered my love of cooking and enjoy my time in my traditional Mexican kitchen with its delightful views of the city and the mountains beyond.

A few days ago I was sitting on my terrace painting a couple of pieces of furniture we'd bought on a trip to Michoacán. The paint was going on in thin coats and I had a moment of the old "hurry up and achieve" panic, but it was more from habit than necessity. Then I remembered, "*poco a poco*." There is no rush. Take it slow and steady and you'll get it all done without stress. I think this is one of the things I love best about Mexico. And it just might be the biggest reason I never intend to live in the United States again.

Cat Calhoun currently resides in San Miguel de Allende where she lives with her wife and two demanding cats. She is a licensed acupuncture professional with a masters degree in acupuncture and oriental medicine. Cat and her wife, DeLora, write a blog about moving to and living in Mexico and the personal and spiritual transformations that have ensued. Read more at http://www.mexiconofilters.com.

22. "NYC to CDMX"

Diana Kurland
Mexico City, Distrito Federal

To say why I left America, or, actually, to say why I moved to Mexico, we need to go way back to where I was born and raised: the San Fernando Valley, a 45-minute drive northwest of Los Angeles, California. I lived a lower middle-class life with my mother, a schoolteacher, born and raised in Scotland, and my father, who was from Brooklyn and worked as a salesman in a department store. I had mostly white friends except for a couple of girlfriends of Mexican descent. These girls never spoke Spanish to us, at school or after. They did speak Spanish, but only at home with their parents and grandparents, as the climate at the time and even today in some places is that the U.S. is an English-speaking country and it was, and is, the only language that should be spoken in public.

In middle school, starting in seventh grade, students were required to choose a foreign language, either Spanish or French. To me it was obvious only Spanish made sense. So, there I was on day one in Mr. John McClintock's Spanish 1 class. I don't know how any of the other students felt, but I was enthralled! I had a feeling that Spanish was going to be the key to another culture, another world.

I continued my study of Spanish through high school and college. Every class was exciting for me, and I minored in Spanish with a major in sociology. My mother had leftist politics in Scotland and brought me up with concern for the less fortunate, which is how I viewed Mexicans when I was in college in the San Fernando Valley. My friends and I were supportive of Cesar Chávez and his efforts in the farmworker's movement of the late '60s and early '70s.

After graduating from college in 1972, I moved to Boston. For five years I rarely spoke Spanish to anyone. I then returned to California and decided to get my teaching credentials, which I did with a master's in special education (deaf and hard of hearing). Deafness is a minority disability, meaning there were fewer teaching positions available when I graduated. So when I saw a big ad in the local newspaper seeking bilingual teachers for the Oakland Public School District I applied, was evaluated as to my ability to speak and write Spanish and was hired to teach first grade. I was thrilled!

That first year was difficult, as I was learning how to teach and doing it in two languages. What I remember distinctly was how sweet and respectful my young students were. Their parents, often illiterate in their native language, had high aspirations for their children. As the "teacher" I was often invited to family get-togethers. I taught in the students' primary language while providing an hour a day in English. This was one of a number of different ways bilingual education was taught in the California schools. A third of the class were English speakers.

After three years of teaching in Oakland, I moved with my children to Albuquerque, New Mexico. Surprisingly, there was no bilingual education there, and I taught my Mexican-American students only in English. When I would get an occasional child from Mexico I would use Spanish with them.

I taught kindergarten and first grade in the poorest part of Albuquerque. In terms of grids, that was the Southwest, where there were chickens and even an occasional horse in the yard. I felt like I was in Mexico and had some of my best teaching years there.

I moved with my children back to California in 1998 and taught again in Oakland. In 2005, after I'd received my nursing degree, I began working as a nurse at Highland Hospital, where I saw some of my former families from my teaching years.

In 2009 I moved to NYC with my youngest child, who'd been accepted to Pratt Institute to study fashion design. I stayed in Manhattan for the next seven years, working as a nurse in the psychiatric ER and then detox at Kings Country Hospital. There I encountered some Spanish-speaking people, mostly from Cuba, the Dominican Republic and Puerto Rico, and I was the go-to nurse on my units when they needed a translator. I loved that and was fond of the patients I took care of.

By 2016 I was of retirement age but continued working an additional year when my daughter gave birth to my first granddaughter. I wanted to be around her for a little while. Retirement in New York was out of the question, though, due to the high cost of living. Plus I'd grown weary of the very cold winters there.

The only country I considered for my retirement was Mexico. This was because Mexico was close to the United States, where I have family in both New York and Oregon. In addition, the weather is, for the most part, warm and sunny, which was like California where I grew up and is what I prefer. Cost of living was, of course, a major factor as well. I have Social Security and a pension which allows me to live well in Mexico and not have to constantly worry about money as I did in the States, even when I was working. And, finally, though these reasons are all about equal, there was the Mexican culture; the language, the art and architecture, the music, the food and the warmth of the people, even toward strangers.

About a year prior to moving, I went to Mexico to look around. I visited Oaxaca and loved it but felt like it was so indigenous that I would never feel I belonged. Puerto Escondido seemed really poor to me, with lots of people begging on the street, and I didn't want to be a "wealthy," relatively speaking, expat in their midst. Plus the waves there were super-strong so my plan to swim daily didn't seem realistic. The only other time I'd been in Mexico was when I was 20, for a short visit to Mazatlán; a friend got stung by a scorpion so the trip was aborted after two days, as he insisted he needed an American doctor. I'm sure he didn't. Mexico City seemed good; I stayed in two different, beautiful Airbnb's. But I thought I wanted a smaller town or *pueblo*, and Mexico City seemed too big and congested for me.

My moving to Mexico was not difficult. I gave notice on my

rented apartment, and I had not owned a car since 2009 when I moved to New York. All my banking was essentially done online. It really just felt like I was going on vacation, the difference being I wasn't coming back.

In telling friends and family my plans I was met with a lot of resistance. If I had a dollar for every time I mentioned Mexico and got a negative reaction, I'd be rich! "Aren't you afraid to go there?" "Aren't there a lot of shootings and drug warfare?" "What about 'the wall'—will you be able to get out if you want to?" "How can you just go and leave your grandchildren?" (I now had four, what with my son's children in Portland, Oregon.) I was undeterred. Mexico was my place; of that I was certain. Where to live was the question.

I went in April of 2017 and was happy to be gone from America, where the electorate thought Donald Trump was their messiah. Even now, it's very hard to read about all that's happening in the U.S. because of him and his cohorts. The 2016 election was a nightmare for many of us Americans and even now following U.S. politics is very upsetting.

I did find the first couple of months here very difficult. I felt like such an outsider. Even though I speak Spanish, I'm tall and blonde and stuck out like a sore thumb. I first stayed a few weeks in the Roma Sur neighborhood in Mexico City, then went to Playa del Carmen with an eye to living there. In August of 2017 I went to Europe for two months, which had always been my plan for when I was first retired. I came back to Mexico City and tried out Coyoacan, a neighborhood famous for Frida Kahlo and Diego Rivera, who had lived there. Supposedly it also had a "bohemian" vibe. I found it to be too small and not especially "bohemian." I then visited San Miguel de Allende, but just to see it, with no real intention of making it my home. Too many expats, too many tourists. I must say, though, that it's an extremely beautiful town.

Next I decided to book an Airbnb for a month in Guanajuato, as it seemed like a great place to live: a university town, colorful houses built on the hillsides, a yearly international festival of art, music and theatre. But after a week of being there and dealing with the *callejones*—steep alleyways up to the houses—and feeling it to be just too small a town for me, I came back to Mexico City to give it a second look. There I was captured again by its architecture, variety of museums and endless things to do and see.

I was extremely lucky to find an apartment in the very same building in Mexico City where I'd previously stayed in an Airbnb for five weeks. I'm in a beautiful Art Deco *colonia* (neighborhood), of which Mexico City has 16. There are two parks here where one can see "dog school" happening on any given day. Generally there's one teacher and 8-10 dogs all lying out in a row waiting for instruction. The teacher works with one dog at a time. Dogs are very loved and cared for here, unlike in the smaller *pueblos*.

By this time I'd also been back to New York and to the Mexican consulate and now had my Temporary Resident visa. Moving was not particularly difficult; I gave away, sold or boxed up my things for storage. To this day I still have 33 boxes in storage in Manhattan. Obviously I didn't need what's in them but now I do want my books and certain clothes and kitchenware, so I'll have them sent soon.

In a few years, if I tire of this amazing big city, I plan to move to the beach, to a small fishing village north of Puerto Vallarta.

I've yet, in almost two years, to have a visitor, friend or family, come from the States. Old stereotypes die hard. It does bother me that no one has come here to visit me and see Mexico for itself. I have to say most of my friends are younger than I am and not retired, and so they don't have that much vacation time. And they tend to go their home countries of Haiti, Trinidad and Jamaica. My family members have jobs and kids and other considerations. And since I go frequently to visit them they don't feel properly motivated to come here, I imagine.

I moved here knowing no one. I didn't even have any knowledge of Facebook groups here which, by the way, have been very helpful in getting used furniture, finding out about events and allowing me to find new friends. I figured if things didn't work out, such as if I was terribly lonely, I'd have to consider moving back to the States. I've made friends here with both expats and locals, and I've also looked into volunteering for two different organizations.

My days are spent shopping at Mercado Medellin or the little

Mercado Michoacán near me for fruit and vegetables. I also go every week to El Pendulo, a *cafebreria* (café / bookstore) with live music on weekends. It's fantastic! There are four of them in Mexico City, each a little different from the others. I buy books in English and short novels in Spanish. I meet with my Mexican landlord twice a week for breakfast or lunch and we speak exclusively in Spanish. I pay for the meals, as he has been acting as my Spanish teacher to help improve my conversational skills. I also have a weekly piano lesson with a teacher who comes to my apartment.

Mexico is like a dream, with huge plants, brilliant colors and a calm, life-affirming culture, despite the media's portrayal of the Mexican people. I'm looking forward to traveling throughout Mexico, particularly north to Monterrey and southeast to Chiapas.

I return to the States every three months or so to visit my three children and four—soon to be five! —grandchildren. When I go, I bring Mexican candies, bilingual books and other things. I'm teaching my three-year-old granddaughter a little Spanish, as well.

I've never looked back and intend to stay here forever.

Diana Kurland was born and raised in Southern California. She started learning Spanish in seventh grade and loved it from day one. She has always felt a great affinity for Mexican people and their culture. Diana retired to Mexico in 2017 from New York, where she was a registered nurse. Prior to that, she was an elementary school teacher, and she is now planning to write bilingual children's books. Her life in Mexico City is full of learning to play piano, taking painting classes and visiting all the sights of this great, metropolitan city including the pyramids, museums, art exhibits, musical events, cafés, shops and restaurants. She visits her family in New York and Portland, Oregon about every three months.

23. "Finding My Heart & Soul"

Judy Whitaker
El Golfo Santa Clara, Sonora

Thinking back, I guess I was in my 30s. (Wow, that seems like a really long time ago!) I'm 69 now, turning 70 this year. I tell people I used to think 70 was old until I got here. Then, I was young and carefree. The world was my oyster (as they say). I was living in south Florida and recently divorced. I'd just closed my first real estate transaction and had the opportunity to travel somewhere for a week.

I'd never traveled outside of the United States by myself so I decided to go to Mexico. I found a travel agency (back then there wasn't internet to book it yourself) that offered a very scheduled trip to Mérida, Quintana Roo, Mexico. To be perfectly honest, I really had no idea where I was going, I just knew I would see pyramids and that was what I was after. I'd always been fascinated by pyramids and Mexico was the closest, so off I went. Traveling by myself (remember I was in my 30s), I was fearless.

From the moment I landed in Merida I was hooked. Merida is so beautiful, with old, unbelievable churches, cobblestone streets, all sorts of vendors, fantastic street food and wonderful hotels.

I toured Chichen Itza, Uxmal and several other pyramids within a day's drive from Mérida. I also explored the city; horse-drawn carriages were my preferred means of travel. I found a driver who spoke some English, and I had a little book with Spanish phrases that I used very slowly. I was able to get my thoughts across and everyone seemed amused with me trying to speak their language, especially the way I said "Mérida." I later found out I was pronouncing it like the Spanish word for "s**t."

I just felt like I belonged there, in Mexico. There was a peace in my soul. I felt so at peace, so calm, no stress, true bliss. Just at peace.

I later traveled to Cancun and Cozumel, where I ended up buying a condo in 1982 that I owned for 10 years. I was living in Atlanta, and the three-hour flight to get there cost less than $100 round-trip. I decided then that if I was ever able to, I would retire in Mexico. I knew I had to see more of this amazing country. The people were so welcoming, and even though my Spanish was minimal, it seemed I could somehow always communicate what I needed to. I have found in my travels to other countries, and also within the U.S., that if you mind your manners and are polite and kind, people will treat you with respect. This was so true and easy in Mexico.

In my 40s I lived in Colorado and it was easy to travel to other border cities: Juaréz, Laredo, Matamoros, Nogales. All of these cities were interesting but none of them called to me. The border cities were very busy with so many Americans and lots of vendors trying to make the almighty buck. They all seemed to be moving at the same pace as the U.S.

When I was in my 50s my father passed, and my mother and I moved to Yuma, Arizona. I got my real estate license again and began working 60-hour weeks. I knew I needed to find a place to retire; time seemed to be flying by. Soon I would be 60 and we all know that's old! So I began to explore the Baja. My mother loved to travel, so off we went. In the back of my mind I thought maybe the reason she and I had ended up in Yuma was because my ultimate goal—to never see snow again and retire in Mexico—might only be a short day's drive away.

We traveled first to San Felipe. That's when I found out my mother knew all the words to the song "El Rancho Grande." I'd never heard that song before but now it's one of my favorites. One time we ordered tacos and she told me they just weren't right. "Tacos should have hamburger meat and cheddar cheese," she said. On the way home from San Felipe we begged the bus driver to stop so we could buy some huge clay pots to place around our pool in Yuma. He humored us and stopped. Trying to get the pots home from the bus station took three trips, because they were so heavy, but they did look lovely around the pool. When people asked where we got them, we would tell our stories about San Felipe and Mom would always sing "El Rancho Grande." She was a good singer. That was fun.

But San Felipe just had too many people; it was too developed, not the beach I was looking for. A few months later we went to Ensenada. Again, too big, too expensive, not the beach I wanted. (But excellent wine and lobster.) Rosarito had too many Americans and too many trailers. We had lived in a trailer when I was young and I knew it wasn't right for me.

Mexicali also had so many people that I thought I was in the U.S., plus the traffic was terrible and really scary. Tecate had no beach and was way too cold, La Rumorosa was about the right size but had no beach and once again was way too cold. Puerto Penasco had the perfect beach but lots of high-rise condos. The traffic was crazy and there were too many beach vendors there too.

I was looking for a place like Cozumel was in the early '80s. At that time it was a sleepy town that still had unpaved streets. The main industry was scuba diving, so there were Americans coming in to dive. I think once a week or so a cruise ship would dock, but the passengers were only there for a few hours. We all knew to never shop when there was a ship in, because the prices of everything would be higher!

Once you got outside of town you seemed to step back in time. Most houses had no electricity, so no washers or dryers. There was laundry hanging across the yards everywhere. It always amazed me how they could get the white clothes so white. (It still does.)

I was selling real estate in Yuma, and a Mexican friend I worked with, Eduardo, told me about El Golfo Santa Clara. The locals in Yuma had been going there for years, and everyone seemed to know about El Golfo. They said to go to San Luis, Arizona, 10 miles south of Yuma, go through the town, cross the Mexican border, then south to the end of the highway. I had my doubts, though, since I'd never heard of this small village.

For the next few years I was working a lot and I really didn't get the chance to travel much. I spent a week in Hawaii; it seemed like just another island. Then, two weeks in Paris. I have to admit I do have a soft spot in my heart for Paris, but it was just too expensive.

It took me a couple of years, but one weekend when my daughter was in Yuma we decided to see if we could find the town. In 2002, El Golfo was not on any maps. The trip was long, with really bad roads. I later found out it was only 90 miles from Yuma, but it took 3-½ hours. When we drove into town, we could see the ocean from the highway and my daughter looked at me and said, "This is it, isn't it?" She's been to Cozumel many times when I owned the condo there. I said, "I think it might be." We both laughed.

El Golfo's streets were unpaved, with no traffic lights and just two stop signs. We would find out there was no cell service, no ATM and just one gas station. A couple of very small markets and one OXXO provided everything we needed for the beach, i.e., beer and chips. After looking for a long time, we finally found a tiny hotel with eight rooms. Ours looked right out to the beach. It felt amazing. We listened to the surf all night long.

In 2006 my mother passed, and that seemed like a sign for me to move on to the next chapter in my life. I sold my house in Yuma and bought a house in El Golfo. Buying a house in Mexico was a bit of a challenge but I got through it.

I was lucky enough to meet another single gal, Teresa, who had lived in El Golfo since 1995. We became fast friends. It really was nice to know another woman who was living on her own. I didn't feel like I was such a "wild woman." She owned and operated a *cantina* (a bar), called El Capitán, and everyone seemed to know her. She helped me with setting up my electric and other services. She had also moved from Yuma and we found that we even had some mutual friends.

In 2006, Americans didn't need a passport to go back and forth to the U.S. from Baja. When that rule changed, lots of Americans stopped coming to this sleepy fishing village. Now you have to have a passport and apply for a Mexican visa to stay in Mexico. I find just getting a tourist visa for six months is my best bet.

El Golfo does get very busy during Semana Santa, the week between Good Friday and Easter. Tourists and visitors raise the population as high as 40,000, up from the regular head count of about 4,000 (which I always say includes dogs and children). We have 30 miles of virgin beach, and ATVs, four-wheel drive trucks and sand rails drive and camp on the beach. It's truly unbelievable. The first year I was here I didn't know what to make of all the people. Now I stock up on groceries, lock my gate and stay in my little compound. I guess I've become a bit of a hermit.

Twelve years after I moved here, El Golfo now has two gas stations, three OXXOs, several grocery stores, paved streets, street lights and most everything I need. The trip from the border only takes 45 minutes on the new coastal highway, which goes from San Luis, Mexico to Puerto Penasco. El Golfo is halfway in-between. I'm easily able to go to the U.S. for any shopping or doctors, since I have Medicare now.

Although El Golfo is only 45 minutes from the border the weather here is so different from weather in Arizona. My friend and I always watch the outside temperature in her car as we drive back home from Yuma. It can sometimes be 105 degrees at the border and we watch the temperature go down as we get closer to El Golfo. We've seen it be up to 20 degrees cooler here because we're at sea level and the ocean breezes cool everything. It's just amazing.

The cost of living is so much less in Mexico with the exchange of the dollar to pesos; right now it's almost two to one. My electric bill last month was $21 dollars. My water and trash costs about $10 a month, for as much water as I can use. I run my air conditioner at night right before I go to bed, then turn it off and only use a fan. I buy most of my groceries at a local market and if I want something special, they'll order it for me. They also let me run an account that I pay once a month (when my Social Security check comes in). I can also use my debit card there so it's really quite easy. I must admit gas is more expensive here, but then I really don't go anywhere. Instead of driving I often ride the bus; they're very comfortable, with WiFi and TVs.

I have many friends in Puerto Penasco, so when I feel the need to go to a resort I can always go there and live like an American on vacation: swim in the big pools, relax in the jacuzzi and enjoy the night life. They in turn come over here to get away from it all: All that beautiful beach, lots of seashells and no people.

It took me a long time to slow down. In the U.S. we're all so used to living on a schedule and moving very fast compared to Mexico. I've now lived in El Golfo for 12 years; I think that makes me a local. Maybe the only difference is that so many of the locals seem to be related. I do have family who think I've totally lost my mind, but they're the ones who never leave the comfort of the U.S. They think Mexico is nothing but drug dealers and murderers. Not in my town.

I now live day to day; I never know what might happen tomorrow. I just know it will be peaceful and happy. I guess I'm on Mexican time now; everything can be done *mañana*, tomorrow. As the saying goes, "Don't worry, be happy."

I don't think Mexico is for everyone. I hear people say they have to have something to do, that they could never completely retire. Maybe I'm the exception. I've found great satisfaction in just helping my neighbors and Mexican friends however I can.

I've also found I don't need all the material things I seemed to need in the U.S., like big box stores, four Walmarts within 10 miles and gas stations on every corner. I'm trying to be a minimalist now. My wardrobe is down to just black and white—it just makes things simple. Flip-flops are my shoe of choice; they go with everything.

I eat lots of fresh produce now, no processed food, and fish caught fresh from the ocean, before it ever hits the fridge. My health is better than ever. Stress is a word that's not in my vocabulary. I haven't worn a watch in years. Until last week I didn't even have a cell phone, just my house phone. I bought one just to take pictures.

I live by myself, and I do find that sometimes I'm a little lonely. I solved that problem though—I now have two tiny Chihuahuas. They seem to always agree with me and they have no political views.

So I guess I really did find my soul here. The beach is my "happy place." I especially enjoy the spectacular sunsets. I'm at peace, with a smile on my face every day. *Todo es bueno!* "It's all good!" (My first Spanish phrase.)

Judy Whitaker is retired and has lived full-time in El Golfo Santa

Clara since 2006. She was a real estate broker in Florida, Colorado, Nebraska and Arizona. Judy now enjoys days on the beach, her passion of cooking, video games and catching up on T.V. shows she didn't get to watch while she was working. She also has two teacup Chihuahuas that entertain her on a daily basis. Judy has a daughter and granddaughter in Atlanta, which she calls home.

24. "Home Is Where The Heart Is"

Carole Muschel
Guanajuato City, Guanajuato
& Mazatlán, Sinaloa

It was the year 2000, almost the millennium. I was doing paper-work at a desk in an Oakland, California hospital NICU and met a nurse-midwife doing rounds. We started to chat, and when I told her I was going to Guatemala, MaryBeth said she'd just returned from there. She described a small shop in Antigua where she'd bought some beautiful writing pads and asked me to bring her some more. This was the beginning of a long, close friendship that has continued across borders and for many years.

MaryBeth's clients in California were Spanish-speaking, so she spent a lot of time in Mexico taking immersion classes to learn the language. She encouraged me to travel around Mexico to discover what a vast, interesting country it was and consider it as a potential place to retire. My husband and I decided to follow her suggestion as we always knew that we wanted to experience living abroad somewhere.

Although we were both successful in our careers and had a good quality of life, originally in New York state and later in Northern California, we felt disconnected from the pace of life in the U.S. We'd even lived for 15 years on an off-the-grid "hippie farm" in Mendocino County, just to get away from the treadmill of city life. That was a special time for us. In that simple, bucolic environment, we discovered our spirituality, and were introduced to sweat lodges at the Native American reservations that surrounded our farm.

We made multiple trips to Mexico to see if life there would meet our dreams, visiting the Yucatán, Mexico City, Oaxaca, Puerto Escondido, Puebla, Mérida, Veracruz, Puerto Vallarta and Zihuatanejo, searching for "our" place. We even had one suitcase filled with kitchen supplies: an electric fry pan, electric steamer, spices and implements to do our own cooking as we traveled. We still had the mindset that we needed these things to maintain our mostly vegetarian U.S. diet routine.

For some reason I'd been enchanted with the word "Zihuatanejo" and thought I wanted to live there. But once we got there, I didn't like the town; it wasn't what I'd dreamed about. Plus the rental we'd booked didn't have our reservation and we had to wander the streets looking for an alternative; not a good start. We ended up in a small rooftop penthouse with laundry hanging everywhere from the other units below.

I can't tell you how disappointed I was. While in Zihua, we befriended several other Americans who were also unhappy with the town. Since we were heading to Mazatlán next—our last stop on a month-long trip—they asked us to keep in touch and let them know if we liked it, and then perhaps they'd visit next year.

When we arrived in Mazatlán, late at night, we were totally exhausted from all the hours of traveling by bus. Our first impression was of the Zona Dorada, the busy, crowded hotel zone. We'd planned to hail a taxi from the bus station but didn't see any. Finally we asked someone how to get a taxi. He pointed to what looked like an electric golf cart, called a *pulmonia*, and said these were Mazatlán's unique taxis. The driver had a difficult time finding our rental *casita* in the dark but finally we got there.

The next morning, when we ventured out to the main street, we were shocked to see a concrete jungle with high-rise buildings that looked like they could be anywhere. It didn't feel like the Mexico we were looking for. Instinctively we got on the first bus and headed downtown. When we found the Centro Histórico, with its beautiful old buildings and charming shops and restaurants, right on the beach, we decided to explore the area more. Encouraged by the fact that at that time Mazatlán was a three-hour, non-stop flight from San Francisco, we began to think it might be the ideal location to begin our life in Mexico.

The following winter we returned to Mazatlán and rented an apartment for four months at the Villa Serena, near the Plazuela Machado. We discovered a diverse expat community, and we met many others like ourselves, which was comforting as we all spoke English and were trying to learn Spanish.

As the financial markets in the U.S. crashed, we watched our savings dwindle. We decided it would be a good time to take what was left of our savings and buy a home in Mazatlán in case the country continued on its downward spiral. We contacted a real estate agent and told him we were looking to buy a house, but after seeing the options, we instead spontaneously purchased an apartment. It had two bedrooms, one bathroom and a balcony overlooking the ocean, and was the second building in from the beach in Olas Altas, in the heart of the Old Town. The apartment was fully furnished and turnkey ready. We didn't investigate the neighborhood or what it took to live in Mexico—we just followed our hearts.

As we slowly retired, we spent as much time as we could in our future home. I retired first and was able to spend four to five months each winter in our Mazatlán apartment, but my husband was still working full-time and could only vacation a few weeks a year

We made new friends, many of them "snowbirds" from Canada and the U.S. Our small apartment complex was mainly Mexican Nationals, and we gradually developed close friendships with some of our neighbors, which has greatly enhanced our love of Mazatlán. We're delighted by the greetings of "*buenos dias!*" we hear as we walk on the oceanfront *malecon* each morning, by the "*buen provecho*" said to us at restaurants, and by the many children's activities we see happening at the plazas, while parents stroll around shopping at the art vendors or eating *al fresco*.

When my husband finally retired, we realized that Mazatlán was way too hot and humid to stay in for many months of the summer and fall, so we began a search for a more comfortable climate. I had long had a desire to visit Guanajuato, so we took a 12-hour bus ride to check out this historic city in the mountains. Again we spontaneously fell in love with another beautiful Mexican city.

There was something about the mountains and views there that reminded us of our idyllic life on our farm in Mendocino. It also seemed like a perfect complement to our coastal home in Mazatlán.

Guanajuato is a very cultured city with a famous university, an international music festival, many beautiful old theaters and interesting museums. There's so much history here and the residents are so proud of their city. There's also a much smaller expat community than we were used to, which was fine. We felt like this would be more of a "real" Mexican experience.

Our first rental was up one of the many *callejones* (alleys), in the center of downtown. Our driver stopped at a small plaza and parked, unloading our many suitcases. He directed us to start climbing up a nearby alley, each of us loaded down with luggage. We huffed and puffed up the steep street. *Callejones* are for walking only and most are unbelievably steep and uneven underfoot. No vehicles travel up these streets, only people and burros—yes, burros—that are still used to transport heavy items. And the altitude of almost 7,000 feet had us out of breath as we climbed up to our house. On the way, we encountered an elderly man with his dog slowly ascending alongside of us. We later learned he was 92 years old and had lived on this hill his entire life.

As our house manager rapidly chatted away at us we just stood there puzzled, realizing we needed to greatly (and quickly!) improve our Spanish. Guanajuato has fewer English speakers than our other home in Mazatlán, where we were "spoiled" by so many people speaking English. But we were both excited to be in this very Spanish-speaking city. Acquaintances recommended a university student named Luz who taught Spanish on the side, so I contacted her after we settled in. She now comes weekly and gives my husband and I separate one-on-one lessons.

I was so nervous at my first class, thinking that after 12 years in Mexico I should know more, but when she was sitting across from me at my kitchen table, her friendly, easy, manner calmed me. She said we'd begin by communicating, just making small talk. She switched back and forth between English and Spanish so I could follow her questions. One of her first questions was, "Why did I pick Guanajuato to live?"

I tried to explain there'd been a strong pull to see Guanajuato ever since I first heard about this beautiful mountain city bursting with Mexican history. It took nine years of curiosity while we were living in Mazatlán until we decided to come and see for ourselves. When we finally emerged from the bus at the station, we found ourselves in a very industrial area surrounded by hotels and businesses. It looked nothing like the jaw-dropping beauty we'd seen on YouTube videos.

But our waiting driver, the manager of the house we'd rented through Craig's List, said we were outside of the actual town. We drove over rising hills for about five minutes, then descended into a maze of stone tunnels built under the city many years ago. When we came back out into daylight, I suddenly saw the magnificent views of the city of Guanajuato. Downtown was barely five streets wide in a ravine surrounded by high hills. The hillsides were decorated by colorful buildings stacked haphazardly up every possible side. The views were everything I'd imagined—Guanajuato looked like photos of Italian mountain towns I'd read about in travel magazines.

As we wandered around the main street, we discovered a good coffee shop, a produce store and many health food stores. We fell in love with the winding streets, the European architecture and the many lovely plazas. I didn't need to travel all the way to Europe to live in these magical surroundings. In Mexico there are designated *Pueblos Magicos*, "Magical Towns," and Guanajuato is justifiably one of them.

We decided to make more of a commitment to living here so we began to search for a long-term rental. We've met many expats who have their home base here but are world travelers. This appeals to our lifestyle, so when we found our new rental home up on the *panoramica*, with magnificent views looking down at the city and across at the opposite hills, we were ready to settle here for the summer and fall months.

Now, almost 13 years later, we have two residences in our adopted country, Mazatlán and Guanajuato. Our U.S. family and friends have begun to visit us in both places, so we stay connected to our loved ones. We feel so fortunate to have developed a full life in Mexico. Last winter we became permanent residents, fulfilling our dreams of experiencing daily life outside the U.S. Each time we visit the U.S. we can't wait to come back home to Mexico!

Carole Muschel's curiosity about other countries was established at a young age because of her father's constant traveling for work. After receiving her nursing degree and getting married in upstate New York, she moved first to "The Big Apple" and then to Northern California and the Bay Area, where her self-esteem blossomed and she discovered creative talents she didn't know she had. Carole received a master's degree in creation spirituality from Naropa University in Oakland, and for her thesis combined cognitive behavioral therapy with the Tarot, which she continues to use for inspiration. After many years of traveling throughout Mexico, she and her husband realized their dream of living in another country by retiring to Mazatlán's Centro Histórico in 2006. For the past two years they've split their time between the coastal beauty of Mazatlán and the magical mountain town of Guanajuato.

25. "How to Trip & Fall Gracefully"

Linda Laino
San Miguel de Allende, Guanajuato

I fell in love with Mexico on my first trip in 1989. I was on my honeymoon and travelled around by bus for a month with my new husband. Mérida in the Yucatán was our first stop, and when we arrived, it was a blissful sensorial shock to my system. The language fell melodious into my ears. The smells flowed through and out my pores. The vivid color threatened to burst my retinas. All of the "foreignness" intrigued me and I absorbed it like my sweat-soaked tank top in the jungle of Quintana Roo.

My month-long initiation prompted me to dream, *If I ever get the chance to move to Mexico, I will.* My "chance" came in 2012, in the form of a job teaching English language arts at a new high school in San Miguel de Allende, the colonial jewel in the heart of the country. For most of my life as a visual artist, I had sustained myself in part by teaching. Coincidentally, my mother-in-law and her husband, both writers, lived in San Miguel for 15 years. Long known as a mecca for artists and writers, I visited them there twice in the 1990s. The charming town worked its famous magic and it felt meant to be that I should be offered a job in that very same place.

When I informed my then-85-year-old mother that I would be moving to Mexico, she asked, "Why in the world would you do that?" To my way of thinking, "the world" *was* the reason. Since I am an artist, I have often looked to other cultures for my muse in color, pattern, inventiveness and traditional craftsmanship. My mother's question was no doubt motivated by losing her middle daughter to great distance, but living in another country was always something that intrigued me. I never quite understood where the desire came from, as I certainly did not grow up with any sort of travel in my childhood. Aside from one trip to Disney World with my family when I was 12, the Jersey shore every summer was the only destination that took me out of my native Philadelphia. My father, who travelled the world as a young marine, however, often dreamed of travel in his later years. He always encouraged me to wander, and unlike my mother, he reveled in my decision and gave me his blessing. Even though that initial teaching job turned out to be not what I wanted, it allowed me to move to Mexico and continue the love affair.

After that initial visit in 1989 and perhaps laying some unconscious foundation, back in the U.S. I began to study Spanish. This endeavor was accelerated after I made the decision to move. I was fortunate to find a native Spaniard who gave small weekly classes in her home. She helped me approach this seemingly daunting task with discipline and enthusiasm. Learning a new language has been challenging but undoubtedly has created new pathways in my brain (and heart). I also firmly believe learning the language is essential to begin to understand the culture in earnest. How could I learn about Mexico, if I couldn't speak to its people? My observation is that if you can speak the language, or at least attempt to, you're treated more as a welcome guest. The language keeps me on my toes and gives me great joy. I'm constantly fascinated to compare how two languages can express the same thing so differently.

When I first moved to San Miguel de Allende, I kept a *diario* that turned into a newsletter I sent to my friends and family. I was intent on capturing my observations and reactions in order to more fully understand my transition. Newness was everywhere and I was navigating *sola*, so that aloneness needed to be processed as well, and writing was my way in. Most of this diary took place during my first few weeks here. These short vignettes offer a glimpse into what it feels like to be an *extranjera*. And here I have to acknowledge that it doesn't feel strange anymore. Like the hot chilis I regularly enjoy, Mexico has permeated a few layers of me and continues to lodge itself deep under my skin. Having said that (and because this is beloved but unpredictable Mexico), I continue to adapt and sometimes be baffled by many things. I try to never forget that I'm a guest in this beautiful country and to have respect for the customs and way of life, however inconvenient they are at times. Finding humor in all situations is a helpful tool for survival here.

Everyone talks about the same things that drew them to Mexico, and in particular, San Miguel de Allende: the people, the climate, the culture, the food, the beauty—not to mention a lifestyle *mas económico*. I, of course, second everything on that list and more. But those of us who've lived here a little while understand that in the end it isn't about the things on that list, but what happens *around* all of those things. In other words: the experience, the exchange, the connection. And this Mexico has in abundance.

Reviewing these excerpts of writing from my current perspective reveals states of mind that were sometimes naive, sometimes stressed and sometimes awed in those first weeks. There's a thread of patience woven throughout. They also allow me to see how since then, I've not only adapted and survived, but grown and thrived in some very real and profound ways.

August 11, 2012

After many trips around town—there have to be many because I can only carry so many things at once—I landed in my new apartment, which I tried to begin to see as a friendly place. Without a car, I'm at the mercy of strong arms and legs and fortitude. Every day seems to be a mission of finding things. Yesterday, I found la papelería, a place to buy notebooks and a binder that I so desperately needed for school. But did I buy the binder I so desperately needed? No. This is the other conundrum about finding a store that has what you need. It's not always convenient to buy the thing when you're there because then you must carry it around to the rest of your errands, or have to make a trip home to drop the thing off. Is it beginning to be understood how much time everything takes here? Have I mentioned that in general, I am not a very patient person? This will become part of my practice: Not only want less but get used to waiting for it. As Vero, one of my cheeky new colleagues, said yesterday, "If you don't develop patience in this country, you will shoot yourself in the head."

Once I accomplished all my errands for the day, I arrived at my new apartment to begin unpacking. This brought an unexpected bout of the mini-blues after I discovered the glass in the frames holding my favorite pictures of Ryder, my son, had broken in the move. I decided I needed to be around people, and remembering my previous invitation, I took myself out to the Canto Mio Café to hear my new friend Fernando sing his romantic ballads. He told me he played at 9 o'clock and so I arrived around 8:30 at the small café, where the only other guests were a table of six obviously enjoying a party. Fernando was nowhere in sight and after being assured by the waiter that he was indeed scheduled to play, I sat down alone at a table and ordered a glass of wine. Within minutes, someone from the group called over "Come and join us, would you like to? You are all alone!" I was so delightfully surprised that of course I accepted. After friendly introductions (and being seated next to the very handsome Ricardo), suddenly there was a plate of food in front of me that they insisted I eat, lest I insult the host. I was overwhelmed with the generosity of these kind strangers who completely took me into their evening party.

The music began with a different singer; sad, acoustic love songs that somehow seemed to suit my mood. Fernando with his friendly face finally arrived and seemed happy that I had made it out to hear him play. A couple of days earlier, I'd enjoyed hearing him practice at the guest house where we met. His singing voice feels like a comfortable caress that you don't want to squander. After Fernando's set, another musician played and, judging from the ovation he received he must have been a well-known poet and "old-timer" of San Miguel. He first read a long poem, accompanied by acoustic guitar, dedicated to his sister. I couldn't understand all of it, but the passion and love and expression in the way he delivered it made my eyes fill with tears. I even told him this as we were leaving and he hugged me goodbye. I could tell he was moved by my confession. There's no lack of, nor embarrassment of, emotion in this culture. It is a place where tears flow as easily as laughter and are indeed recognized as coming from the same place.

The generosity and friendliness of the Mexican people is often referred to. As a culture, they're used to living with sometimes several generations under one roof. Family is extremely important. The fact that someone is alone seems odd and sad to them. The natural tendency to share is rampant here, and in my personal experience, that's a quality that has humbled me many times.

There's a man named Julio who appears to be in his 60s, who often sells avocados close to my apartment. I pass him on my way home. He's quite sweet and affable, and I've always bought at least one avocado and stopped to chat with him for a few minutes. I hadn't seen him in quite a while, and today, there he was when I turned the corner. I walked up to greet him and give him a hug. When I asked where he'd been, he related how he was doing his other work of patching and painting walls. We chatted a bit more about which was easier or harder work, and even though I really didn't need one, I chose my avocado. When I asked ¿*Cuánto cuesta?* he waved his hand in the air and flashed his broad smile. "*Nada Señora, es un regalito.*" It was a gift. After I gushed my thanks, I thought about insisting he take my money. Poor Julio selling avocados on the hot and dusty corner surely needed that $10 pesos more than I did. It occurred to me that I didn't want to insult his generosity. So instead, I thanked him profusely and saw how much it pleased him to give it to me. We forget that the poor want to give also, even if their pockets dictate they shouldn't. A sage reminder in a town that sadly for some, produces conditions ripe for begging.

When asked, "What's your favorite thing about living in Mexico?" I invariably say the street life. The street is the place to witness all of the emotion described above, as well as all the stuff of life itself. I'm so used to seeing so much happening on the streets that I fail to fathom how in the world I survived a childhood growing up in the barren, lifeless suburbs of Philadelphia. Here, the architecture, with its emphasis on courtyards and roof gardens, assures that even at home, you're living outside most of the day. On the street there is food (naturally), dancing, passionate kissing, music and singing, gatherings, plazas (!), selling, children playing and artisans working. Some shops are so small the artisans sometimes overflow into the street. I regularly see men weaving chair seats sitting outside on the high stone sidewalks. Being surrounded by liveliness in this manner creates connection, to be sure, but also a sense of the surreal. I truly never know what or who I'm going to encounter when I walk out my door, which is often a delight. And by the way, Fernando—my first friend in San Miguel—and I are still friends. We travel in the same circles, and now I see him with his beautiful young family, Claire and little Chloe.

August 12, 2012

The hunt and hope for internet was on. At the suggestion of our landlady, Vicky, my new upstairs neighbor, and I are going to share the internet. We decided we needed to get a little "squeaky" with our service provider. Having some experience in this area, Natasha, who had lived and worked in Guadalajara for a long time, offered to go with us. As we were headed to the bus, she joked, "OK, what's our strategy? Gringa bitches, or shall we put on a little lipstick?" We opted for the latter and off we went back to Megacable where we found the sweet man who took our order and pesos on Friday. With his shining eyes and friendly smile, he assured us that tomorrow for sure, el técnico would be there. He even gave us his name and personal cell phone, just in case. OK, we will see.

I learned a long time ago that Mexicans really hate to disappoint. They don't like to say no. This appears to be very nice. And it is. It's meant with the utmost sincerity at the time. The bad news is that some people will promise you everything, but in the end it's merely a suggestion which they may not be able to actually deliver. (Romancers included, by the way). Some would rather send you on a wild goose chase with directions, for example, than say they don't know where something is. I think you have to decide this is charming or once again, as Vero says, "…you will shoot yourself in the head."

August 13, 2012

How can the same people who are associated with the hammock, the most siesta-inducing piece of "furniture" on the planet, also be responsible for some of the most un-user-friendly seating known to man? The chairs in my new apartment defy fitting the curve of anyone's back. This paradox seems to match the Mexican people's dual personality of a joyful and spontaneous view of life, but also their fierce stoicism when faced with the most incredible adversity. They're an ingenious people who seem to have an outside-the-box resourceful solution to any problem you might come up with. And if they don't, they simply shrug and don't worry about it. The afore-mentioned patience I'm trying to develop comes in spades here. I've never seen people be rude, inconsiderate or boorish in any way. (So much kissing and hugging!) They go about their daily lives for the most part with politeness, kindness and grace.

Even my ever-so-slightly jaded attitude six years later would say this is still true. On the other hand, people are people everywhere, and some days you simply don't get the best of them. I don't think I'm doing my Mexican friends any favors by lumping all of them together stereotypically as "smiling, joyful souls." There's plenty of frustration here, for both *extranjeros* and locals. We all seem, however, to acquire patience, like a collective ooze that drapes over the population like smoke and when nothing goes according to plan, it lulls us all into uttering with acceptance, *así es la vida.* Things eventually work out one way or another.

August 18, 2012

I was recently reminded why I do (and must!) look down whenever I'm walking in this town. A new friend took a bad fall caused by an unseen boulder in her path. She broke her arm in a few places and apparently had some bleeding in her brain due to hitting her head pretty hard. Yikes. Indeed, I'm often tripping on something, and the terrain is uneven at best and pretty treacherous at worst, with huge, sudden drop-offs in the sidewalk or just dangerously large holes to fall into. These accidents happen frequently enough here that someone coined the phrase the "City of Fallen Women" when referring to San Miguel. (I've grown to seriously dislike this phrase). It's quite hard to be a graceful walker though, and the women who brave heels in this town leave me in awe.

Yesterday I bought a lamp. Isn't that exciting news? I can't tell you how incredibly happy it made me, to have some ambient light in my apartment. Mostly I'd been using candles. While lovely, these old eyes were given quite the strain trying to read by them. This new life has made me grateful for small accomplishments and small gifts, many unexpected. The slowness of time, the walking, the doing without, has been quite a lesson in not taking anything for granted.

When the desire to purchase something arose, my working-class father used to ask: "Do I need it? Can I afford it? Can I get along without it?" Having heard that for most of my life, it finally made sense to me here in Mexico. These days I no longer find it desirable to complicate my daily life with so many possessions. Six years ago I unburdened myself of so much stuff in order to make this move. I live by choice in a very small apartment, so I can't accumulate too much. I've learned what many are gravitating toward these days: It really is the ephemeral that makes us happy, and not all the "things." I would say that living in Mexico has allowed me (sometimes forcibly) to be grateful for those "small accomplishments," the kindness of strangers and the occasional domestic find that makes life a bit brighter.

August 19, 2012

My practice of accepting impermanence is sorely being tested. This morning I woke to no internet and no water—hot or cold. I'm beginning to understand what I've heard from many friends, Mexican and otherwise: Services can be spotty and unreliable. For the moment, I have my comfortable bed, a cup of good coffee and an incredible view. I think I'm adapting.

Last night, Vicky upstairs accidentally turned the gas off on her water heater instead of turning it up. Since this is new to both of us, I couldn't remember how to re-light the thing. After we risked blowing ourselves off the roof by all manner of knob-turning and button-pushing with a lit match, I offered my shower for her to use. As she was showering I could hear her laughing hysterically, saying the pressure was so horrible, someone may as well have been spitting on her. It's true. I've considered cutting all my hair off in order to reduce the amount of time needed for rinsing off shampoo.

Americans don't like to wait for anything, have you noticed? We're incensed when we can't have what we want—service or product—now. I've witnessed some foreigners here acting belligerent and rude when they're inconvenienced in some way. In contrast, I've begun to develop an instinct to adapt. Things go wrong. People don't show up. You're confused (a lot). Impermanence is a quality deeply rooted in the Mexican culture, most illustrated during Day of the Dead. I believe impermanence and adaptation are close cousins. When things fall apart, you need to either change or deal. Be prepared for nothing to go your way. And here's the trick: not lose your shit over it.

August 21, 2012

Most of the shops in San Miguel are about the size of a big walk-in closet. This shopping experience suits me just fine, as I've never been fond of the U.S. mega-stores. This also means that these "tiendas de la esquina" are not big on selection either. This also, for the most part, suits me just fine. I never thought we needed 20 different kinds of toothpaste anyway. Having said that, some of these tienditas are like Mary Poppins' carpet bag. You ask for something obscure that you clearly don't see anywhere, and usually they'll pull it out of somewhere for you.

At the immigration office—which is quite small—there are only two men who hold your fate. As we take a number, Vero prays to get the kind, handsome bureaucrat on the left, because, as she complains, "One day I yelled at the other guy and now he hates me." Somehow, I think these things are important when you're trying to deal with bureaucracy. I can't tell you how many procedures and papers have passed through me by now. As Vero was dealing with the not-so-nice guy (prayer not answered), Vicky and I had to go across the street to get our photos taken for resident ID cards. I sat on the little stool and after I was instructed to take off my earrings, the sweet young man with the camera came towards me and oh-so-gently tucked the tendrils of hair around my ears and off my forehead before he took my picture. It was one of the tenderest moments I've ever shared with a stranger.

When we returned, Vero had moved over to the desk of the kind, handsome bureaucrat. I thought she probably yelled at the other one again. (She is a fiery Argentine.) At the end of the day, I was told that sometime in the near future—as yet to be determined—I will have an official temporary resident card.

Having just been bestowed my permanent residency, I can state that dealing with *migración* is still not an easy task. My whole process took three months, with at least 10 trips to *migración*, two trips to Hacienda (the tax office) and two trips to the accountant, as well as visits to a couple of banks—in order to make payments to *migración*—thrown in. These offices are not on my "beaten path" so there are cabs involved or very long walks. There are limited office hours. There also seems to be some reluctance to give you ALL of the papers and instructions you need at one time. Just when you think you're all set, there's always "one more paper" needed in order to complete the process. When they were finally stamping my papers (they love to stamp), I was roused out of a malaise I've developed, reserved for waiting in tiny airless offices. By that time, I was so over the process I couldn't even celebrate being over the process.

I'm sure it's the same for foreigners everywhere and I have no doubt it's worse in the U.S. and probably more so these days. But it's the expat's price of doing business, so to speak. It helps to see it as something like theater.

September 16, 2012

Time, for me, has almost stopped. One month of life here has felt like six. I'm not sure what that implies but I do find myself slowing down. México is teaching me that things are not always what they seem and reminds me daily to be open to surprises, without judgment. And that's a very good thing.

Ever since I moved to Mexico, my friends and family have asked, "When are you coming 'home?'" My mother might have continued to ask as much if, sadly, she hadn't died four months after I arrived. Being far from loved ones is one of the hardest decisions I've had to make. But my relationship to time is becoming very Mexican, very fluid. As someone who has struggled to ignore the clock, México has taught me to not project too much into the future and instead, simply to enjoy what's in front of me. A planned day of busy-busy can easily change into a day of lazy-lazy and I flow with it. *¿Quién sabe?* has become my mantra. Who knows what will happen, and indeed, anything at all can.

To immerse yourself in another culture, in the end, is to immerse further into yourself. After all, we only discover our truest nature bit by bit when we're in the presence of "other." Famed mythologist Joseph Campbell refers frequently to the function of ritual being something that "pitches you out," not something that "wraps you back in where you've been all the time." To travel, experience and live in another country is to perform a kind of ritual. It's an ongoing process to beat a path to ourselves by embracing foreignness.

What better way to walk that path than to wander the streets of an ancient, cobbled town, where you might run into the occasional student, neighbor or friend, pick up one of Julio's avocados, buy a *beso del diablo* ice cream or a small bouquet of gardenias, maybe get a shoe shine. And if you're lucky, you just might come across some surreal or unexpected spectacle or happening that manages to "pitch you out" and therefore, wake you up.

Linda Laino is an artist, writer and teacher who has been making art in one form or another for more than 35 years. Holding an M.F.A. from Virginia Commonwealth University, she enjoys playing with words as much as form and color. Since 2012, she has resided in San Miguel de Allende, Mexico, where the surreal atmosphere and sensuous colors have wormed their way into her paintings. Finding beautiful things on the ground is a favorite pastime. Her art can be seen at www.lindalaino.com. Some of her essays and poetry can be found in "Elephant Journal," The New Engagement," "Sheila-Na-Gig Journal," "Life in 10 Miinutes," and on her blog, https://www.wordsandpictures. lindalaino.com/

26. "Why Mexico?"

Holly Hunter
Mayto Beach, Jalisco

I've had a history with this amazing country since my early youth. My first trip was as a wide-eyed eight-year-old in 1963, traveling to Mexico City with my mother. I remember standing at the bottom of the grand staircase at the Hotel Maria Isabel as a beautiful bride and her groom made their way down to the limo that would whisk them away to the "Happily Ever After." I immediately fell in love with a romantic version of Mexico; later I came to appreciate the warmth and generosity of the people, the music, art, food and culture, many times richer than nearly all of the 48 other countries I've visited since.

Proximity to the U.S. makes it possible to drive back to visit friends and family every year, another consideration in the decision to expatriate to Mexico.

In 2004, as a nearly 50-year-old "empty nester" living in frigid New England, I was open to something new and interesting. When I signed up for a week-long Financial Life Planning course with George Kinder to boost my business as a Certified Financial Planner—I owned a financial planning firm and managed the assets of 80 families—I had no idea attending that workshop would change the course of my life forever. I returned home from Kinder's class with the crazy notion of buying a *casita* on a little piece of land in Mexico near a beach, a place to go to warm up in the winter. This was in response to the life-planning question from the course: "What would you do with your life if you had all the money you would ever need?"

My subconscious had also been influenced by International Living Magazine. I began subscribing back in the early '80s, way before the internet, and I still have the hard copies that used to come in the mail every month. For decades I'd savored the stories of others who traveled to foreign lands, seeking adventure or an alternative lifestyle, and who found their Paradise in the process.

I approached my husband Dan with my idea and surprisingly, he was open to it. We decided to spend our next vacation in Mexico, renting a car and sleeping in a tent to explore the possibilities. We ruled out the Gulf Coast due to humidity, mosquitos, hurricanes and the heat, even though the Yucatán had the best direct flights for us from Boston and amazing beaches. We also determined that we needed to be within two hours of an international airport for access back to the U.S. for our work.

We settled on the west coast, on the Pacific Ocean within striking distance of Puerto Vallarta, a well-known and highly praised expat vacation and retirement destination. Dan and I were instantly drawn to Sayulita, a little surfing village an hour north of Puerto Vallarta, with its quaint cafés and the eclectic English library offering Spanish classes. The problem was that everyone was attracted to Sayulita, and there was nothing in our price range, which at that time was under $100,000 USD. We drove north to our two-hour self-imposed distance limit from the airport in P.V., exploring towns like Lo de Marcos and Guayabitos, but didn't find the same welcoming vibe we had in Sayulita.

So we headed south. Midway between Puerto Vallarta and Manzanillo, we found the wonderful community of Chamela, a short jaunt to the exclusive, high-end Costa Careyes, where we would have settled if we'd been able to find a house in our price range. Feeling distraught, we studied the map and decided to explore a peninsula just south of Puerto Vallarta where there were no roads, in the hope that other sun-seekers had not yet arrived and driven prices up.

Lost on a horrible dirt road, we began to see small, hand-painted signs for Hotel Mayto. I remember saying sarcastically to my husband, "My ass there's a hotel out here in the middle of nowhere!" I spoke a little Spanish, and we stopped and asked a local if the road was passable. He asked if our car was a rental. We replied that it was, and he said it was fine, go ahead. Reluctantly we navigated the deep, loose sand and occasional boulder-size rocks in the road for more than an hour.

The road finally ended at the most beautiful beach we'd ever seen. Dan and I got out of the car, pinching ourselves as we looked in both directions at the beautiful landscape around us. It was an absolutely pristine beach, with not a soul on it, wide and curving with a mountain range backdrop like something from a movie set. We couldn't believe it.

The Hotel Mayto was indeed in business, offering a fresh seafood lunch under a palapa roof overlooking the ocean and pool. While enjoying our meal, I overheard a couple discussing real estate in English and decided to stop and ask a few questions as Dan went to settle our check. At that moment, an older man arrived to pick up a take-out order and asked Dan if we were looking for property. Dan replied that yes, we were, and he immediately invited us to see his land that was just behind the hotel, about 300 yards from the ocean. The landowner, who introduced himself as Esteban, had ironically been away for four months in a tiny village near Sayulita and had just returned that day; having no food in his fridge he'd come to the hotel to pick up something to eat at the exact moment we were settling up to leave. Had any one of us not been hungry at that instant our collective fates would have been very different. Touring the property with Esteban we were intrigued, but it was way more land than we needed and the house was a real dump. I was also concerned about the remote location and lack of community, meaning people who looked like me and spoke English. We left with the promise that we would think it over and get back to him.

After our visit we drove to the nearby fishing village of Tehuamixtle to find a room for the night. As we drove down to the waterfront, a very handsome band of *mariachis* in pink ruffled shirts came out from a nearby restaurant, surrounded our car and began to serenade me. Although I'm not one who's normally open to signs from the universe, I had to admit that perhaps this was indeed "Paradise Found" after all.

We awoke before dawn and quickly headed over to meet

Esteban, leaving behind a couple who'd just arrived at the hotel the night before to look at possibly buying the same ranch. We kept him out all day and saw every inch of the 100 acres, returning to find a note on the door from the other couple who'd come to see the land and who were sorry to have missed him. There were actually two parcels, and Esteban gave us the choice of which we preferred to purchase; his plan was to live on the other. At that time, the smaller 40-acre piece with the house was $200,000 USD and the larger parcel without a building was $150,000 USD. Although the parcel we chose was double what we intended to spend and 160 times bigger than we wanted, we made a deal for $175,000. Our agreement gave us nine months to close, which in the U.S. would have been more than enough time.

We were soon to learn that purchasing land in *Ejido* ownership (an archaic system of communal land holdings common in Mexico) and having it privatized was a daunting task, in addition to the insanity of trying to rush the Mexican government. Ultimately the purchase was to become a three-year lesson in patience and emotional roller coaster rides before we finally acquired full ownership. There were several times during the process when the deal nearly fell through for a variety of reasons, not the least of which was Esteban's heart attack, a higher offer from a famous Mexican opera singer and the mounting *mordidas*—"little bites"— that various public officials required in order to keep the paperwork moving forward.

Every opportunity between the winter of 2005 and 2009 we came to the ranch. We dreamed of it when we weren't there. On one of our visits we had our pick-up truck camper that Dan had driven down perched on our hill overlooking the most beautiful beach in Mexico, and I thought "Living in this 40-year-old camper, at one with nature, I'm happier than I've ever been." It was an epiphany when I realized that we wouldn't need much money for rice, beans and an occasional tank of gas, which was quite contrary to my financial planning background where we were taught to believe every American needs at least $3 million in savings in order to stop working. (Every million yielding roughly $40,000 USD annually.)

This may be true if you plan on maintaining a high-consumption lifestyle north of the border, but not in Mexico.

Upon returning to Maine, Dan and I spent hours, days and weeks creating spreadsheets and running numbers to see if it was possible to bail out of our high-stress corporate lives, sell everything and head to the ranch. It seemed crazy, and our colleagues, friends and family assured us that it was. Both of us in our late 40s had no right to reject the status quo beliefs that you worked until you earned today's version of the gold watch, nose to the grindstone, until receiving the first Social Security check at age 66-and-a-half. At times it felt like not making it to 66 was a real possibility—if death didn't take me out, a disabling illness was going to.

The stock market crash of 2008 and the resignation of my assistant motivated me to finally jump off the corporate hamster wheel once and for all. My life had become one of quiet desperation, wash-rinse-repeat, and I was living for our trips back to Mexico. The only time I felt I was really alive was on our little patch of Paradise there.

Finally, in 2009, having acquired full legal title to the land, we made the decision to sell our businesses and chase our dream. Dan sold his architectural photography firm to his employees, and I sold my financial planning practice to an outside firm who filed bankruptcy within the first year. (Without fulfilling their financial obligation to me, but that's another story.)

The lesson we learned is that you can run numbers from here to eternity, but what counts is what you have liquid in the bank, how much debt you're carrying and what income you're able to generate. The sale of both of our companies in 2009 allowed us to pay off all the debts we incurred leveraging our home and my office to buy the Mexico properties (we ultimately purchased both parcels). We decided to keep our home in Maine to generate rental income once it was debt-free, as we were both many years from collecting Social Security. We also wanted a hedge, a place to return to with our tails between our legs in the event that moving to Mexico turned out to be a huge mistake.

Originally our plan was to create a campground at what we now called Rancho Sol y Mar to cover maintenance expenses and provide income to the local community through employment at the ranch and potential tours. We loved the folks we'd met camping around Mexico and thought it would be a great and easy project. Having created successful businesses in the U.S., though, was not a guarantee we could duplicate it in Mexico, and we didn't. The roads to Mayto were so poor that no one in a larger RV could make it to our lovely campground, and the few stragglers we received were in vans or tents for brief stays at $10 a night.

Next we thought perhaps not focusing on RVs and instead creating a guest house was the way to go, to at least generate enough income to keep the jungle from taking over. We hosted dozens of volunteers who helped us create the compressed earth block guest house, which sleeps 16 in four rooms. We also began to focus on sustainability at that time, using natural building materials, solar energy and composting toilets. Dan and I had both been motivated by Lester Brown's book, "Plan B," which outlines and explains with solid data the challenges we're facing on the planet through the destruction of rainforests, burning of fossil fuels and mismanagement of water resources. In 2014 we hosted a Cob Building Retreat (building with clay, sand and straw) which provided the basic structure for our new home on the hill, and a Permaculture Workshop in 2016 which taught us how to be better stewards of the land. We carefully subdivided the acreage, providing each of our five children with ocean-view lots of their own. Our daughter Hillary has built a home on her lot at the ranch and visits whenever she can.

We get by on the rents from our house in Maine, early withdrawals from my retirement account and the Social Security check that I just began receiving. In addition, Dan's mother passed away two years ago, leaving a small inheritance which we invested in a condo in Puerto Vallarta to generate more income through rentals. The cost of living is very reasonable while we stay in Mexico; it's the trips up north and my travel that have been expensive.

The move to Mayto was initially very challenging on all fronts. We had no phone service and no internet for nearly 10 of the 13 years since our purchase. We had to drive two hours each way to access email and make important calls, an additional reason why we had to sell our businesses since it was impossible to service clients without adequate technology. I also found myself feeling lonely without English-speaking folks with similar interests in my small village.

Daily life at the ranch includes milking the goats, making cheese or yogurt, caring for the chickens and ducks and tending the garden. We have a steady stream of visitors and friends at our guest house now and are finally able to stay connected with family via internet. Having the condo in Puerto Vallarta has added another dimension that includes a wonderful group of friends that I see whenever the condo isn't rented. The money I'm able to save not buying impulse or luxury items like nice clothes, expensive groceries and eating out has allowed me to travel around Mexico and also attend workshops here and in the United States to learn about everything from cheese-making and salsa dancing to yoga, meditation and studying Spanish. My life is fuller and richer today than any I could have imagined living a conventional retiree's lifestyle in the United States.

Holly Hunter started out life living a heady existence as a jet-setter summering in Martha's Vineyard, traveling the world, partying with politicians and celebrities. Mother of four, she also owned a financial planning firm. At age 50 she decided it was time to make a new life for herself. With husband Dan Gair she set out on a new adventure. Together they developed Rancho Sol y Mar, a sustainability education center on the Pacific Coast of Mexico. (http://www.ranchosolymar.com/RanchoSolyMar/Rancho_Sol_y_Mar.html) Embracing her new life, Holly learned the art of cheesemaking while tending her herd of goats. Find their book, "The Mexico Diaries, A Sustainable Adventure," an account of settling in Mexico, replete with narcos, scorpions, snakes, goat wrangling and an unusual cast of characters, on Amazon.

27. "Just. Like. That."

Gabriella M. Lindsay
Mazatlán, Sinaloa

Sometimes it takes death to realize you're not really living. For years my husband and I had talked about moving to México. You see, after my mother and father expatriated to a beautiful colonial city by the sea called Mazatlán, we started visiting and fell in love with the charm, the culture and the people. It was there, right in the sands of the Pacific, that we were married, and we vowed that one day, someday, we would return to live.

Of course, life happened. Three kids in three years, two cars, the white picket fence, the whole nine yards. We were living the "American Dream" that we're all so desperately and vehemently sold. And we bought it. And we loved it.

Until we didn't.

Both my husband and I were working more than full-time jobs. Me as an Assistant Principal, he as a Post-Doctoral Fellow at a university. We were raising three amazing children, both running entrepreneurial side-hustles, volunteering at our church and trying within all of that to have some semblance of a social life. That last part we were failing at miserably.

Despite our careers, despite our entrepreneurial ventures, we were still struggling to make ends meet. We were coming home tired, frustrated and disheartened. What were we working so hard to achieve? What was all of this 'stuff' for? The house, the cars, the student loans, everything was a series of bills to pay. This was not what we envisioned for ourselves.

We continued to dream, however. We would say, wouldn't it be great to just let it all go ... move away ... start a new life? It was a beautiful dream indeed. Unfortunately, we always circled back to, "But who does this? We can't do this! That's not what we're supposed to do." So, we accepted the "go-to-school, get-a-job, work-'til-you're-old, retire" mentality that we're all so familiar with.

Our dreams were not for us. They were the dreams of someone else. Someone who didn't have loans to repay, children to raise or careers to build. No, our dreams would have to wait until another day.

So, we continued on. Day in and day out, hustle and grind, lather, rinse, repeat.

That is, until reality, in the form of major heartbreak, hit.

I recall it vivid as day. It was a Wednesday afternoon in February 2016. My kiddos were down for their nap and I was just about to settle into a snack and my favorite Netflix show when my phone rang. It was a Mexican number. I started to answer but the caller hung up. Just as I was about to call back, my husband called me. I picked up immediately as the phone was there in my hand. "Gabi, um, I have some news. Um, it's about your mom. Gabi, um, your mom died. I'm so sorry, honey. I'm leaving work, I'll be home soon."

I slid to the floor. As his words sank in, the other line on my phone rang. It was my sister, confirming what my husband had just told me. She was there, at my mother's apartment, with my dad, my brother-in-law, a friend, my mom's upstairs neighbors, assorted medical staff and a funeral director. I could hear the chaos in the background, but I remember her clear voice, restating what my husband had just told me.

I had just talked to my mom on Monday, told her I would call again on Wednesday evening, and here we were, Wednesday afternoon, and she was gone.

Just. Like. That.

The rest of the evening was a bit of a blur. It included my husband returning home, cancelling the fitness class I was supposed to teach at the church that evening, buying us two red-eye plane tickets, sending the kids over to his sister's house for a few hours, calling his mother to come on the next plane from Los Angeles, calling his cousin to babysit that evening and helping me pack a carry-on bag with essentials.

We were headed to Mazatlán to bury my mother.

I cried on and off during the flight and embarrassingly wailed the majority of our layover in Texas. I remember watching a woman sitting across from me at the gate looking at me with sympathy in her eyes and I remember hoping that she was going on an enjoyable trip. A honeymoon, or off to a wedding or simply on a well-deserved vacation. It was the longest day of travel ever.

We spent the next two weeks clearing my mom's apartment, making funeral arrangements, visiting the various offices necessary in order to properly document an American Death Abroad. Visiting the funeral home was the hardest. Identifying her body, conversing with the funeral director who was trying his absolute best to understand my broken Spanish and talk to me as much as he could in English. It was a long two weeks.

During that time, just my husband and I, we talked and I cried and we talked some more and we realized that perhaps it was indeed time. Time to start living the lives we wanted. The lives we deserved. Morbid as it seems, my mother's passing truly put into perspective the idea that tomorrow is not promised and that the "someday" we had been talking about since our wedding (then six years earlier) may never come. We had to change that "someday" to today.

Upon our return home, we knew what we had to do. We had to take the leap. We had to make a plan. We had to do what we felt in our hearts we needed to do. We booked plane tickets to return to Mazatlán in late June with the kids in tow. We would do some on-the-ground reconnaissance to see if we could actually, really, truly live in Mazatlán.

Ask any expat and they will tell you: The vacation experience is nothing like the living experience. And so we went, determined to get as much of the living experience as we could. We loved every minute. So much so, that after seeing a few homes, we signed a lease on a family home. When we returned to Chicago, we put our "forever home" on the market, bought five one-way tickets back to Mazatlán and began downsizing.

On October 15, 2016, my family of five boarded an airplane with 10 suitcases, eight carry-on bags, a whole lot of hope, excitement and a bit of trepidation and took off into our new lives as expats living in Mazatlán. We weren't sure how it would turn out, but what we did know is that we could no longer live wondering, "what if?" We could no longer live according to the rules we were handed. We had dreamed about it, we had prayed about it, it was in our hearts to do it and so, we did.

Upon arrival we quickly busied ourselves settling in; getting appliances, setting up utilities, finding our way around. I'll admit, for the first month or so, I wondered if we had made a terrible mistake. Tomorrow, I quickly came to realize, never really meant tomorrow; rather, whenever someone could do it, and I became concerned that indeed we would never have internet or gas or clean running water. My husband took it all in stride as he typically does, and helped our family navigate the transition.

Despite my plans to homeschool, when we were introduced to a nearby school that accepted kids as young as three years old, we quickly enrolled our kiddos so they could learn Spanish and we could get some time to work on our businesses. Managing homeschooling and business-building simultaneously just was not my jam. Plus, we figured this would be an excellent opportunity for the kids to acquire a new language and make friends their age. This decision turned out to be just like the decision we made to move to México in the first place: Perfect.

Between *futból* tournaments, ballet performances, school assemblies, parent-teacher events and online client consults, we were busy bees raising our kids and balancing all that comes along with expat life. As a result of this, we've learned to move with more patience, more understanding and to grant others (and ourselves) a bit more grace. Our lives have slowed down, which has given us the opportunity to savor the important moments; something we were unable to do in the States.

As we quickly approach the two-year mark since we embarked on this expat adventure, I look back and realize that this has been one of the best decisions I've made in life. My three children, who were just three, four and five when we left, are now fully fluent in Spanish, comfortably holding conversations with adults and kids alike, can read in both languages and are quickly becoming adapted to the cultural norms of those around them. They are true third-culture kids in every sense of the word.

As for my husband and I, we're living life with more freedom and energy than we did before. We now have time to spend with one another, with the kiddos and with friends. We're both working in our passion areas and we're beholden to no one's timeclock but our own. It's been liberating and empowering to say the least. Knowing that we have the power to choose has been both a humbling and encouraging experience for us both.

We left America because we wanted more. We left because we knew that there was something out there beyond the everyday. We left because we wanted cultural experiences for our children that we could not provide in the U.S. We left because my Black husband and our two Black sons needed a chance to live without fear for their lives. We left because our freedom, our happiness, our livelihood and our discovery of self was important to us and we knew that we would not find it where we were.

We sought and we found.

But we had to leave America first.

Our family now resides on the beautiful island of Antigua in the West Indies. We are recent transplants, having only been here for three weeks at the time of writing. We have found Antigua to have many qualities and characteristics similar to those of Mexico and for that we are grateful. The people are warm, the beaches inviting, and unlike in the U.S., our children are appreciated, doted on and loved immensely by those around us.

Leaving America has most certainly been a blessing to our family. On the rare occasion we return stateside to visit family, we are often shocked at both the pace of life as well as the materialism we see. Living abroad gives you a different perspective. One that encourages growth, compassion, and a deeper understanding of your truest, highest self. We left America to discover something new and in return we found ourselves.

Gabriella M. Lindsay is a wife, mother of three, serial entrepreneur and a life management expert. A woman of faith, it is her passion and calling to teach women how to live a life by design by stepping into their ultimate purpose and greatness. She does this by employing organizational systems, business development and mindset enhancement strategies through programs, coaching and digital products. Gabriella and her family sold-it-all to move from Chicago, Illinois to the beachside paradise of Mazatlán, México in October 2016. There, her children attended a local school while Gabriella and her husband Vernon ran their entrepreneurial businesses online. She and her family currently reside on the Caribbean island of Antigua. She enjoys cold chai rooibos tea at her favorite oceanfront café and has a penchant for chicken tacos and rum cake. Gabriella and her family are active bloggers and have a vlog channel on YouTube. Learn more about them at https://www.lavidalindsay.com.

Acknowledgments

Nancy, Glen, Carole, Gail, Dianne, Carol—Thank you for always being there for me, with an opinion, a comment, your friendship, and most of all, encouragement, to do this book. It wouldn't have happened without you all!

Lo de Marcos, Nayarit—The deep joy and healing that came from your beauty and tranquility is immeasurable. I will be forever grateful for my time with you.

About the Author

Janet Blaser has been a storyteller her entire life. She considers herself fortunate that her career as a journalist, editor and publisher involved her with great food, amazing places, fascinating people and unique events. Her work has appeared in numerous travel and expat publications as well as newspapers and magazines in and around Santa Cruz, California.

Originally from New York, she spent most of her adult life in Santa Cruz until moving to Mazatlán, Mexico in 2006. There she started M!, an English monthly magazine, and also founded the Mercado Organico de Mazatlán, a weekly open-air market where local farmers sell their organically grown produce and products.

She currently lives happily in a tiny town on the coast in Nayarit, Mexico, where she writes, gardens, surfs and is practicing the art of relaxation. Janet counts among her many blessings three wonderful children as well as a trio of delightful grandchildren.

Join the expat community, read more of Janet's work and follow the book tour:
- Facebook: https://web.facebook.com/whyweleftamerica/
- Website: www.whyweleftamerica.com
- Contact her directly at whyweleftamerica@gmail.com